ECONOMICS IN THE TWENTY-FIRST CENTURY

A CRITICAL PERSPECTIVE

Economics has always been nicknamed the "dismal science," but today the field seems a little more dismal than usual as governments, social movements, and even students complain that the discipline is failing to make sense of the major economic problems of today.

In *Economics in the Twenty-First Century*, Robert Chernomas and Ian Hudson demonstrate how today's top young economists continue to lead the field in the wrong direction. The recent winners of the John Bates Clark medal, economics' "baby Nobel," have won that award for studying important issues such as economic development, income inequality, crime, and health. Examining this research, Chernomas and Hudson show that this work focuses on individual choice, ignores the systematic role of power in the economic system, and leads to solutions that are of limited effectiveness at best and harmful at worst.

An accessible summary of the latest debates in economics, *Economics in the Twenty-First Century* takes on what is missing from mainstream economics, why it matters, and how the discipline can better address the key concerns of our era.

ROBERT CHERNOMAS is a professor in the Department of Economics at the University of Manitoba.

IAN HUDSON is a professor in the Department of Economics at the University of Manitoba.

T0339167

 **UTP insights**

UTP Insights is an innovative collection of brief books offering accessible introductions to the ideas that shape our world. Each volume in the series focuses on a contemporary issue, offering a fresh perspective anchored in scholarship. Spanning a broad range of disciplines in the social sciences and humanities, the books in the UTP Insights series contribute to public discourse and debate and provide a valuable resource for instructors and students.

Books in the Series

- Robert Chernomas and Ian Hudson, *Economics in the Twenty-First Century: A Critical Perspective*
- Roland Paris and Taylor Owen (eds.), *The World Won't Wait: Why Canada Needs to Rethink Its International Policies*
- Stephen M. Saideman, *Adapting in the Dust: Lessons Learned from Canada's War in Afghanistan*
- Michael R. Marrus, *Lessons of the Holocaust*
- Bessma Momani, *Arab Dawn: Arab Youth and the Demographic Dividend They Will Bring*
- William Watson, *The Inequality Trap: Fighting Capitalism Instead of Poverty*
- Phil Ryan, *After the New Atheist Debate*
- Paul Evans, *Engaging China: Myth, Aspiration, and Strategy in Canadian Policy from Trudeau to Harper.*

ECONOMICS IN THE TWENTY-FIRST CENTURY

A Critical Perspective

Robert Chernomas and Ian Hudson

UNIVERSITY OF TORONTO PRESS
Toronto Buffalo London

ISBN 978-1-4426-4942-2 (cloth)
ISBN 978-1-4426-2677-5 (paper)

Library and Archives Canada Cataloguing in Publication

Chernomas, Robert, author
Economics in the twenty-first century: a critical perspective/Robert
Chernomas and Ian Hudson.

(UTP insights)
Includes bibliographical references and index.
ISBN 978-1-4426-4942-2 (cloth). – ISBN 978-1-4426-2677-5 (paper)

1. Economics.   I. Hudson, Ian, 1967–, author   II. Title.   III. Series:
UTP insights

HB171.C52 2016   330.9051   C2016-900390-6

University of Toronto Press acknowledges the financial assistance to its
publishing program of the Canada Council for the Arts and the Ontario Arts
Council, an agency of the Government of Ontario.

Canada Council **Conseil des Arts**
for the Arts **du Canada**

ONTARIO ARTS COUNCIL
CONSEIL DES ARTS DE L'ONTARIO
an Ontario government agency
un organisme du gouvernement de l'Ontario

Funded by the   Financé par le
Government   gouvernement
of Canada   du Canada

For the late Robert Heilbroner

He went beyond the call when I was a new graduate student and years later advised me it was time to write books. RC

The Worldly Philosophers inspired me to become an economist. IH

Contents

Acknowledgments   ix

1 Introduction   3

2 Development and Growth   22

3 Labor, Income, and Inequality in the United States   49

4 Health, Healthcare, and the Individual   79

5 Crime   106

6 Two Kinds of Crises   126

7 Conclusion   147

Notes   157

Index   185

Acknowledgments

In writing this book we have been very fortunate to have benefited from the supportive people at the University of Toronto Press. We owe a particular debt to Jennifer DiDomenico, who carefully steered us through the publication process and provided thoughtful suggestions that greatly improved the book.

We also had considerable help from others along the way. Fletcher Baragar and Mark Hudson provided invaluable advice on a couple of the chapters. The manuscript passed through the hands of two unknown referees who were reassuringly positive about the general direction of the research and also made some valuable suggestions for improvement.

Finally, we received financial assistance for writing the book from the Global Political Economy Research Fund in the Faculty of Arts at the University of Manitoba, which we used to hire Breann Whitby and Musah Khalid, who did sterling work as research assistants.

ECONOMICS IN THE TWENTY-FIRST CENTURY

chapter one

Introduction

Economics has the awkward distinction of being both the most influential and most reviled of the social sciences. The economic crisis that started in 2008 does not appear to have caused the discipline's influence to wane, but it has expanded the number of its critics. Even the queen of England memorably entered the fray, enquiring how it was possible that no one in the profession noticed the downturn coming.[1] The original, understandable, indictment of the profession's lack of ability to predict or explain the economic meltdown rapidly spread to a wider criticism. Students were walking out of first-year economics courses and signing petitions lamenting the poor quality of their economics education. Respectable media outlets like the *New York Times* in the United States and Canada's *Globe and Mail* were conducting scathing investigations into the discipline under headlines like "Economics Has Met the Enemy, and It Is Economics."[2] Broadly speaking, the growing criticism from outside (and occasionally inside) economics centered on how the discipline lacked realism and used technique as an end in itself, instead of engaging with concrete economic realities and accepting a pluralism of approaches adapted to the complexity of economic problems. A fundamental component of this perceived lack of realism is the lack of attention by the mainstream of the discipline to inquire about the economic influence of the most powerful people, institutions, and corporations that dominate the decision making of the twenty-first century.

This book explores whether this criticism should be applied to the work of the new generation of economic superstars, who have established significant influence both inside and outside the discipline. The John Bates Clark (JBC) medal is given to the American economist under forty "judged to have made the most significant contribution to economic thought and knowledge," and is generally considered the second most prestigious in the profession (after the Nobel Prize, which it sometimes foreshadows). We will examine the work of those who have won the award (given out biannually prior to 2010 and annually thereafter) from 2001 to 2013 (see table 1.1). The winners of the JBC are significant because they represent the future of economics as defined by the discipline itself. The selection of winners reveals the type of methods and subject areas that the discipline deems meritorious. This might not be of particular importance if economists had no sway on the world outside the "academic scribblers" beavering away in ivory-tower obscurity, but this is not the case. Economists significantly influence both broad public opinion and public policy. Indeed, JBC award winners have already done so. For example, Steven Levitt, the 2003 JBC winner, co-authored *Freakonomics*, which sold millions of copies and spent a remarkable two years on the *New York Times* bestseller list. Esther Duflo, the 2010 JBC award winner, and 2011 Financial Times/Goldman Sachs business book of the year award winner, was the subject of a *Telegraph* article asking, "Can this woman change the world?" What these economists study, and the manner in which they conduct their research matters, both inside and outside the ivory tower.

Who Was John Bates Clark?

Clark (1847–1938) was an American economist at Columbia University. He was one of the original founders of the American Economic Association and its president from 1893 to 1895. Perhaps reflecting his education in the European schools of Zurich and Heidelberg, he started out his career as a critic of capitalism, but for most of his academic life he defended the merits of the competitive economy. Clark's most famous contribution is his marginal productivity theory of income distribution (more on this in chapter 3), which argued that in competitive markets people are paid the value of their productivity. In more colloquial terms, people get paid what they are worth. This theory, which is a specific example of his more general "faith in the virtues of competitive markets," meant that Clark has largely been characterized (or caricatured) as an apologist for laissez-faire capitalism.[3] While he may have been an apologist, he was a thoughtful and reflective one. Clark was conscious of the role of economic theory and economic policy in fostering a society that people felt was fair:

> The welfare of the laboring classes depends on whether they get much or little; but their attitude toward the other classes – and, therefore, the stability of the social state depends chiefly on the question, whether the amount that they get, be it large or small, is what they produce. If they create a small amount of wealth and get the whole of it, they may not seek to revolutionize society; but if it were to appear that they produce an ample amount and get only a part of it, many of them would become revolutionists, and all would have the right to do so.[4]

Table 1.1 John Bates Clark Medal winners 2001–13

Recipient	Institution	Year
Matthew Rabin	University of California, Berkeley	2001
Steven Levitt	University of Chicago	2003
Daron Acemoglu	MIT	2005
Susan C. Athey	MIT	2007
Emmanuel Saez	University of California, Berkeley	2009
Esther Duflo	MIT	2010
Jonathan Levin	Stanford University	2011
Amy Finkelstein	MIT	2012
Raj Chetty	Harvard University	2013

The "Old" Mainstream

Up until this generation of economists, the "old" mainstream rested on four pillars. First, rational self-interested maximization is the assumption that people use the information available to weigh the costs and benefits of every activity and undertake those that are the most beneficial. To take one example (to which we will return), people decide to commit crimes by calculating the costs, like incarceration and loss of legitimate income, and the benefits, like the income from a theft or the satisfaction of a murder. This is the often derided *homo economicus*, the rational calculator who attempts to maximize his or her own benefits.

Second, mainstream economics has focused on the individual as the center of inquiry. Economic predictions are made based on how individuals respond to their constraints and incentives. So, for example, consumer behavior can be predicted by how individuals respond to price changes given their preferences for a product. This emphasis on the individual can be contrasted with using class as the unit of analysis, as was done by classical economists like Adam Smith, Thomas Malthus, and David Ricardo, and is currently done by non-mainstream economists like those who work in the post-Keynesian and Marxist traditions. Focusing on class stresses that individuals can be combined into groups with similar economic interests and that these groups can be expected to absolutely and relatively prosper or suffer depending on economic trends and policies.

As an example of an analysis focusing on classes in society that differs from old mainstream analysis, we can look at the theory of comparative advantage in international trade. Most old mainstream economists argued that if nations specialize by producing what they can make most efficiently, and trade with other nations for the goods that they are less capable of producing, all trading nations will be better off than if they did not trade. It is this theory that underpins mainstream economics' support of free trade between countries. A concrete example of this is when Walmart sources its products from low-wage nations, like China, reducing consumer prices in the United States. Yet, this simple model abstracts from the winners and losers in free trade. Trade specialist Paul Krugman argues that competition from low-wage nations has driven down the incomes of less-educated American workers. "And no, cheap consumer goods at Wal-Mart aren't adequate compensation."[5] Still, free trade helped Walmart become one of the largest and most profitable corporations in the world by allowing them to purchase their products from the lowest-cost countries. According to the Economic Policy Institute, free trade has contributed to rising income inequality, suppressed real wages for production workers, weakened unions, and reduced fringe benefits.[6] There is a "class effect" from free trade. Business owners benefit and workers, especially those who are in occupations that compete with low-wage countries, lose.

Third, mainstream economics relies on formal mathematical modeling. This is justified by its ability to produce rigor, by which economists mean logically consistent conclusions derived from an explicit set of assumptions. A contentious issue with formal modeling is that it must, by definition, choose which aspects of reality to include and which to exclude. When abstracting from a world of infinite potential variables, the theorist must decide which are the most salient and which it is possible to exclude without significant cost to the ability to predict or explain. Old mainstream economics has typically chosen to model human behavior as individuals with no class or power, who behave in a rational manner to maximize their interests, and who do not make systematic errors when making economic decisions. In these models, the owners of Walmart, the Walton family, and John Q. Public have similar goals and behave in a similar manner. The only real difference is that the Waltons' income permits them a greater range of consumption choices. However, in reality the Waltons' wealth does not stem only from cheap sourcing from the developing world, but also from the tremendous power that comes with the massive scale of their operations, which they have used to dictate prices and alter the terms of trade with their suppliers and workers. Despite the fact that the Waltons have considerable political and economic clout, both because of their sizeable financial resources and the inherent power that comes from the fact that business decisions have a massive impact on the broader economy, most mainstream economic models abstract from the fact that the Waltons (and other large corporations) have more influence on how the economy works than do their customers or employees.

Finally, the quest for scientific truth is undertaken using econometrics – statistical techniques that determine whether variables are related to each other. If economists want to determine whether the minimum wage impacts unemployment, researchers would over time, or across different regions (or both in panel data), use unemployment as the dependent variable to be explained by the appropriately named explanatory variables (things that could reasonably be expected to influence unemployment), one of which would be changes in the minimum wage. If changes in the minimum wage are statistically related to changes in unemployment, independently of the other explanatory variables, then economists conclude that the minimum wage influences unemployment rates. This appears straightforward, but after numerous econometric tests, economists still disagree about the impact of minimum wages on unemployment.[7] The problem is that discovering incontrovertible evidence based on the very messy real world is inherently difficult even with advanced econometric techniques. Further, as was the case with modeling, the conclusions from econometric testing depend a great deal on choices made by the investigator – the choice of the econometric technique to be used, of the explanatory variables, and of the data, to name but a few. Economics is hardly the only social science to engage in these kinds of statistical techniques. They have become commonplace in most other disciplines as well. However, it was economics that largely introduced these techniques that put the science in social science. Econometric testing also has a centrality in economics that it does not hold in other social sciences. Indeed, as economists expand beyond their traditional subject areas, it is this method of enquiry that may come to define the discipline.

Critics of the Economic Mainstream

The old economic mainstream, and its four pillars, has been subject to long-standing criticisms. One stream of criticism revolved around the economic method. Broadly speaking, the concern of these critics focused on the perceived tendency in economics to lose itself in abstract modeling, econometric technique, and unrealistic assumptions that rendered it incapable of addressing real-world economic issues. The problem here is one of emphasis. Critics in this tradition are not arguing that all modeling is useless. Modeling can illuminate real-world phenomena, but in economics it has evolved into an end unto itself. This is a concern that has long been expressed but remains unaddressed. A 1988 commission to review graduate training set up by the American Economic Association expressed concern that it was churning out *"idiot savants"* who were narrowly brilliant in terms of technique but were completely ignorant of actual economic issues.[8] One of the more long-standing critics in this vein is Tony Lawson of Cambridge University, who argues that what he considers to be the discipline's numerous failings stem from its insistence on "mathematical deductivist reasoning" as the benchmark language.[9] The inability of almost all the mainstream economists to foresee the economic crisis of 2008 (and in many cases, actively arguing that the policies in place made an economic crisis nigh on impossible) brought some big economic names into the Lawson camp. Columbia University economist Jeffrey Sachs, argued that the reliance on modeling has distracted economists' attention from the "underlying mechanisms in the economy."[10] Willem Buiter, who taught at the London School of Economics and Yale and is currently the chief economist at Citigroup, argued that the emphasis on mathematical rigor, and the unrealistic assumptions that were needed to make models solvable, left macroeconomists woefully unable to address the 2008 crisis, describing the state of the discipline as "self-referential, inward-looking distractions at best." As a result of the emphasis on modeling and mathematical tractability, concern with anything approaching the actual economy, especially the possibility of the economy being under stress, meant that the profession was unable to predict the crisis.[11]

An alternative criticism of mainstream economics is that, at least since the 1980s, it has grown increasingly enamored of free markets and suspicious of the state.[12] The "free market" criticism gained increased traction after the 2008 economic crisis, which many commentators attributed, at least in part, to a withdrawal of state oversight in the financial sector, a policy justified by economic theory.[13] Even Alan Greenspan, one of the champions of deregulation of the US financial system leading up to the 2008 crisis in his capacity as the chair of the Federal Reserve, declared partial culpability on this front, admitting that his faith in free markets was "a flaw."[14] Critics who argue that economics has developed a free market bias have been provided with ample evidence to bolster their argument. Even in the aftershock of the 2008 crisis, which tragically demonstrated the dangers of laissez-faire policy in the financial sector, economics' highest award was given to the more dogmatic proponents of free markets. In 2013, Eugene Fama, the originator of the efficient-markets hypothesis, which "demonstrated" the impossibility of asset market bubbles (the flashpoint of the 2008 crisis), was one of the winners of the Nobel Prize. This would be akin to astronomy awarding its highest prize to someone who "proved" that the sun revolved around the earth.

While both the technique and free market criticisms do reveal considerable flaws in the discipline of economics, they do not explicitly acknowledge the most fundamental gap in how the discipline understands the economy.

What Is Really Missing? The Economic System

In the late 1990s and early 2000s critics of mainstream economics like Sheila Dow[15] and Robert Heilbroner and William Milberg[16] argued that the problem with economics' reliance on the four pillars is that they lead to a lack of attention to the influence of broader social forces – macrofoundations – on the individual.

People do make choices, but a focus on individual choice, rather than the powerful social and economic institutions that shape those choices, pulls a veil over what actually determines economic reality. Humans do not form preferences in a vacuum. They are not handed down by a divine being. Rather they are formed from the earliest moments of infancy through exposure to social conventions and shaped by the dominant institutions. A focus on the individual ignores the fact that individuals are significantly influenced by their social surroundings. According to Heilbroner and Milberg, economics, and all social sciences, should strive to "penetrate the façade of 'the individual' to its social roots."[17] Perhaps most important among these macrofoundations that were being neglected was the role of the economic system itself in shaping behavior and creating power relationships in society. While the methodological critique mentioned earlier in the chapter does contain an important element of truth, the focus on econometrics and mathematical modeling, without an exploration of the social and economic context, is particularly problematic in so far as it is focused on the individual as the primary explanatory agent.

One important example, particularly beloved by mainstream economists, is the abstraction of the market. Economists take the market to be an unconstructed entity beyond human control. As Adam Smith put it, markets inevitably evolve courtesy of the human propensity to "truck, barter, and exchange."[18] In some situations markets may indeed evolve spontaneously through the meeting of buyers and sellers, but this is not, in general, the manner in which they emerge in our economic system. Markets are the result of very deliberate efforts by powerful actors to shape them to suit their interests. Firms attempt to restrict competition to create oligopolies. They lobby governments to create favorable rules on a variety of fronts from labor laws to tax regimes to environmental policies. Markets are, therefore, constructed in very deliberate ways. They are the result of the ability of different economic actors, with different economic interests and power, to create the specific rules that govern markets. Yet this real world of markets is frequently ignored by economists.[19]

The Dow-Heilbroner-Milberg critique can be thought about on two levels. The first, omission, would focus on the JBC economists' choice of research areas. A standard list of important economic goals would likely include stable growth, price stability, full employment, and the efficient allocation of resources. Some might even add to this list environmental sustainability and a reasonably equitable distribution of wealth and income. Yet the JBC medal has not gone to economists who have chosen to direct their attention to either the 2008 economic crises or the connection between the economy and growing environmental deterioration, arguably the most important subjects at this historic conjuncture. This is not because these are not the subject of enquiry of any economists. The 2008 crisis, particularly, launched a fleet of books, so it is not as though JBC winners did not have time to put together an analysis. Rather, the JBC medal is indicative of the kinds of topics that are, or in this case are not, rewarded (discussed later in the chapter).

Yet, it is not implausible that the JBC winners who are the subject of this book could turn their attention to these issues, or that the award might be granted to a researcher in these areas at some point on the future. To be fair, the JBC winners do research many issues of policy importance, like healthcare and economic development. Therefore, the second and more significant level of the critique is commission – the manner in which JBC winners address the issues that they do research. As we go through the economic issues covered by the JBC economists we will evaluate the extent to which they deviate from the old mainstream assumptions criticized by Dow-Heilbroner-Milberg: rational maximizing human behavior (the controversial *homo economicus*), formal modeling techniques, complex econometrics, and a focus on the individual. We would argue that the most damning of these is the use of the individual as the center of analysis, which ignores what Heilbroner-Milberg describe as the "social forces" that influence the individual. The social forces that we are concerned with in this work are not as expansive as those in other disciplines outside economics would, perhaps, include in this term. We are not dealing with the full spectrum of the complexity of human interactions that might fall under the term social forces. Rather, we are interested in the social forces of power and how that power is created and manifested in a capitalist economy. In particular, the question is whether the approach to those crucial issues investigated in the research of the JBC winners, from poverty in the developing world to the merits of progressive taxation, contain an analysis that incorporates the systematic role of the power – particularly, although not exclusively, that of the corporation – in an economic system dependent on private investment for employment, innovation, and growth.

Part of an analysis of the macro-context would involve investigating the specific institutions that make up the unique version of capitalism that exists in different countries. Capitalism is not a homogeneous system, identical in every nation. Most importantly for the purpose of this book, the United States has an exceptional economic structure that stands in stark contrast to more social-democratic nations. As we shall argue throughout this book, the political economy in the United States has resulted in less power for the general population, and more for corporations, than is the case in most other wealthy nations.[20] Comparisons with other nations illuminate the fact that the US political economy is not a natural or inevitable state of affairs. Different structures and power dynamics are possible, and do exist, in other nations. Comparisons are also important for providing instruction about how other nations have tackled similar issues and assess the relative merits of the different approaches. Since most of the research of the JBC winners is concentrated on the United States, there is a potential that it will not acknowledge the fairly unique national context of the United States or compare the United States to other, very different political-economy systems. Although this book does not always and everywhere employ a comparative systems analysis, on issues in which the United States is a particular outlier, like healthcare and crime, it will examine the extent to which JBC winners incorporate the differences between capitalist nations into account as opposed to treating the US system as an inevitable state of affairs.[21]

As authors like Lawson point out, the methods of modern economics do not make a hospitable ground for an analysis of power in the economic system. It is here that we can see the interrelationship between the method and the free market critiques which were presented as distinct earlier in the chapter. One strain of the methodological critique (associated with people like Lawson) is that the economic insistence on mathematical rigor and tractable models does not merely abstract from reality, but creates a specific kind of bias in economic analysis, towards free market results and away from concerns about power and broader social forces on the individual. This connection is identified by those who favor a more ideological explanation for the direction of modern mainstream economics like Dow. In comparing the old mainstream and newer game-theoretic approaches with a feminist, political economy method, Dow argues that simplifying assumptions allow the former to "yield sharp definitive results," while the latter emphasize how the individual is influenced by the social, the evolution of social convention and the interrelationship between economic and social structures.[22] Ignoring social forces, conventions, and economic structures is not ideologically neutral. It disregards the power relationships that exist in an economic system, hiding the impact of broader social forces in the cloak of individual choice.[23]

Economics should not be automatically rebuked for its commitment to seeking chains of reasoning or the mathematical and statistical quest for a rigorous understanding of how the world actually works. However, we will investigate the extent to which the JBC winners tether their technical chains to something that resembles a capitalist economy – something that was not accomplished in the "old" mainstream. To borrow a phrase from Anwar Shaikh, in economics mathematical formalization has not resulted in rigor so much as "rigor mortis."[24]

Economists and Their Training

The latest generation of economists is the progeny of a discipline that has evolved both very specific tools and a particular ideology. The ideological component of the economics discipline is not inevitably a state versus free market division, as Roger Backhouse has suggested (although he has provided some fairly compelling evidence to suggest that the mainstream of economics has veered towards a free market ideology since the 1970s).[25] More fundamentally, it is about the level at which society should be analyzed, with a focus on individual preferences and the incentives that guide them. In numerous studies, people with training in economics tend to be more individualistic and behave less cooperatively than those unfortunates forced to muddle through life without. In game experiments like the Prisoners' Dilemma, economists behave less cooperatively than others. Economists also give less to charity. Students who have completed a mainstream first-year economics course exhibit less honesty in surveys than those who have not. In an article summarizing these results, the authors conclude that the training received in economics, which focuses on individual self-interest and incentives, has helped shape economists' beliefs.[26] Economists tend to look at the world in a certain way. They see, and analyze, the economy as a collection of individuals responding to incentives rather than the individual as part of a broader collective. Economists, more than other disciplines, are trained to believe that, as Margaret Thatcher memorably claimed, "there is no such thing as society. There are individual men and women."[27]

The tools and techniques taught to fledgling economists are driven by what Backhouse termed the "internal dynamics of the economics profession."[28] By this he meant that both training and incentives in the discipline have produced technicians, wedded to the methods of a particular sort of empirical rigor. It is these techniques that are taught in graduate schools. The idea that there is a problematic lack of connection between economics and the economy was reinforced by a survey of economic graduate students from "top-ranking" programs in the early 2000s. In answer to a question asking about what skills would put them on the fast track to economic success only 9 percent thought a "thorough knowledge of the economy" was very important, while 51 percent viewed it as unimportant. By contrast, "being smart in the sense that they are good at problem solving" and "excellence in mathematics" were considered to be very important by 51 and 30 percent of the students respectively. (It is also, perhaps, of concern from the "it's not what you know" perspective that 33 percent of graduate students felt that an "ability to make connections with prominent professors" was very important.)[29]

What is accepted by the discipline in terms of the subject of enquiry and method is enforced through incentives within the academic world. It is success within these boundaries that improves a candidate's chances of landing a good job, getting that much sought-after promotion, and publication in a leading journal. Robert J. Shiller, Nobel Prize–winning economist at Yale, claimed that the discipline suffers from what he called "groupthink," such that once the dominant methods were established, graduate students who bucked the trend found it very difficult to get a an academic job.[30] Few fledgling economists were so brave that they were prepared to risk their future, and so the economic status quo replicated itself. The incentive structure facing those who want to avoid ridicule exists even after a researcher lands that coveted academic appointment. Following what is acceptable to the mainstream increases one's chances of getting published in the leading journals, getting promotion, and earning a reputation as an important scholar.[31] This trend has not changed in the wake of criticism of the discipline following the 2008 crisis, when some degree of critical introspection might have been expected. According to long-time critic of orthodox, mainstream economics James K. Galbraith, academic economists are "like an ostrich with its head in the sand" in their refusal to reconsider their fundamental approach.[32]

Why Power Is Important

The Dow-Heilbroner-Milberg critique focuses on economics' failure to analyze the broad social forces that influence individual behavior. According to this view, the manner in which the economy operates, the social and political systems in which the economy is embedded, and an individual's place in those systems have a profound influence on what economists often, very blithely, refer to as individual preferences and choices. Most important among these influences is the power that exists in both the economic realm and the political system that provides the "rules" by which participants in the economy abide. Power is held and wielded by actors such as corporations, but power is also deeply imbedded in the structures, institutions, and even ideologies of a society. The conditions in which power is present in different economic contexts, how it impacts economic actors, and why this creates problems for modern economic analysis is the subject of the rest of this book. However, it might be useful to provide a brief example of contexts in which power is present in the economic system but overlooked in much economic analysis and why the presence of power matters.

One of the principal arguments in this book is that power in the economic system is primarily held by the corporate world. If power can be associated with size, the world's multinational corporations certainly rank as some of the largest economic entities. Some sense of the size of the largest firms can be seen by comparing the revenues of large companies with the GDP of countries Using this measure, 44 of the top 100 economic entities in 2009 were corporations. Together, these 44 companies earned revenues of $6.4 trillion, over 11 percent of global GDP. Walmart's revenues exceeded the GDPs of 174 countries, including Sweden, Saudi Arabia, and Venezuela. Exxon's were larger than those of Finland or Egypt.[33] The sheer size of corporations creates a number of important sources of power for firms, from their ability to provide jobs in an economy dependent on private sector employment to their financial clout in the political arena, that are often not well represented in modern economic analysis. If companies are too big to fail, they should also be too big for economists to ignore.

Large firms, and the organizations that represent them, have some powerful weapons when it comes to fighting for their economic interests. First, democratically elected governments, and the public that vote for them, will take into consideration the impact of any policy on firms' willingness to invest. After all, it is private investment that creates jobs, tax revenue, and economic prosperity. Investment decisions are made by business on the ability of that investment to turn a profit. The higher the profit that can be realized in a region, the greater the willingness of firms to invest. The need to create an environment conducive to private investment then places limits on the kinds of economic policy that can be considered. Measures like green taxes, universal social programs, or higher corporate taxes may be desirable in the opinion of the citizenry on their own merit, but since they are likely to decrease profits, and investment, they are less likely to be implemented. This power of investment limits the scope of economic policy when the interests of business are at odds with the desires of the broader population.[34] This limit is demonstrated by governments' reluctance to implement policies that would increase the price of emitting greenhouse gasses that are the cause of climate change. UK business secretary Vince Cable explicitly explained this logic in response to a proposed carbon target in 2011: "Agreeing too aggressive a level risks burdening the UK economy, which would be detrimental to UK, undermining the UK's competitiveness and our attractiveness as a place to do business."[35] Yet, the power that the need to attract private investment confers on business is seldom recognized or discussed by mainstream economics except to treat it as a natural and efficient phenomenon.

Second, when corporations organize themselves to promote their common interests, they are especially powerful. They have been especially successful on this front in the United States, where most of the JBC economists focus their research. One method that businesses use to promote their common interests is through influencing economic policy outcomes by spending money in the political process. A particularly transparent example is the American Legislative Exchange Program (ALEC), founded in 1973. ALEC's role is to craft "model" bills and resolutions that can be easily turned into law by sympathetic politicians, mostly at the state level. ALEC's funding comes from the by now usual suspects in the business foundation world, including the Schaife family, heir to the Mellon banking and oil empire, the Coors family of brewing magnates, and oil industry billionaires Charles and David Koch, but also it draws considerable funding from individual firms. Its list of corporate donors is a virtual who's who of corporate America, from General Motors to Bank of America to Microsoft to

McDonalds. Donor firms get veto power over the wording in the legislation cooked up by ALEC.[36] ALEC claims to have introduced a remarkable 3100 individual pieces of legislation in one year (1999–2000). Its recent activities include the Automatic Income Tax Reduction Act, which would provide an automatic biennial tax rate decrease; the Public-Private Fair Competition Act, which would establish whether state agencies compete "unfairly" with the private sector; and the anti-union Right to Work Act, which removes employee's obligation to pay union dues.[37] ALEC's bill pipeline was not confined to these areas, but extended to writing legislation on the environment, public schools, and healthcare. ALEC bills have been successfully adopted, sometimes word for word, at the state level. One might claim that this was politics "by business, for business," rather than any romantic, inclusive notions of "the people."

The degree of influence of corporations and the organizations that represent them is a legitimate question; the fact that their power can be completely ignored without creating some genuine problems for economic analysis is not open for debate. The chapters that follow will examine, in much more detail, specific markets where power has important ramifications and the extent to which this is incorporated in the research of the current generation of leading economists.

The Book

The rest of the book critically analyzes the work of JBC winners. We have taken a topic-by-topic approach so that we can evaluate the collected work of the JBC winners on some of the most important economic issues. This is not meant to be an exhaustive list of all the topics researched by every author. We have chosen the topics for inclusion based primarily on the areas of the JBC winners' most significant publications. When another JBC winner has contributed to these topics, their research has also been included. Chapter 6 deals with what JBC research between 2000 and 2013 has omitted: the two topics that would arguably be considered of universal importance at this juncture in history – the economic and environmental crisis.

Each chapter will follow a similar template. After a brief introduction, the research of economists and other social scientists that do focus on the broad economic context and power relationships will be used to demonstrate the importance of these concepts in understanding the chapter's topic. This will be followed by a summary of the work of the JBC economists. Finally there will be an evaluation of their work. For each issue we will analyze the extent to which the work of the JBC winners includes or leaves out the macro-context that shapes individual decisions, especially the power relationships that largely shape that macro-context.

Chapter 2 examines the economics of development. This is the study of how poorer nations can improve their lot. The two JBC economists that are most closely associated with this area of study are Daron Acemoglu and Esther Duflo.

In chapter 3 we will look at how the JBC economists analyze incomes and economic inequality. Given the importance of this topic, it should be no surprise that a large number of JBC winners have contributed to this issue. While we will examine the work of all the JBC winners who have contributed in this area, we will pay special attention to Raj Chetty, Acemoglu, and Emmanuel Saez, whose names are most closely associated with the debate around social welfare programs and inequality.

Chapter 4 looks at health economics. In this chapter we will examine Matthew Rabin's work on time inconsistency and its negative impacts on health, but we will spend the most time analyzing the work of Amy Finkelstein, who has dedicated her academic career to this one area.

Chapter 5 analyzes Steven Levitt's work on crime. Unlike the other chapters in this book, which contain analysis of more than one JBC winner, Levitt stands in isolation on this topic. Levitt has published in a wide variety of other areas, from education to racism, but his favorite area of research is crime and corruption, which we have focused on here as an example of his general research method.

Finally, chapter 6 looks at the work of JBC winners on economic and environmental crises. This is the topic on which the JBC winners have written the least, which is perhaps revealing of what they consider important thus far in their still young careers. In terms of economic crises, we will look at Jonathan Levin's work on the subprime credit market, and at Acemoglu and Saez's work on economic cycles. Susan Athey's work on timber will be studied in relation to the topic of the environment.

chapter two

Development and Growth

Why are some nations wealthy while others languish? What policies contribute to rapid growth and rising living standards? The founding text of the entire economic discipline, Adam Smith's *An Inquiry into the Nature and Causes of the Wealth of Nations*, was an attempt to answer this question. However, the idea that special attention needed to be paid to policies that would increase living standards in nations that lagged behind those that were more affluent really only emerged after the Second World War. The massive gap in living standards between the largely impoverished former colonies (what was then known as the "third world") and the wealthier, developed countries (the "first world"), along with the growing sentiment that governments had both the ability and the obligation to intervene in the economy generated an entirely new field dedicated to the problems particular to poorer nations. Most development economics wrestled with two interrelated questions: "What is the cause of the lower incomes in the developing world?" and "What should be done to raise living standards up to those of rich countries?"

The two JBC medal–winning authors most closely associated with this long tradition are Daron Acemoglu and Esther Duflo. Acemoglu is a professor at the Massachusetts Institute of Technology. As of 2014 he was one of the most cited economists in the world. His 2012 book *Why Nations Fail: The Origins of Power, Prosperity and Poverty* was shortlisted for the Financial Times and Goldman Sachs Business Book of the Year Award. Acemoglu is prolific, writing on a wide range of topics, but his most influential work is on the connection between colonial rule and development as laid out in his article (along with Simon Johnson and James Robinson) "The Colonial Origins of Comparative Development: An Empirical Investigation."[1]

Duflo, also at MIT, has been the subject of glowing articles with headlines like "Can This Woman Change the World?" for her work applying Random Control Testing (RCT) to development problems.[2] She went Acemoglu one better on the business-book podium when her book, with serial co-author Abhijit Banerjee, *Poor Economics: A Radical Rethinking of the Way to Fight Global Poverty*, won the Financial Times and Goldman Sachs Business Book of the Year Award, and the $48,000 that goes with it, in 2011. In 2009 she received a MacArthur Foundation "genius" fellowship and the ultimate celebrity endorsement when invited to dine not once but twice with Bill Gates.[3]

There is a sizeable army of economists toiling away over the "causes of" and "solutions to" questions about development. This chapter will examine what it is about these two researchers that distinguished them from the rest of the pack. In the process, their research will be evaluated for the extent to which they continue along with the "old" economic mainstream, especially the tendency to ignore the economic context in which individual decisions occur and the powerful institutions that shape that context. In order to accomplish this, we must outline why an analysis of power is important for understanding the political economy of developing economies.

Power in the Modern International Economy

In very broad terms, one answer to the "causes of" national living standards that lag behind the rest of the world is external impediments. The general argument is that the rules of the international economy are stacked against poorer nations, not simply because they are starting at a disadvantage, but because international actors have continuously placed obstacles in their development path. The economic context in which developing nations and their many poor citizens strive to increase their income is shaped by power-ful international organizations, multinational corporations (MNCs), and countries acting on their behalf. Any account of the oppor-tunities and constraints facing those in the developing world that ignores the power of these actors will, at best, be incomplete. The theory of external impediments has a long intellectual history. About the same time that economic development was emerging as a distinct subsection of the discipline, Raul Prebisch,[4] the direc-tor of the Economic Commission of Latin America, released *The Economic Development of Latin America and Its Principal Problems*, which argued that the prices of the primary products exported by the developing world would tend to fall compared to those of the industrial products of the developed world. This would present a structural obstacle for the developing world if it followed a poli-cy of free trade because they would have to export increasingly large quantities of primary products to afford the same quantity of industrial goods. Subsequent scholars in what became known as dependency theory[5] and world systems approaches[6] stressed an unequal relationship between the core, developed nations and the developing periphery. The hallmark of this theory was that the de-velopment of the core nations conditioned the development of the periphery, frequently to the detriment of the latter. The mechanism through which this occurs varied depending on the specific brand of dependency, ranging from the siphoning of profits by MNCs to rules of international trade agreements that disadvantage the de-veloping world trading partners. The unifying theme is that the economies in the developing periphery were heavily influenced by powerful external forces that at least conditioned, and at most stunted, their development.[7]

Léonce Ndikumana and James Boyce's book *Africa's Odious Debts*[8] is very much in this tradition. According to the authors, the conventional accounting, in which Africa is considered a debtor to the rest of the world, is misleadingly incomplete. While it is true that governments in the continent had racked up $177 billion in external debt as of 2008, a more careful calculation would also in-clude net private capital flows. In the thirty-nine years between 1970 and 2008, there was a net capital-flight outflow of $735 billion from the thirty-three sub-Saharan countries for which there is data. If these funds had been invested in assets that earned interest equal to short-term US Treasury bills, the 2008 value would have been $944 billion.[9] A later paper extending this method to four North African countries discovered that a further $450 billion was lost to capital flight between 1970 and 2010, amounting to $619 billion if foregone interest is included.[10] Combining these two studies yields $1.56 trillion in capital that could have been invested in the poorest continent as opposed to fleeing offshore. Far from being a net international debtor, capital actually flowed out of the poorest continent to the rest of the world. Ndikumana and Boyce refer to the connection between external debt and capital flight as a "revolving door," in which loans to African governments are channeled into the corrupt pockets of their leaders and then flow back out of the continent in the form of capital flight.[11]

Is it possible to interpret this outflow (and other damaging policy decisions) as a purely domestic problem, representing nothing more than modern-day pirates plundering the nations that they were supposed to be governing? Maybe, but the looting of Africa by its rich and powerful was directed, supported, and abetted in various ways by those in more affluent continents. Most obviously, governments, especially in the United States, imposed or propped up the very people who were funneling money out of Africa, making this less a tale of domestic dysfunction and more one of external interference.

In his book *Killing Hope*, William Blum documents a conservative fifty-five cases in which US military intervention was used to either protect or install governments.[12] The main criterion for US support was whether governments were amenable to foreign business, particularly US-based MNCs. In a recent example of this, when the United States had a free hand to set economic policy in Iraq after the overthrow of Saddam Hussein, the head of the Coalition Provisional Authority between 2003 and 2004, Paul Bremer, created an economic plan that implemented sweeping pro-business changes. This made a stark contrast with Hussein's economic program, which was marked by state-run companies, foreign ownership restrictions, import quotas (prior to the sanctions), and other government interventions that often curtailed the potential for profit, especially for foreign firms. The plan for implementing post-invasion economic reform was given to a private firm, Bearing Point, which was contracted with the ambitious task of delivering "economic recovery, reform and sustained growth in Iraq."[13] In practice, this meant the immediate firing of 500,000 state employees (not all of whom were in the military, although many certainly were), removing all import restrictions, privatizing state-owned firms, reducing the corporate tax rate from 40 to 20 percent, and eliminating foreign ownership restrictions outside the natural resource sector as well as reinvestment requirements for foreign capital.[14] Tellingly, the Bremer administration was happy to let Hussein's policies restricting trade unions and collective bargaining stand.[15] Iraq's economic policy, like so many in which the United States played a less direct but no less influential role, was designed to suit the interests of a foreign power and the business interests that it so often aids. Although it was not always the case that the United States backed rapacious regimes (South Korea would be one of several counter-examples), the United States was largely instrumental in, at worst, or indifferent to, at best, extensive plundering. Of primary concern was the extent to which developing nations were open to US business. As a result, those in power, and the economic policies that they follow, are often more the result of post-colonial decisions made in Washington or London than in the capitals of the developing world.

Multinational firms can also influence a country's economic development. This can occur in its most obvious form when MNCs act to influence the nature of the government through blatant political manipulation. But in a subtle, much more mundane manner, it happens through economic decisions on things like investment, employment, and tax compliance. In fact, any comprehensive analysis of corporate activity would view both of these approaches as simply different arrows in a firm's profit-making quiver. Firms will attempt to engage with nations on terms as favorable to its profits as possible and will undertake political activities in an effort to maintain those favorable terms. When former US vice-president Dick Cheney was the chief executive of Halliburton, the company illegally bribed Nigerian government officials for access to that country's oil fields. When charged by Nigeria, Halliburton eventually settled the case by paying a $35 million fine (although Cheney went unpunished).[16] A 2004 survey of multinational corporations found that over 17 percent of MNCs headquartered in OECD nations but operating in the developing world *admitted* to using bribery to further their interests.[17] This is not merely a case of government officials extracting payments from an unwilling private sector but a situation where "many firms collude with politicians for their mutual benefit ... at times affecting public policy, and more generally undermining public governance in emerging economies."[18] As development economist Jeffrey Sachs noted, "the next time you hear about a corruption scandal in Africa or another poor region, ask where it started and who is doing the corrupting. Neither the US nor any other 'advanced' country should be pointing the finger at poor countries, for it is often the most powerful global companies that have created the problem."[19] This is not a recent development. A 1980 survey of MNC activity in Peru, Venezuela, Chile, and Zambia recounted numerous instances of MNCs intervening in the political process in myriad ways. For example, the International Petroleum Company in Peru "bribed ministers, corrupted governments and promoted revolutions."[20] This is not to suggest that MNCs have it all their own way in dealing with developing-country governments. Indeed, all four of the nations in this study dramatically constrained the activities of MNCs through taxation, regulations on domestic ownership, or outright nationalization. Yet, the point here is that the pace and pattern of development was heavily influenced by both the business decisions of MNCs and their behavior in the political realm, which was blatant and frequent. "When survival is at stake for an MNC there may be indeed few limits to its political cunning."[21]

International trade and finance institutions have also frequently operated to the detriment of developing nations. The most widespread recent example of this is most likely the policy package of the Washington Consensus, delivered through aid policies of the US government, stabilization policies of the IMF, and donor agencies like USAID, from 1989 to 2004. This sweeping policy package, described by the man who coined the term as a "sensible, if incomplete, reform agenda,"[22] involved controlling inflation, eliminating government deficits, liberalizing trade, removing restrictions on capital flows, privatizing state-owned assets, deregulation, and ensuring property rights.[23] It would be an inaccurate generalization to claim that these policies are inevitably forced on unwilling governments in the developing world. In fact, some developing nation governments have come to embrace the policies in the Consensus. However, as donor and lending agencies, the IMF and USAID were in a position to force even truculent nations by requiring that borrowing countries implemented Consensus-style policies before they would approve loans.[24]

Joseph Stiglitz, the former chief economist at the World Bank, was scathing in his criticism of the IMF and the Consensus. According to Stiglitz, the IMF was the driving force behind the implementation of the Consensus in country after country.[25] Stiglitz argues that the policies of the Washington Consensus have failed the developing world. They "benefit the few at the expense of the many, the well-off at the expense of the poor."[26] GDP growth in Africa and Latin America was anemic over the fifteen-year period between 1990 and 2005. GDP growth in Latin America between 1990 and 2003 was a very modest 2.7 percent per year, while sub-Saharan Africa grew at 2.8 percent, both well below the pre-Consensus decades of the 1960s and 1970s.[27]

Economic historian Ha-Joon Chang argues that the free trade cornerstone of Consensus policy has been detrimental to developing nations. According to Chang, currently affluent nations almost universally made extensive use of industrial protection and promotion during their early stages of growth. Yet these now wealthy nations and the institutions, like the WTO and the IMF, over which they have influence insisted that poorer nations abandon these measures by implementing a comprehensive free trade policy that prevented protecting or fostering infant industries and enforced strict patent protection laws that prevented technological catch-up through reverse engineering.[28] Chang argues that this policy inconsistency amounted to wealthy nations "kicking away the ladder" from poorer nations.

Given the highly controversial nature of these policies, it would seem reasonable to ask why they are so universally prescribed. The most common answer is that it is due to an unshakable belief in the benefits of free markets among international institutions and the G-7 nations, especially the United States, but it may be worth asking who benefits from these policies.[29] First, IMF policies ensured that developed-country creditors had their loans repaid at the expense of the developing country borrowers. Directly, IMF loans were often used by indebted developing nations to pay back developed-country creditors. More indirectly, the policies to earn foreign exchange and reduce government program spending were designed to ensure that money was available to pay off creditors. According to Stiglitz, the IMF program in Thailand and Korea was "great for European and American creditors, but it was not so great for the workers and other taxpayers."[30] Without explicitly stating that the IMF deliberately sets out to protect the interests of the financial world, Stiglitz points out that many of the top executives at the IMF either come from or have moved to the financial sector.[31]

Second, the privatization of state property has provided an opportunity to get valuable assets at knockdown prices. For example, in order to qualify for funding from the World Bank, Uganda was required to undertake a mass sell-off of state assets. Although the value of these assets was estimated at $500 million, the sale only raised a meager $2 million.[32] This is not an isolated case. Identical stories could be told about privatizations from Mexico to Russia. One of the reasons for the low selling price of public assets in these types of privatizations is undoubtedly the desperation of cash-starved states to get their hands on additional finances. However, it is surely not merely coincidence that it is so often the economic elite with close ties to the state that benefit most handsomely.

Liberalization of the financial sector also facilitated the kind of capital flight that Ndikumana and Boyce found in Africa. While this obviously benefits the wealthy Africans who can now more easily move their money around the world, the very banks that the Washington Consensus policies made sure were paid back also benefited. It is these banks, often located in tax havens like the Cayman Islands, where Citigroup has ninety subsidiaries, which earn handsome incomes from eagerly providing a landing place for capital flight. According to Austrian banker Erhard Fürst, foreign deposits in Swiss banks earned negative interest rates, a reversal of the usual bank–depositor payment scheme, meaning that the banks were being paid by their depositors for their role as a safe haven.[33] Capital flight from Africa was aided and abetted by the multinational banks that benefited from the ill-gotten gains of the African elite.

This is not to suggest that internal factors play no role in the relative poverty of low-income nations. However, any analysis that ignores the external structural impediments to the development of many low-income nations in the current international economic system will be limited to telling, at best, a partial truth. Further, this partial truth will conveniently ignore the culpability of profit-seeking international corporations, international institutions, and developed-country governments in this state of affairs.

Duflo: Individual Nudges

Duflo has positioned her work as a sober, scientific alternative to the warring positions in development economics over the usefulness of aid. On one side of this divide is the "aid is beneficial," camp epitomized by Jeffrey Sachs,[34] which claims that development assistance from wealthy nations to their poorer neighbors would finance crucial services, like health and education, that could not be afforded by local sources. On the other side is the "aid is useless" position of people like William Easterly,[35] who argues that the massive amounts of assistance have resulted in very little tangible development, largely because much of it is squandered by corrupt leaders, stolen, or misspent. Duflo's claim is that carefully planned, scientifically tested, small-scale aid interventions based on RCTs can have massive, positive impacts, but much aid does not meet this criterion. According to Duflo, the big lesson from development history so far is the need to research, study, and test – traits that have been in short supply in development economics, which, she argues, suffers from lazy formulaic thinking. The general thrust of Duflo's research is that although the poor can often be "clever in the way they spend what little money they have,"[36] they often make poor choices with disastrous consequences. In the context of Kenyan farmers' reluctance to purchase fertilizer she wrote, "One senses a reluctance of poor people to commit themselves psychologically to a project of making more money."[37] Duflo employs RCT to determine precisely what incentives will most effectively nudge the poor to change their behavior from destructive to constructive.

Duflo applies RCT across a wide range of areas of inquiry, but two of the most common are health and education in the developing world. Poor people often do not take available and affordable options that would improve their health. They do not use chlorine tablets, vaccinations, or mosquito netting, even when they are very cheap and readily available.[38] This is not to say that the poor are necessarily reluctant to spend money on improving their health, since they often do spend money on treatments that are expensive or ineffective. Duflo argues this is because the poor do not have proper information and, naturally, they weigh the short-term costs (like the trip to the probably unstaffed clinic) more than the longer-term benefits. Duflo claims that these resistances are quite "weak," and so small incentives, like a free set of plates or a bag of lentils, will convince people to do what is good for them.

The same logic can be applied to nutrition. The common understanding is that very poor people are malnourished, which leads to poor health and, in turn, limits their ability to get out of poverty. But Duflo argues that people who are malnourished do not spend all of their income on food, or even necessities. Instead, they often buy things like alcohol and tobacco.[39] Nor do they purchase as much nutrition as possible, even with their limited budget, opting instead for more preferred, or customarily consumed, food items.[40] "Households could easily get a lot more calories and other nutrients by spending less on expensive grains (like rice and wheat), sugar and processed foods, and more on leafy vegetables and coarse grains."[41] So, the problem is that the poor actually harm themselves by making sub-par meal choices, especially for children and babies. The solution, tested and certified effective by RCT, to getting nutrients to kids and babies is through such programs as sprinkling micronutrient packages on school lunches and adding nutrients to foods that people like to eat.

Limited educational attainment is explained in much the same way. Duflo highlights two very different problems. The first is the issue of teacher attendance. While most analysis rests on getting the children to come to school, Duflo argues that it is far more important for the teachers to show up. The reason for the high instructor absenteeism is that teachers are guaranteed a salary whether they show up or not and there is little threat of dismissal for taking a less than rigorous attitude to their own attendance. One RCT-tested solution is to monitor teacher attendance using cameras and create a payment structure that is a nonlinear function of how frequently they are on the job. Creating incentives for teachers increased attendance by 21 percentage points and improved student test scores.[42] The second problem stems from a misunderstanding about where the highest returns to education arise in the developing world. The largest gains from additional education come at the lowest levels – from basic literacy skills and primary school. However, teachers and families act as though the returns are greatest at higher levels. Teachers will focus their attention on the best students at the higher levels. Students' families tend to concentrate their education investment on one child's education, frequently, at the expense of the others.[43]

The overarching message from Duflo's work is that small changes can have very large effects. In her own words, the poor often lack crucial information. They "bear too much responsibility for their own lives"[44] in the sense that they have to constantly act to make the right choices, like remembering to put chlorine tablets in water. The impediments to poverty alleviation are "less to do with some grand conspiracy of the elites to maintain their hold on the economy and more to do with some avoidable flaw in the design of policies."[45] The flip side of this claim for Duflo is that focusing on "concrete problems" is superior to answering "big picture" questions, which are both overwhelming and, to a certain degree, irrelevant.[46] Solving the big picture questions is overwhelming because there are no real answers to these debates, as is illustrated in the

Sachs versus Easterly dispute about aid. It is irrelevant because it is possible to greatly improve the lives of the poor "without changing the existing social and political structures."[47]

Dramatic improvements can then be made in eliminating poverty by making it easier for the poor to make the right decisions through well thought out and thoroughly RCT-tested incentives. As Duflo unapologetically points out, this is quite paternalistic. The implication of these recommendations is that the reason that people are poor is that they have been making poor decisions and that the programs designed to alleviate their poverty have been poorly designed. Poor decisions and poor programs make poor people.

An Evaluation of Duflo: The Limits of Individual Incentives

Although RCT is very much the flavor of the month in development circles, it is not without its critics. Although there are a number of more narrow, what might be called technical, criticisms to RCT, it is not these that we would argue are the most important.[48] Rather, we would like to focus on two more wide-ranging concerns.

First, although the authors are very insistent about scientific testing of what changes people's behavior, they are prepared to be a bit more speculative about the reasons for the behavior change, which can lead to some very misleading conclusions. For example, a Duflo RCT study found that offering people two pounds of dal for each visit, and a set of plates for completing the treatment course, increased immunization rates sevenfold, from 6 to 38 percent (which, it should be noted, is still very low).[49] Duflo argues that the reason for the success of the incentive was that it overcame people's natural tendency to weigh present costs more heavily than future benefits.[50] An alternative explanation is that poor people might be hungry and that, for them, this might be a fairly sizeable gift. The authors try to dismiss this by pointing out that the dal is only worth about half a day's wage,[51] which might be interpreted alternatively as sizeable incentive. As the former director of the United Kingdom's Overseas Development Institute Simon

Maxwell explains, "The reason is not because they are hungry. Instead, the reason (hypothesized not tested) is 'time inconsistency.'"[52] Duflo draws the same conclusions, with the same problems, when discussing why the poor have low saving rates, which is explained as a penchant for time inconsistency. People are unwilling to sacrifice today's delights to save for tomorrow. The straightforward alternative argument is that the poor do not save very much because they are too poor.

Despite Duflo's frequent entreaties that the poor are not to blame for their predicament, this unfounded, and untested, speculation about people's motives creates the impression that, left to their own devices, the poor behave like Aesop's grasshopper. Although Duflo and Thomas Malthus differ in that Duflo argues that the rich also suffer from time inconsistency but can afford it, while Malthus argues that the rich are better able to plan for the future, Duflo's analysis of the problems of the poor sounds disconcertingly similar to Malthus's words: "The labouring poor, to use a vulgar expression, seem always to live from hand to mouth. Their present wants employ their whole attention, and they seldom think of the future. Even when they have an opportunity of saving they seldom exercise it, but all that is beyond their present necessities goes, generally speaking, to the ale house."[53] For Duflo, despite the fact that both the poor and the rich suffer from the impatience of the grasshopper, it is much more of a debilitating problem for those with limited resources. The solution for Duflo does not appear to be to increase their resources but to teach them to live better within their meager means.

The second, and more worrying, difficulty with Duflo's work, and RCT in general, is that it greatly limits the questions posed by development economics. As Richard Easterly pointed out, "RCT has led development researchers to lower their ambitions."[54] This is well illustrated by the difficulties that Duflo gets into in her analysis of entrepreneurship. Her careful analysis of studies on micro-lending revealed that the poor were not particularly entrepreneurial. They do not make investments that would improve their future incomes. The stated reason – although, again, testing on this hypothesis is in short supply – is that these investments would not improve their income very much and so people do not think it is worth the effort. What they really want is a safe, secure job.[55] It is here that RCT gets into trouble. How does one increase the number of safe, secure jobs? These are not the type of policy decisions that RCT, so far at least, is capable of evaluating. In order to come up with some policy answers to this crucial question, Duflo offers a laundry list of massive, large-scale interventions from South Korea–style government direction to better urban planning in order to increase mobility to the cities where better jobs reside.[56] These recommendations have not been through the rigors of RCT, nor, most likely, is this even possible. The problem here is not with Duflo's recommendations, which we would argue are actually fairly reasonable, but rather that the method of RCT could not hope to furnish an answer to the question "How did the wealthy nations raise their standards of living?"

The limit to Duflo and RCT's small-scale, individual approach is that it ignores the historical example of nations that found broader, societal solutions to development problems. Duflo's discussion on health is, again, an important example. Duflo correctly identifies diarrhea from unsafe drinking water as a major cause of infant mortality. She argues that a low-cost solution is to have families add chlorine bleach, which will purify the water at a very low cost. RCT can be useful in devising a method to induce families' participation.[57] Convincing impoverished families to purify their water supply individually was not the manner in which the currently more affluent nations dramatically improved their health outcomes. When they were at much lower income levels in the late 1800s and early 1900s countries like the United Kingdom and the United States, due to poor water quality and sanitation, faced similar difficulties of high child mortality that were solved by public health measures often involving large-scale infrastructure projects. In the United States, early 1900s public works projects included sewage systems, providing fresh drinking water, and draining swamps, which are what most people associate with public health. The US also enacted broader social measures to improve the working and living conditions of the general public – from a social welfare system to rules on occupational safety and health.[58] Ndikumana and

Boyce argue that the health problems in Africa are due to "a lack of resources." According to their calculations, had the hundreds of billions funneled out of sub-Saharan Africa been spent on public health, it would have prevented "77,000 excess infant deaths per year."[59] This kind of solution cannot be examined using RCT because it focuses on a broad social change rather than on nudging the individual.

While Duflo's method makes some grand promises about how testing and facts need to overcome the ignorance and ideology that she claims is prevalent in development economics, RCT contains biases and limits of its own. Crucially, it ignores the context in which individuals operate. In doing so it hides the role played by powerful actors in the international economic system and the broad policy solutions to development problems that were so successful in developed countries. According to New School economist Sanjay Reddy, RCT results in "severely limiting the questions that can be asked and shoring up a practical philosophy that is quiescent in relation to many important questions that cannot readily be analyzed using the authors' favoured method. These include questions related to the structure and dynamics of markets, governmental institutions, macroeconomic policies, the workings of social classes, castes, and networks, and so forth."[60] Duflo's RCT may provide some answers to small-scale, limited questions but it ignores the effects of powerful international players, from multinational corporations to the US military, which dramatically narrow the choices available to the vast majority of the citizens of poorer nations whom she wants to nudge towards more rational choices. Duflo may be throwing lifejackets to those in the water, but would it not be better to prevent the boat from sinking?

Acemoglu: Genuine Time Inconsistency

Duflo attempts to answer the question "How can we lift people out of poverty?" but is less keen on investigating the wider institutional reasons that people are poor. The same could not be said about Daron Acemoglu (along with James Robinson, who plays

Banerjee's co-author role), who is most famous for his work attempting to explain, as his book title suggests, why nations fail.[61] Also, in stark contrast to Duflo, who favors small-scale interventions without examining the big picture, Acemoglu has a broad, sweeping explanation for the failure of nations that rests on poor institutions, which are a legacy of colonization.

Acemoglu argues that the roots of economic success or failure can be found deeper than what he claims are the surface causes that previous researchers had identified, like agricultural productivity or saving rates. These things may be important, but they are not causes. Rather, they are caused by the appropriate institutional structure. For Acemoglu, good institutions, like those in South Korea or the United States, are inclusive. They "feature secure private property, an unbiased system of law, and a provision of public services that provides a level playing field in which people can exchange and contract; it must also permit the entry of new business and let people choose their careers."[62] Poor economic performance is caused by failure to follow this straightforward policy prescription. Africa is a cautionary tale: "Property rights have been insecure and very inefficiently organized, markets have not functioned well, states have been weak and political systems have not provided public goods."[63] The greatest threat to property rights and markets is a predatory state in which government levies high and arbitrary taxes or expropriates land and property. This uncertainty reduces individuals' willingness to save and invest and is the root cause of low productivity, saving, and growth. Low educational attainment can be explained by the lack of incentive for people to get educated and the unwillingness of an extractive government to fund education.[64]

The root of poverty is found in rapacious states that enrich their member elites at the expense of their population. The question, then, is how did these kinds of destructive states come about? Much of the blame lies with the lasting legacy of colonialism.

While extractive institutions certainly existed in today's impoverished nations before the arrival of Europeans, colonial states often created rules designed to dispossess the native population and transfer resources from the colony to the home nation. This is not true of all colonies, however. Acemoglu argues that there is a crucial distinction between "settler" colonies, which had large European populations, and those where Europeans faced high mortality rates, and would not settle. In settler colonies, like the United States, Canada, Australia, and New Zealand, the settlers set up institutions that enforced the rule of law and encouraged investment (at least for themselves – they were less committed to the property rights of the native populations). At the other extreme, as in the Congo or the Gold Coast, they set up extractive states with the intention of transferring resources rapidly to the colonizing nation.[65] Further, the detrimental, predatory institutions set up by colonizers persisted well after independence because colonialism created political structures that inhibited growth and heterogeneous nations that were difficult to govern.[66]

The wealthy European nations, by contrast, owe their success to institutions that are beneficial to economic growth. "Political institutions placing limits and constraints on state power are essential for the incentives to undertake investments and for sustained economic growth."[67] Acemoglu and his usual co-authors note that the rise of Europe between 1500 and 1850 was concentrated in the Atlantic ports. They argue that not only was this due to the obvious mechanism of an increase in profits because of the lucrative colonial trade, but also, crucially, that the growing political strength of the emerging merchant class in the non-absolutist nations of the Netherlands and England resulted in increasing protections of private property rights from expropriation by the monarchy. In the English example, during both the Civil War and the Glorious Revolution merchants sided with those who wished to decrease the rights of the monarchy. Anti-monarchy victories in these conflicts resulted in "major checks on royal power and strengthened the rights of merchants."[68] In countries in which strong merchant classes were able to protect property rights by limiting the monarchy's privileges to grant monopolies and impose arbitrary taxes, economic growth followed.

The list of inclusive, non-extractive states is long and remarkably diverse, able to encompass widely varied development paths such as those of the United States, South Korea, and Lula's Brazil. Although Acemoglu's stress is certainly on the security of property rights, this should not be mistaken as favoring a free hand for business. Part of what constitutes inclusive economic policy is a limit to the power of large business, especially in the crony capitalist form that Acemoglu sees emerging in the United States currently. Markets are, therefore, not sufficient to ensure inclusiveness. They can tend to concentration, resulting in the rise of political and economic elites. One of the more inclusive, and therefore, beneficial periods in US development was when the anti-trust movement of the Progressive period in the early 1900s limited the power of the robber barons.[69] More currently, the rise of the Worker's Party in Brazil, from its creation of "participatory budgeting" in Porto Alegre to Lula's presidential election in 2002, was based on a broad coalition of social movements that sought to remove political and economic power from the hands of the military elite and their business allies and return it to Brazilians. Acemoglu notes that the rise of the Worker's Party corresponded to a period of strong economic growth, declining inequality, and much higher educational attainment in the country.[70]

Yet equality is not unequivocally beneficial. In a more current twist on the importance of incentives and private property rights, Acemoglu argues that what he terms "cutthroat" capitalist nations (the United States), with greater inequality, are more innovative than "cuddly" countries (Scandinavia) with stronger redistributive institutions. The argument is that the greater the gap between successful and unsuccessful entrepreneurs, the greater the innovation. For an individual country, redistributive institutions, like unions or social democracy, that improve the consumption of those at the lower end of the income distribution scale may result in increasing welfare. However, although cuddly Scandinavian capitalism may be appealing to an individual nation, since it is the United States' version of cutthroat capitalism that drives innovation in the world economy, the comfort of the cuddly is only possible through free riding on the inequality of the cutthroat. Acemoglu's evidence is that in the much more unequal United States, people work longer hours and file more patents per capita than in Scandinavian countries.[71] Therefore, if we were all Scandinavians, the world would be a poorer place.

An Evaluation of Acemoglu: Current International Events and the Innovative State

Arguing that colonialism has been a problem for the colonized is a welcome improvement on much economic analysis of the problems of development, which has often been ahistorical and free of context. Acemoglu is no doubt correct in arguing that the colonial experience left much of the developing world at a considerable, and persistent, disadvantage. However welcome Acemoglu's focus on the pernicious institutional legacy of colonialism may be, it overlooks much of what is currently hindering impoverished nations and places too much emphasis on property rights as the driver of economic success.

First, as an explanation of "why nations fail" it omits the more current external factors that have had a detrimental impact on developing nations that were outlined at the beginning of this chapter. While Acemoglu is very clear that the current predatory governments are a lasting legacy of colonization, the reason that nations fail appears to be the shortcomings of the state in the former non-settler colonies. Yet it is not only the governing elite that siphon off wealth from the impoverished citizens of the developing world. Nor is it often true that the governing elite are a result of a political process, democratic or otherwise, internal to former colonies. The opening segment of this chapter dedicated considerable ink to demonstrating that a variety of post-colonial institutions have played a crucial role in hindering the growth of poor nations. However, to illustrate why this point is so important we might use one of Acemoglu's own examples – Mobutu's reign in the Congo.

Acemoglu argues that the precolonial Congo was ruled by an absolutist king whose personal wealth stemmed from extracting income from his unfortunate subjects through slavery and arbitrary, exorbitant, taxation. The extractive institutions created no incentive for the population to save and invest since any increases in income would simply be taxed away. The negative impact of the king was such that people moved as far away from established roads and markets as possible to avoid the reach of their grabbing ruler. The arrival of the Europeans replaced the domestic despot with an even more gluttonous foreign one – most famously, the Belgians under King Leopold II. According to Acemoglu, on achieving independence, the extractive "institutions, incentives and performance reproduced itself" under the rule of Mobutu.[72] So it is extractive institutions that keep the Congo poor.

It is true that extractive institutions kept the Congo poor, but confining the post-colonial extractive institutions to the obviously parasitic domestic elite headed by Mobutu leaves much of the tale untold. Mobutu came to power after the previous democratically elected prime minister, Patrice Lumumba, was overthrown following a civil war in which the mineral-rich province of Katanga, supported by the Belgian government and mining companies like Union Minière, fought for independence. Lumumba's overthrow and subsequent death by firing squad was actively sought, financed, and supervised by not only the Belgians but also the United Kingdom and the United States (who attempted a CIA-inspired assassination using poisoned toothpaste). The United States then supported Mobutu during his reign from 1965 to 1997, during which he managed to amass a personal fortune of somewhere between $50 million, by his own reckoning, and $5 billion, according to the US State Department (one could argue that not all this money was squandered – Mobutu was the financial backer of the famous 1974 "Rumble in the Jungle" heavyweight championship between Muhammad Ali and George Foreman), while the average income in his country was 60 cents a day.[73] Not only was the United States involved in financing Mobutu's lengthy stay in power, in the late 1980s it also pressured the IMF and World Bank to extend $275 million in additional loans to the Congo over the objections of senior staff, who correctly predicted that there was very little chance that the country would ever be able to repay the loan given the rapacious nature of its current government.[74] Mobutu's predatory regime was not merely a legacy of colonial institutions but was put in place and supported by foreign firms and governments.

The Mobutu example is not an anomaly in *Why Nations Fail*. There is little mention of any post-colonial, negative, external influences on impoverished nations. The *Why Nations Fail* index has no listing for MNCs, foreign direct investment, or a role for the US military and espionage in shaping the fortunes of developing countries anywhere in the world. Yet, as we highlighted earlier in the chapter, MNCs extracted significant income from the developing world. Further, as was the case in the Congo and so many other countries, MNCs actively intervened in the domestic politics of the developing world. It is, therefore, inaccurate to paint the governments of developing countries as the sole culprit in extraction and corruption.

The IMF does merit some mention in *Why Nations Fail* – in five of the 462 pages. The problem with the IMF is that its "sensible" policies were "not adopted, not implemented, or implemented in name only."[75] The abysmal economic performance of countries that had IMF policies foisted on them in the wake of the debt crisis was not the fault of the policies themselves, but because "their intent was subverted or politicians used other ways to blunt their impact."[76] *Why Nations Fail* suggests that the real problem with the IMF was that, as outsiders, they failed to understand that their reasonable policies would be subverted by extractive governments. As was pointed out at the beginning of this chapter, the problem with the IMF was that an external body was imposing free market policies that were much more successful in ensuring that debt repayments continued to flow to creditors than in improving the economies of debtor nations. This is not to suggest that Acemoglu is always enamored of IMF policies. As part of an uncomfortably antagonistic response to Sach's[77] review of *Why Nations Fail*, in *Foreign Affairs*, Acemoglu and Robinson claim that Sachs

> seemed to think that IMF style adjustment policies (combined with repression of any opposition) he advocated in Bolivia were the secret to growth. Actually, perhaps he is right in some twisted way. After the reforms Sachs advocated got all of them fired, Bolivian tin miners went off to the Chapare Valley in eastern Bolivia to grow coca. That's what helped provide the social basis of the coca growers union, which then became a key political base for now president Evo Morales and his MAS party. As we argued in a previous post ... there might be some hope that the

MAS party is changing Bolivian institutions in an inclusive direction. So perhaps Sachs has played an important role in this, but of course not through the mechanism he had in mind.[78]

The IMF and the other current international economic institutions that have contributed to the poverty of the developing world are largely ignored by Acemoglu except when they are a handy stick with which to bruise an unkind reviewer. Developed-country influence on the developing world is not limited to the admittedly horrific legacy of long-dead generations, but is a current, ongoing phenomenon.[79] Acemoglu's focus on the persistent detrimental legacy of colonialism is no doubt a component of the explanation for the gap between rich and poor nations. It is also a welcome inclusion of historical and comparative analysis, albeit not one that will be unfamiliar to economists outside the mainstream. Yet, crucially, it ignores the most powerful contemporary determinants of the economic trajectories of developing nations.

Acemoglu's attachment to property rights as the main driver of economic success has been criticized as dangerously one-dimensional.[80] It downplays the crucial role that governments often play in innovation and growth. Although Acemoglu certainly advocates for "inclusive" economic and political institutions that level the playing field like those in Porto Alegre, even arguing for rules that would favor strong unions because of their important role in the democratic process,[81] the overarching message is that the role of government is to ensure property rights while avoiding the kind of crony capitalism that results in too much power for too few businesses. Yet other scholars have argued that many successful nations have relied extensively on a much more active state than that which is implied by Acemoglu. Ironically, this is particularly true of the nations that are currently strong advocates of non-intervention like the United States and United Kingdom. Both of these nations used tariffs and subsidies during their early industrializing period to foster the growth of particular sectors.[82] An active state can also be important in creating innovation according to Mariana Mazzucato's book *The Entrepreneurial State*. Contrary to the popular myth that the dynamism of the private sector can be contrasted with the moribund, bureaucratic government, many of the most important inventions, from pharmaceuticals to electronics, owe an often unacknowledged debt to the state. Just to take one example, the high-tech poster child Apple benefitted substantially from groundbreaking public innovation. It was the government that undertook the initial research that created the Internet, touch-screens, GPS, and voice-activated "assistants" like Siri, which are so vital to Apple's products.[83] According to Mazzucato, US venture capitalists waited for the state to take the big risks in research and development, and after companies like Apple adopted these publically funded technologies they hid their profits in tax havens, undermining the state's capacity for future innovation.

Mazzucato's arguments are a more recent take on those of Lester Thurow, the former dean of MIT's Sloan School of Management, who argued in *The Future of Capitalism* that private firms in a competitive environment will underinvest in research and development for several reasons.[84] First, research, especially at its more basic levels, is a positive externality. Spillover benefits mean that the social benefits are much greater than the private remunerations to the innovating firm. Second, private firms will not invest in research and development because they tend to have short-term time horizons. Corporations that must maintain shareholders' rates of return in a competitive environment cannot afford to undertake costly current investments for long-run payoffs. Since the return to basic, as opposed to applied, science is both longer term and more uncertain, it is unlikely that private firms in the United States would undertake this type of research. Because governments tend to be more indifferent as to who reaps the benefits from investments in innovation, nor is it focused on its own rate of profit, the state must play an essential role in the long-term investment in capitalist economies. According to Thurow, the claim that innovation occurs due to intense competition in a profit-maximizing corporate system is very misleading.

While Acemoglu's choice of exemplar nations includes those that have employed activist governments, the focus on property rights creates the impression that it is the private sector that generates innovation and prosperity, when, in fact, the role of government in most wealthy nations has been far more interventionist, using protectionist policies to foster domestic firms and spending billions in research funding to provide innovative technology for companies.

Finally, it is worth contesting Acemoglu's claim that cutthroat capitalism, with more inequality, is more innovative than the cuddly version. The logic behind this is that innovators need to be provided with the incentive of insecure incomes. Acemoglu's evidence for this is that in one model cutthroat nation, the United States, workers put in longer hours and residents have registered more patents per capita than in the more cuddly Scandinavian countries.[85] It is true that US workers toil longer than their wealthy-country counterparts. By the mid-2000s it was not uncommon in the United States for men to work more than 60 hours a week and women to work more than 50. A growing number of people took on two or three jobs. All told, by the 2000s, the typical American worker worked more than 2200 hours a year – 350 hours more than the average European, more hours even than the typically industrious Japanese. This was many more hours than the typical American middle-class family had worked in 1979 – 500 hours longer, a full 12 weeks more. Americans now sleep between one and two hours less than they did in the 1960s.[86] However, the connection between working hours and innovation is not immediately obvious. The number of hours worked by an increasingly income-constrained US labor force appears to be more a measure of desperation due to stagnant wages and unprecedented personal debt than of innovation. As will be suggested by JBC winner Saez (and his sometimes co-author Piketty) in chapter 3 of this book, there are two Americas, where a cutthroat existence is the norm for the vast majority and a cuddly one for the corporate wealthy. It is the American business class that is coddled with huge government subsidies, tax incentives, and public-sector funded research. They are better off than their fellow classmates in Scandinavia.

Even the superior patent per capita measure is fairly limited. If Acemoglu had chosen an alternative, like the World Economic Forum's (WEF) annual Global Competitiveness Report ranking of nations' innovation, his conclusions might have been different. The WEF is funded and populated by the world's largest corporations.

In the 2013–14 report, Finland ranked first, Sweden sixth, and the US seventh on innovation.[87] Further, to the extent that the United States is an innovative nation, one could question whether this should be attributed to its insecure and unequal income distribution, as Acemolgu has done, or to the entrepreneurial role of its government, as Mazzucato has suggested. Many scholars perhaps most famously Richard Wilkinson and Kate Pickett in *The Spirit Level* – have pointed out that inequality of outcome is a problem. Unequal nations fare more poorly than those that are equal on myriad social indicators, including health, education, social mobility, and violence.[88] According to Wilkinson, "if you want to live the American dream, you should move to Finland or Denmark."[89] Given the uncertainty associated with both Acemoglu's measures and sources, innovation would seem to be an unwise justification for the difficulties that come with pronounced inequality.

Conclusion

Duflo departs from some of the four pillars of the old mainstream. She does not engage in complicated mathematical modeling, and explicitly argues that people do not actually act in a rationally maximizing manner. Although she does not do particularly complicated econometrics, her focus on RCT trials demonstrates her dedication to the importance of scientific testing in the social sciences. Finally, her focus on altering individual behavior through subtle incentives is in keeping with maintaining the individual as the center of analysis.

Duflo's research can be usefully compared to throwing life jackets to the passengers of the *Titanic*. While her conclusions are narrowly correct, in a more profound sense they are very misleading because they ignore the social roots – macrofoundations – of so much poverty. People are not impoverished in much of the developing world because of their own misguided actions, but because of broad economic structures that systematically create impediments to their prosperity. It was the South that bore a disproportionate burden of repeated debt crises. Frequently, developing-country regimes that supported the transfer of wealth from the South to the North were supported by developed-country firms and governments. Yet rather than focus on these structural problems, Duflo uses social experiments to determine that a bag of lentils provides an incentive for a poor-country mother to travel to get her child immunized. Throwing life jackets is preferable to letting people drown, but a far better solution would be to keep people out of the water. Duflo's RCT solutions redirect attention away from analysis of the power structures that determine whether the economic ship is likely to sink or stay afloat.

In his work on development, Acemoglu departs, perhaps, more noticeably than any other JBC winner from the four pillars of the old mainstream. He often goes without formal modeling. Although he incorporates statistical testing, it is not the focus of his method, which is often much more historical. Acemoglu does not focus on the individual as the primary unit of analysis. Instead, he pays attention to the broad social and historical context in which individual actors operate and acknowledges the role that power can play, at least that of colonializers over their colonies.

In contrast to Duflo, and most of the other JBC winners, Acemoglu's analysis does explicitly focus on the evolution of institutions as an explanation of economic success or failure. He argues that slow economic growth in the developing world is caused by poorly functioning institutions that are an enduring legacy of colonial systems that were set up to extract resources. Yet his view of institutional failure is limited to developing-country governments failing to create a strong system of property rights and expropriating income for its own benefit. His analysis does not acknowledge the crucial continuing role of the international economic system in creating impediments for development through contemporary multinational corporations, developed-country governments, and international institutions like the IMF. Further, his claim that an equal nation can only thrive by free riding on the technological innovation of the more unequal cutthroat country fails to distinguish between who is cuddled and whose throat in being cut in the United States. It also may not be a very accurate gauge of what promotes growth, prosperity, and equality.

It would be difficult to argue that the external power of multi-national corporations, the IMF, and current foreign governments did not have a significant, if not determining, influence on the development of many poor countries. Yet it would be difficult to find any mention of these post-colonial external factors in either Duflo or Acemoglu. Duflo's focus on small-scale interventions leaves the larger structures in which those interventions take place unquestioned and unchallenged. Yet a crucial factor in the transformation of the currently wealthy countries was precisely the type of big-picture policies that led to the public health movement. Acemoglu does not fit nicely into the tradition of neglecting the social and economic macrofoundations that was criticized by Dow, Heilbroner, and Milberg. He does pay attention to the big picture. However, his focus on colonialism and its legacy in creating extractive developing-country governments neglects the current macrofoundations by ignoring the modern international institutions that create arguably the most significant impediments to the development of poorer nations.

chapter three

Labor, Income, and Inequality in the United States

There's class warfare, all right, but it's my class, the rich class, that's making war, and we're winning.

Warren Buffett[1]

Humans have occupied the earth for tens of thousands of years. For the vast bulk of that time, income as we think of it in the contemporary era did not exist. Access to food, clothes, shelter, and other resources in pre-capitalist societies was to a large extent determined by means other than the market. It is only in the capitalist era that market income came to decide how necessities and luxuries were distributed among members of society. Income and its distribution in capitalism, along with its accumulation in the form of wealth, can have significant effects on mental and physical well-being, social mobility, productivity, and economic growth. As capitalism has evolved, different nations have moderated their dependence on the market for income to varying degrees. Broadly speaking, the more social democratic the country the less income from the market matters with respect to an individual's access to the necessities of life. The difference between nations' dependence on the market for income determination has been intellectually mirrored by economists, who have engaged in an energetic debate about what determines income, the extent to which this should be left to the market, and what would constitute a fair distribution in society.

In the second decade of the twenty-first century, one of the main manifestations of this debate is a discussion of whether the growing income inequality in many nations is problematic. Hardly a day goes by without the subject of inequality of income (and wealth) making the headlines somewhere. Thomas Piketty's 685-page tome *Capital in the Twenty-First Century* became a surprise best-seller (1.5 million copies sold) by attempting to explain why inequality is inherent in capitalism.[2] The sudden obsession with inequality must come as something of a welcome frustration to academics like the perspicacious heterodox economist James Galbraith. He was analyzing inequality long before it became something of a cause célèbre among people like economics Nobel Prize winners Joseph Stiglitz and Paul Krugman, who seem to have become radicalized by the transformation of the economic landscape that we will describe in the next section.[3] Even some of the 2015 Republican candidates for president of the United States decided it was an issue that could not be ignored. Jeb Bush and Paul Ryan recognized inequality as a key campaign issue, although Piketty described their sudden concern and proposed solutions as "hypocrisy."[4]

With best-selling books, political parties from across the ideological spectrum, the media, and academics having jumped into the fray, it is no great surprise that a large number of JBC winners have touched on the topics of how income is determined, whether its distribution is fair, and what policies should govern it (although for some these topics are more central than others). We will introduce the JBC authors and analyze their work later in the chapter, but first we will provide a brief outline of why power and economic context are important in any analysis of income determination and division.

Power and Context: The Labor Market after the Second World War

There are two very different ways to characterize the labor market. The first, used by the old mainstream, sees it as a voluntary, mutually advantageous exchange among equals. The second, and we would argue more realistic, views it as a venue where the conflicting interests of powerful employers contest with those of employees dependent on wage income for their livelihood. In the latter tradition, economists Samuel Bowles, David Gordon, and Thomas Weisskopf once wrote that profits are the spoils of a three-front war that firms must continuously wage with their workforce, the government, and other companies.[5] The outcome of the battlefront between firms and their workforce not only influences profits but simultaneously determines labor income. As we saw in chapter 2 on development, incomes in any society depend in part on the rate of economic growth in that country. As productivity per person increases, more income is created. The "front" to which Bowles, Gordon, and Weisskopf refer is the division of productivity growth between workers and the firms that employ them. While this conflict takes place on an individual level every time a worker takes a job or negotiates a contract, the conditions under which that bargain occurs depends crucially on the overall economic context and the rules surrounding the labor market. This context is very different between nations, and indeed, even within the United States in different periods. The thirty years after 1980 were drastically changed from those preceding.

The "Golden Age" of US capitalism, between the late 1940s and the late 1960s, was characterized by rapid capital accumulation, high rates of profit, high levels of investment, rapid productivity growth, low inflation, low unemployment, and rising real wages. The failures of the free market during the Great Depression and the economic success of government military spending during the Second World War created a political climate where growth and full employment became the responsibility of the state. The US government sought to reduce severe economic instability using monetary and fiscal policy, including progressive taxes and unemployment insurance, to avoid severe downturns. This period marked the dramatic expansion of the welfare state to mitigate the inequities and hardship resulting from the market distribution of income, but these programs had the additional effect of strengthening the bargaining position of labor because a guaranteed income, even a meager one, in the absence of a job diminished the threat of unemployment.

The period immediately after the Second World War was also one of intense labor-management strife, which forced corporations to seek some kind of accord with the militant labor unions. Labor accepted corporate control over production, technology, plant location, marketing, and the labor process in exchange for job security, rising wages, and union recognition. Unions delivered an orderly and disciplined labor force and corporations rewarded workers with a share of the income gains made possible from productivity growth. Low unemployment, a relatively generous social safety net, and strong unions created an economic context in which workers had a degree of power in the labor market.[6]

The "Golden Age" did not last. The 1970s were characterized by a falling rate of profit, a productivity slowdown, accelerating inflation, rising unemployment, and eventually stagnating investment and an end to growth in real wages. In the United States, business and government responded to this economic malaise by turning to policy prescriptions designed to cut costs to firms in an effort to restore profits.[7]

In terms of labor costs, one method by which this was accomplished in the 1980s and early 1990s was high-interest monetary policy, which decreased consumption and investment. In the resulting high-unemployment environment, workers quit less, worked harder, and received lower wages as they were forced to compete with one another for increasingly scarce jobs.[8] The United Kingdom followed a similarly high-interest-rate policy at the same time under Margaret Thatcher's Conservative government. Alan Budd, adviser to the Conservative government and professor of economics at the London Business School argued, in astonishingly candid terms, that the contractionary monetary policy was seen by the Thatcher government as "a very good way to raise unemployment. And raising unemployment was an extremely desirable way of reducing the strength of the working classes ... What was engineered – in Marxist terms – was a crisis of capitalism which re-created the reserve army of labor, and has allowed the capitalist to make high profits ever since."[9]

The position of labor was further weakened by deliberate policy choices and increasing international competition. At both the state and national level, governments in the United States whittled away policies that protected labor, like unemployment insurance and rules surrounding the right to unionize. At the same time, labor-intensive manufacturing processes were increasingly located in emerging economies, creating a less secure workforce in the United States.[10] Writing in the late 2000s for the *New York Times*, Krugman, once a staunch denier that trade created a "race to the bottom" for wages, argued: "When we import labor-intensive manufactured goods from the third world instead of making them here, the result is reduced demand for less-educated American workers, which leads in turn to lower wages for these workers."[11]

It was these combined forces that helped improve the profitability of US firms after the 1980s. In fact, it is possible to argue that the restoration of business profitability came at the expense of the labor force. The chair of the Federal Reserve between 1987 and 2006, Alan Greenspan, argued as much in his testimony before the US senate, although he put a much more positive spin on the outcome:

> As I see it, heightened job insecurity explains a significant part of the restraint on compensation and the consequent muted price inflation ... The continued reluctance of workers to leave their jobs to seek other employment as the labor market has tightened provides further evidence of such concern, as does the tendency toward longer labor union contracts ... The continued decline in the state of the private workforce in labor unions has likely made wages more responsive to market forces ... Owing in part to the subdued behavior of wages, profits and rates of return on capital has risen to high levels.[12]

It was Greenspan's "traumatized worker" that enabled the US economy to function at low unemployment rates from the late 1990s on without allowing wages to cut into profits.

A return to profitability based on these policies had predictable consequences on the income of the vast majority of the labor force in the United States. Between 1979 and 2007 the real average hourly earnings of nonsupervisory workers fell by 3.7 percent. This marked a genuine transformation in the income of US workers, whose real earnings had increased 2.35 percent per year from 1948 to 1973. Given the remarkable remaking of the US labor market after the 1980s, it is no surprise that firms fared considerably better. The after-tax rate of profit in the nonfinancial corporate business sector increased by 20.4 percent between 1979 and 2007. Predictably, inequality, which had decreased after the Great Depression of the 1930s, increased dramatically after the 1980s. The share of total income going to the richest 1 percent of the population stood at 23.9 percent in 1928. It fell to about 10 percent in the post–Second World War period, but ballooned to 23.5 percent in 2007. In 1978 the average pay of a CEO from a large corporation was 29 times more than the average worker's. By 2007 that ratio rose to 352.[13]

Another way to illustrate how the labor market context after the 1980s changed the distribution of income between workers and firms is to compare the growth in hourly wages with the growth in labor productivity (the value produced by one worker in one hour). Figure 3.1 traces the growth of real hourly compensation, which includes the value of benefits as well as wages, and productivity. Prior to the early 1970s, compensation grew almost perfectly in line with productivity increases. In the early 1970s a gap begins to appear and, starting in the 1980s, the difference between the two grows increasingly large. What this suggests is that workers are receiving an increasingly small share of the value that is being produced in the economy. In a telling calculation that helps drive home the impact of what workers have lost, the Center on Wisconsin Strategy found that had wages tracked productivity between 1979 and 2004 as they had in the 30 years prior to 1979, the median hourly wage in Wisconsin would have been about $22.00 an hour as opposed to its actual level of $14.00.[14] The overall conclusion is that before 1980 the gains from productivity were being divided more equally between workers and firms. Post 1980, profits have been bolstered by increasing the proportion of the productivity gains that have gone to business.

To maintain household income, families have toiled longer hours for their meager pay. Employees in the United States work more hours per year than in any of the other wealthy countries, even the one-time epitome of work dedication, the Japanese. According to Robert Reich, professor of public policy at the University of

Figure 3.1 Productivity growth and real hourly compensation growth, non-farm business sector, 1947–2009

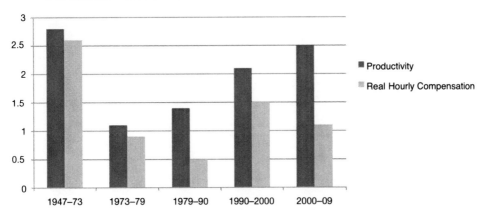

Note: Labor productivity is output, adjusted for price changes, divided by hours worked at all jobs. Real hourly compensation is the hourly cost to businesses, adjusted for price changes, of wages, salaries, and benefits paid to workers.
Source: US Bureau of Labor Statistics, The Economics Daily, available at http://www.bls.gov/opub/ted/2011/ted_20110224_data.htm.

California, Berkeley and former secretary of labor, American families worked twelve weeks (500 hours) more in the late 2000s than they did in 1979. This is not only about increasing female participation in the labor market. Americans now sleep between one and two hours less than they did in the 1960s.[15]

In an effort to maintain their consumption level despite stagnant or declining wages, American workers increasingly resorted to credit. As figure 3.2 shows, household debt in the United States rose sharply in the two decades prior to the economic crisis of 2008. By the mid-1990s households became net debtors, meaning that they borrowed more than they saved, a gap that became increasingly large through this period. Between 1990 and 2008 the ratio of total household credit (that is, both consumer and mortgage debt) to disposable income rose from 0.84 to 1.3. Workers' families, defined as one in which the head worked for someone

Figure 3.2 US household* and corporate net lending, 1960–2007 ($ billions)

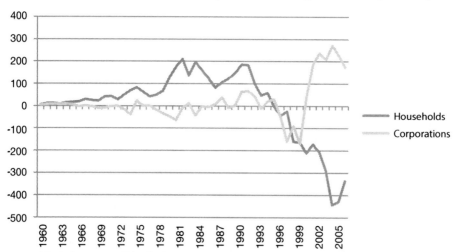

* Includes non-profit institutions serving households.
Source: F. Baragar and R. Chernomas, "Profits from Production and Profits from Ex-
change: Financialization, Household Debt and Profitability in 21st-Century Capitalism,"
Science & Society 76(3) (2012): 328. Calculated from US Department of Commerce,
Bureau of Economic Analysis, "Integrated Macroeconomic Accounts for the United
States" (2010), table S2.

else, had a higher incidence of debt than all families. While
77 percent of all families held some debt in 2007, 86.2 percent of
workers' families did so. Workers' households also had a higher
incidence of debt in the form of installment loans (58% compared
to 49%) and credit-card balances (54% to 46%) relative to all households taken together.[16] In the short term, this trend was beneficial
for many businesses. Instead of maintaining consumption through
the cost-increasing method of raising wages, firms were able to use
the interest-earning technique of lending. It also means that the interest on the loans represent an additional transfer of income from
the laboring debtor to the lending firm. As a result, the financial
sector grew in size and became much more profitable.

The shift in power in the macroeconomic context surrounding
the labor market in the United States since the 1980s has resulted in

a remarkable gap between workers' productivity and their wages. In the already relatively unequal United States income distribution has become even more tilted towards the very rich. American workers' compensatory response has been to work the longest workweek in the industrialized world and, until the economic collapse of 2008, to take on crushing debt, resulting in extraordinarily precarious economic circumstances for many families. Any explanation of income determination and distribution in society that does not include an analysis of this macro-context is at best incomplete and, at worst, a misleading distortion of the facts.

JBC Winners, the Labor Market, and Causes of Income Disparity

How do those who have won the JBC prize characterize the labor market? To what extent do they follow in the tradition of the old mainstream, in which an emphasis on individual analysis and rational maximization led to a characterization of the labor market as a place where individuals meet in a mutually advantageous exchange between relative equals? This approach downplayed or ignored the broad macro-environment that formed the overarching conditions in which this exchange takes place, especially the relative power between employers and their workers created by these macro-foundations.

A larger number of JBC winners have written on this topic than on our other subjects, but some, like Emmanuel Saez, are more closely associated with the labor market and income distribution than others. We will start with those who are less focused on the labor market and move to those who are almost exclusively dedicated to it.

Levin: Relationships

Although Levin may not have quite the public acclaim of other JBC winners like Levitt or Acemoglu, he is one of the most lauded young economists in the discipline today. After winning the JBC award in 2011 he was proclaimed a "Young Global Leader" at the World Economic Forum in 2012 and given a John Simon Guggenheim Memorial Fellowship in 2014. Much of Levin's work focuses on how information asymmetry (when one person in an exchange has more information than the other) impacts the functioning of specific markets. He has applied this idea not only to the labor market but also to the subprime credit market and timber auctions, among others.

In the labor market, Levin continues a well-established tradition of using what are called principal-agent models, with imperfect information. In these models, the firm (principal) is dependent on the effort of the worker (agent) for its profits. However, the firm cannot accurately observe the worker's effort, so it can't distinguish between hard-working and shirking employees. The general literature revolves around finding out how firms can elicit the desired amount of effort from their workers by offering the correct incentive structures.

Levin's additional wrinkle to this tradition has been to argue that in many labor market circumstances firms and workers have a "relational contract," in which employers and employees rely on an informal agreement about rules that are difficult to formalize.[17] While labor contracts contain many formal components, from the rate of pay to holiday time and insurance benefits, many other elements are not so explicitly spelled out. For example, opportunities for promotion or the likelihood of layoffs in a downturn are unlikely to be formalized, but firms and their workers may have an unstated understanding of how the firm is likely to behave towards its workforce.

As an example, one paper of Levin's examines whether, and in what circumstances, firms should make a relational commitment (like the promise not to lay off their workers in a slow period) to all their employees or only a select subset.[18] According to Levin, the advantage of the universal commitment is that it will improve worker motivation and induce greater effort. The predictable downside is the reduced flexibility for the firm during downturns. Levin argues that firms that renege on a universal relational commitment will find that their remaining, and now disgruntled, employees will decrease their work effort, making the firm less profitable. Levin argues that, among the conditions under which a universal commitment is undesirable, when the economic environment is unstable, firms are better off only extending the relational commitment to a select group of the workforce, through the use of temporary workers, for example.

An Evaluation of Levin

On one level, Levin's work offers conclusions that are reasonable, if unremarkable. It follows closely in the old mainstream practice of individual-level analysis, maximization (albeit with imperfect information), and mathematical modeling. Also in keeping with this tradition, his work suffers from its lack of attention to a broader context, especially the role of unemployment and labor market rules. Although he contrasts firm and worker strategies when the economic context is stable or turbulent, Levin's work assumes that the reaction of workers to a firm's commitment can be asserted without reference to broader labor market conditions. To see why this is a problem, take Levin's claim that when firms break a universal relational commitment by laying off employees, those disgruntled workers left at the company will reduce their work effort. It is possible that this might be true when the consequences of getting terminated are small, as would be the case when unemployment was low or there were particularly generous unemployment benefits. However, when workers are more desperate to keep their existing jobs, for example, when unemployment is high (as would most likely be the case when firms are breaking their relational commitment by laying off workers), the threat of job loss may well result in an increase in productivity as workers compete with each other to avoid the sack. What Levin neglects is that workers largely fear being unemployed, which confers labor market power to employers. This power will wax and wane depending on the broader conditions that surround the labor market – conditions that have deteriorated for workers since 1980.

Rabin: Fairness

Matthew Rabin is the impressively titled Pershing Square Professor of Behavioral Economics at Harvard. Like Duflo and Saez, he was awarded a MacArthur "genius" fellowship. He was an early pioneer of behavioral economics, which incorporates insights from psychology to modify the old mainstream economic assumptions about human behavior – the heavily criticized self-interested, rational, maximizing *homo economicus*. Rabin has altered this assumption about how people behave in a variety of ways that are germane to later chapters, but for the purposes of the discussion of the labor market his most relevant research adopts the behavioral idea that people care about fairness in addition to their own self-interest.

Rabin's conception of fairness is the relatively straightforward notion of tit for tat. If someone is nice to you, you will be nice back, even at a material cost to yourself. If someone is mean to you, you will seek to hurt them in return, again even if doing so hurts you. Rabin incorporates this idea into a game-theoretic approach that can be applied in a variety of exchanges, including those of the labor market. Like Levin, he follows the convention of modeling the labor market as a repeated game between firms and their workers, where workers choose a level of effort and firms choose a benefit level to compensate the worker. Rabin's contribution is to allow both the firm and the worker to care about the fairness of their exchange. So if the firm gives the worker a bonus, the worker will find it fair to reciprocate with more effort and vice versa. The big conclusion is that concerns about fairness can lead workers and firms to reciprocate their way to a high-effort, high-benefit relationship as long as "neither is too tempted by material concerns to cheat."[19]

An Evaluation of Rabin

Although Rabin has broadened the old mainstream assumptions about how people behave, he still maintains the focus on the individual and formalized mathematical modeling. Further, concepts as complicated and contextually influenced as fairness are still reduced to a very narrow definition (hurt me, I'll hurt you; help me, I'll help you) that could have been formulated by two kids sharing the back seat of a car. Leaving aside the problematic, but most likely correctable, assumption that firms are in a position to care about fairness rather than profits, fairness in society is surely a more nuanced, contested, and culturally influenced concept than that formulated by Rabin. A more careful definition of fairness, which moves beyond this curiously individualistic conception, would include people's concern for each other well beyond the confines of an immediate personal exchange.

Rabin's formulation of fairness is unable to explain why people's ideas of fairness vary over time, across cultures, and even between different groups in any given society. To take just one example of how the definition of fairness is influenced by a person's background and social position, people with MBAs and those "well educated in economics" are more likely than others to believe that social inequality is "inevitable" and that free market outcomes are fair.[20] What is fair in any society is a socially constructed idea that is subject to a contest between groups with different material interests over what society defines as equitable. Part of the reason for the labor market trends highlighted earlier in the chapter is that well-funded think tanks have made a concerted and successful effort to convince the US public that reducing the government's role in redistributing income and implementing rules that benefit workers (like minimum wages) are unfair as well as inefficient.[21] Other nations have expressed a preference for a definition of fairness that is much more egalitarian. Social democratic nations have repeatedly voted for universal social programs along with redistributive tax and transfer policies that suggest a very different social definition of fairness than that prevailing in the United States.

Other nations clearly prefer a broader conception of fairness than Rabin's narrowly individual definition.

Chetty: Taxes, UI, and Mobility

Like Rabin, Raj Chetty is best known for his ability to incorporate what are seen as more reasonable assumptions about human behavior. His work applies these insights, along with the traditional tools of modeling and econometrics to macro, big-picture areas, concentrating on three broad topics: taxation, social insurance, and social mobility. His devotion to the old pillars of mathematical modeling and econometrics is revealed in an article in the *Wall Street Journal* in which he claimed that he took up economics because he liked "the idea of applying mathematical rigor to important social problems."[22] As appears to be so often the case with JBC winners, Chetty earned a MacArthur "genius" fellowship to go alongside a slew of other awards, including the international version of the JBC, the Calvó-Armengol International Prize in Economics (Duflo was the first winner).

His work on taxation largely focuses on how taxes change people's behavior. He has done this with a variety of tax types, from dividend taxation[23] to the discovery that policies that require active decisions to increase savings (like tax subsidies) are far less effective than passive programs that require no action by savers (like automatic employer contributions).[24] However, perhaps the most germane to this chapter is his work using Danish tax records to investigate the connection between income taxes and labor supply. He does attempt to inject some realistic macro-facts into his modeling. Firms bargain with unions over wages and work hours. Workers unsatisfied with their employment conditions face search costs when looking for a new job. However, some of the standard, puzzling assumptions about the labor market remain. Most problematically, in equilibrium, "all workers are employed,"[25] an assumption that flies in the face of jobless rates in most nations and suggests that unemployment is not a common structural feature of the economy. Chetty and his co-authors apply this model to

Denmark and find that a noticeably large group of workers have incomes just below the level at which the top marginal rate kicks in. They argue that this is evidence that firms tailored their wage and hours offers to meet the desires of workers who were unwilling to work longer hours, because it would push them into a higher tax bracket. Further, the reduction in overall work hours associated with a higher marginal tax rate is caused not only by those individual workers who actively choose to curtail their time at work to avoid the higher tax rate, but also through more widespread effects as societal expectations and institutions around working hours change.[26]

Chetty also mounts a defence of unemployment insurance (UI) that challenges the standard canard of moral hazard (that any income from the state for the out-of-work will increase unemployment because workers will take a more leisurely approach to their job search). He does this in two different ways. The first is his alternative explanation for the fact that many people wait until their unemployment benefits expire before ending their spell of unemployment. Previously, this had been interpreted as the moral hazard associated with social insurance. However, using Austrian data, Chetty found that ending unemployment often meant exiting the labor market rather than finding a job, which is obviously not a sign of moral hazard. If only those who actually find employment when their benefits expire are counted, the estimates of the magnitude of moral hazard are considerably reduced.[27] The second tack is a reinterpretation of evidence that shows that UI contributes to longer unemployment spells. While this had typically been viewed through the negative lens of moral hazard, Chetty argues, more positively, that drawing on UI while unemployed also allows workers to maintain their consumption (the liquidity effect), avoiding the need to take unsuitable employment in a desperate rush back to work. The question is whether the utility-increasing liquidity effect or moral hazard dominates. He finds that at current rates, around 60 percent of the increase in unemployment length caused by UI is due to the beneficial liquidity effect, which improves the match between workers and jobs. Conceivably, the liquidity effect could be provided by the private sector, which could offer insurance in the event of loss of employment or credit until the worker finds another job. However, these services are not provided privately, making government UI necessary. This interpretation implies that UI is actually welfare enhancing, since it allows workers the time to find appropriate employment rather than forcing them to take the first job they are offered in order to keep the wolves from the door.[28]

Finally, and most recently, Chetty examined one of the most fundamental issues of fairness in any society, social mobility. The ability for anyone to go from rags to riches is a crucial justification for income inequality since it implies that there is equality of opportunity even if equality of outcome is absent. Chetty (as part of a team that includes Saez) finds that intergenerational mobility (as measured by the connection between a child's income and their parents' income and the connection between attending college and their parents' income) did not get worse in the United States between 1971 and 1993, although the increase in income inequality has made the consequences of being stuck in an intergenerational low-income trap more severe.[29] The same team also examined the substantial range in intergenerational mobility within the United States. For children born between 1980 and 1982, the probability of someone whose parents were in the bottom income quintile ending up in the top income quintile was only around 4.5 percent in Charlotte and Atlanta. However, those chances increased to over 12 percent in San Francisco and San Jose. While the authors are careful to stress that they have not established any causal relationships, lower mobility is associated with segregation, income inequality, poor school quality, lack of social capital, and single parenthood.[30]

An Evaluation of Chetty

Chetty's work does take on some of what we have described as the broad macro-issues like progressive taxation, the social safety net, and equality of opportunity. Yet, he does so in a curiously limited manner. His research uses modeling and statistical techniques that resonate with fellow economists (and are in keeping with the old mainstream), but thus far his use of these techniques has neglected how social policies alter the power relationships in the labor market. His work on UI is a good example. The problem with Chetty's liquidity justification is that the obvious solution to his role for UI might simply be to improve the private credit or insurance market for workers rather than resort to government-provided UI. However, this ignores the critical role of UI in the labor market. Guaranteed income for the unemployed increases the power of workers to influence wages and working conditions in the labor market and helps stabilize demand. Yet, these crucial roles are obscured.

Further, Chetty's work on social mobility fails to make the obvious comparisons between the United States and other nations. In noting that social mobility varies widely between different regions in the United States, he and his colleagues argue that "the main lesson of our analysis is that intergenerational mobility is a local problem, one that could potentially be tackled using place-based policies."[31] This emphasis on the United States may be in line with the focus of their study, but intergenerational mobility is not just a local problem. If that were the case, the United States would not rank so abysmally low in this regard when compared to other nations. In a study that measured the connection between the incomes of sons and that of their fathers in twelve OECD nations, the United States had the third strongest relationship, behind only Italy and the United Kingdom. In the United States over 45 percent of the wage advantage that high-wage fathers have over their low-wage counterparts is passed on to their sons, but this number is less than 20 percent in five of the OECD countries in the study (Canada, Finland, Australia, Norway, and Denmark – where it is only 15 percent).[32] Further, economist Miles Corak has found that there is a very strong connection between levels of inequality and barriers to intergenerational mobility. Greater inequality means that family income plays a larger role in determining income for the next generation.[33] A more complete explanation of social mobility in the United States must take into consideration the factors that make it perform so poorly as a nation, one of which is the level of its inequality, which is decidedly not a local phenomenon.

Finally, Chetty's tax study is based on a model that assumes there is basically no unemployment. In doing this, Chetty is following a time-honored tradition in economic modeling of the labor market, but it is one that flies in the face of even a casual glance at unemployment rates in almost every nation, including Denmark, the country Chetty is examining. Chetty attempts to justify this by claiming that for the year of his study, "the unemployment rate in 2000 in Denmark was 5.4%, among the lowest in Europe."[34] However, between 1980 and 2014, the unemployment rate in Denmark averaged 7 percent. Although the unemployment rate has been very low recently (it was 4 percent in 2014 and hit a low of 1.7 percent in 2008), between 1980 and the early 1990s, the unemployment rate ranged from a low of 8 percent to a peak of 13 percent in 1994.[35] These unemployment rates do not square easily with the assertion of full employment.

The employment context is important because, as we have stressed previously, high unemployment rates tilt power in the labor market towards firms and away from workers. At the beginning of this chapter we noted how unemployment played a crucial role in moderating the demands of workers in the United States, especially in the 1980s and early 1990s. This role is not isolated to this particular period. In the long sweep of history, the US capitalist economy has only enjoyed one prolonged spell of anything remotely close to full employment, the "golden age" that lasted for about thirty years after the Second World War. In all other periods, unemployment has been a frequent and, for workers, unwelcome visitor. Any labor market analysis that ignores this structural reality downplays the power that is created by unemployment.

Acemoglu Again: Unemployment, UI, Minimum Wages, Inequality, and Growth

In the last chapter we analyzed Acemoglu's research on development and innovation, which argued that private property rights and a cutthroat competitive society were crucial for economic growth. Acemoglu's rocket to economic stardom was largely fueled by his work on the centrality of institutions, but his research on the labor market and incomes would be a successful career for most economists. In contrast to his historically and comparatively based research on institutions, his work in the labor market fits squarely in the old mainstream tradition that has been termed the New Keynesian approach, which is the use of mathematical techniques to create a formal justification for Keynes's insight that economic downturns, and their accompanying unemployment, are actually possible. While one might think that a casual glance at historical unemployment trends would have been sufficient proof that full employment is seldom realized, economists, Acemoglu among them, have long sought to create formal models that can mirror real-world macro-fluctuations.

The hallmark of most of these models is that some "friction" needs to exist in the labor market that prevents wages from being sufficiently flexible downwards in the face of some negative economic shock. In one Acemoglu article, the friction is the always popular information asymmetry between workers and employers. While employers fully understand the value of labor at all times, workers do not. When the economy suffers an adverse shock, such as a decline in productivity, an unexpected slump in demand, or even Keynes's "animal spirits," the value of labor will fall. Employers will immediately know this, but the severity of the shock is only gradually understood by the more ignorant workers. As a result, workers' wage demands at the bargaining table are unrealistically high relative to their productivity, creating unemployment when workers are unwilling to work for what they incorrectly perceive to be a lowball wage offer.[36] The straightforward interpretation of this chain of events is that workers are unemployed because they are unwilling to work at the "correct" value of their labor after the economic shock.

Acemoglu has also weighed in on the growth in income inequality that was documented in the first section of this chapter. He argues that the main cause of growing inequality is "skill-biased technical change." His analysis starts out with the promising premise that the adoption of technology responds to profit incentives. The supply of educated workers has increased considerably in the last sixty years, creating a short-term decrease in the skill premi-um between high- and low-wage workers. However, in the longer term, the relatively lower wages of the highly skilled induces firms to invest in technology that complements these workers so that over time their productivity rises, increasing the difference between their wages and those of the less skilled. Acemoglu claims that this is the primary source of growing inequality in the United States.[37]

Acemoglu then uses this core idea to explain the differences in inequality between nations and analyze some of the factors that have been commonly associated with greater inequality. He argues that the difference between the unequal United States and the rela-tively egalitarian Germany is the latter's greater commitment to training lower-skilled workers.[38] He also argues that the skill bias to technical change can be exacerbated by international trade, which would suggest that studies that fail to include the increase in com-plementary technology for skilled workers brought on by trade will underestimate the impact of trade on inequality.[39] He makes a similar argument about de-unionization. We have pointed out that declining union membership and workers' growing trauma-tization has been a factor in the limited wage gains in the United States. Acemoglu argues that as high-skill workers have seen their relative wages increase because of the introduction of skill-biased technology their support for unions has been undermined. The de-unionization that results from what others might term declining solidarity eliminates the wage compression imposed by unions, exacerbating the inequality caused by skill-biased technology.[40]

Acemoglu and his partner in property-rights fame, James Robinson, have also weighed in on the growing income shares of the top 1 percent highlighted by Saez (see below for more detail). They argue that growing inequality is not inherently a problem and that increasing taxes on the rich to combat inequality can "choke off incentives." The real problem, they claim, is that the decline of quality mass schooling has reduced the equality of opportunity. More problematically, economic inequality has enabled the very rich to spend some of their fortunes creating political inequal-ity that has been used to tilt the policy landscape in favor of the wealthy in ways that reduce the opportunities for everyone else.[41]

Like Chetty, Acemoglu's work on the labor market involves using modeling and econometrics to justify the kind of government intervention that a free market economist would write off as unnecessary at best and debilitating at worst. Also like Chetty, he argues that unemployment insurance might actually increase economic efficiency. His logic is that if workers are risk averse, they will trade off lower wages for greater employment security. Firms respond to their low-wage workforce with lower capital intensity, which slows long-term economic growth. By providing workers with income when they do not have a job, unemployment insurance encourages them to seek higher-wage jobs despite the accompanying decreased job security. Firms with a higher-wage workforce will increase the amount of capital they use, increasing productivity. So, unemployment insurance increases wages and productivity, but also increases unemployment. Acemoglu notes that while this creates a case for unemployment insurance, it does not necessarily create a case for government intervention, since "it does not explain why the private sector cannot offer unemployment insurance."[42]

Acemoglu does something similar with the minimum wage, a long time bête noir of free market economists, who argue that it actually makes the poor worse off by reducing the number of jobs that will be offered to low-wage workers. Acemoglu puts a much more positive spin on the minimum wage, arguing that it reduces the profitability of hiring low-wage workers, encouraging firms to hire higher-wage workers and invest in more capital, which will cause more good jobs to be created and increase overall productivity.[43]

An Evaluation of Acemoglu

Acemoglu's work on incomes and the labor market is much more in keeping with the old mainstream techniques of formal modeling and statistical testing than his work on institutions and development. Like Chetty, Acemoglu has taken on some of the big, broad macro-issues. However, like Chetty he has done so in a manner that backgrounds the role of the economic system. His discussion of unemployment is superior to Chetty's labor market model in that Acemoglu admits that prolonged unemployment is possible. Yet, his search model contains the awkward implication that workers choose not to work at the wage they are offered. This is patently not what occurs in economic downturns where the problem is not workers refusing employment, but their being involuntarily laid off by firms. The obvious solution to unemployment in Acemoglu's model would be to improve the information available to workers about their actual productivity so that they would be willing to take lower-wage work. As we mentioned with Chetty, this ignores the crucial role that unemployment plays in ensuring profitability in the economic system. As we saw in the 1980s, when wages are cutting into profits, reduced investment and the resulting unemployment will put downward pressure on wages, which restores profitability. So unemployment is a structural feature in our economic system, no matter how frictionless the labor market.

Acemoglu's discussion of unions and inequality suffers from the same limitations. While he is correct in connecting the decline in unions to the increase in inequality, his claim – that this decline is due to international trade exacerbating skill-biased technical change that increases the returns to high-skilled workers and decreases their support for unions – is incomplete at best. Unions declined not only because of decreasing interest in their existence by workers, but also owing to a macro-context that was increasingly hostile to unions. The myriad reasons for the decline in unionism in the United States are too lengthy to detail here in any great depth, but they must surely include the role played by international trade facilitating the move of the manufacturing sector (an industry with a high union density) to low-wage nations and the successful attempt by employers to shed themselves of the burden of unions. Firms moved production facilities out of regions with high union density and aggressively lobbied for changes in labor laws that made it more difficult to form and maintain unions.[44] Again, Acemoglu's oversight concerns the constraints of the economic system itself. Firms cannot operate in a high-cost environment when lower-cost locations are available. By pushing up workers' wages and reducing management control of the workplace, unions often increase firms' costs. It is the negative impact of unions on firms, and firms' inevitable response, that contributed to the decline in unionization in the United States. Perhaps this obfuscation of the role of the economic system itself should not come as a complete surprise. In a *New York Times* interview Acemoglu stated that "the term 'capitalist' is not my favorite."[45]

Acemoglu's skill-biased technical change is also incomplete. The big changes in inequality are not between skilled and unskilled workers. Rather, incomes have grown fairly sluggishly well up the income spectrum, into what, by pretty much any definition, would be described as skilled workers. The big gains have been made at the very top of the income distribution in the top 1 percent. Further, the higher up the income spectrum one goes, the larger the gains. This data does not support a skill-biased explanation, which would benefit a much larger segment of the population. This point is reinforced by Paul Krugman, who uses Congressional Budget office data to show that the income shares of the 81st to 99th percentile of the population remained constant, at 35 percent, between 1979 and 2007. As we outlined in the first section of this chapter, during the same period, the income share of the richest 1 percent increased from 10 percent to over 20 percent. Further, the shares going to the top 0.1 percent, the truly rarefied air of the super-rich have increased most of all. According to Krugman, it is simply incorrect "to be saying that the important inequality issue is college graduates versus non-graduates ... Income inequality in America really is about oligarchs versus everyone else."[46]

The skill-biased explanation is a much more comforting and inclusive tale than the story told at the beginning of the chapter, since more people (and those who have the merit to acquire the proper skills) are included in the prosperity. It also suggests that the rise in inequality is a neutral, market response to changing returns to skills rather than the result of the very deliberate policy actions and corporate tactics detailed at the beginning of the chapter. Finally, as Krugman has pointed out, the solution to the skill-biased basis

for inequality is to increase educational attainment, a policy recommendation which is as banal and uncontroversial as it is likely
to be unsuccessful given the massive changes to the labor market
that have driven inequality in the United States.[47]

Like Levin, Rabin, and Chetty, Acemoglu ignores the power over
employment and state policies wielded by business as well as the
effect of unemployment on workers. They treat the macroeconomy
as a level playing field where equals decide whether to work or take
leisure time, hire or invest, ignoring the real power of business to
decide how many will work for how much. Chetty and Acemoglu
justify government intervention in social insurance and minimum
wages, but they fail to acknowledge how these policies alter the
powerful labor market position of firms, and, therefore, why business might be staunchly opposed to their well-meaning reforms.

Saez: Inequality, Its Causes, and Some Solutions

Like many of the other JBC winners, Emmanuel Saez is one half of
an almost inseparable partnership. He and his frequent co-author,
Thomas Pikkety, have become the name in income distribution.
In contrast to other duos, Saez's partner, Piketty, has become perhaps the more famous of the two after the publication of his solo
work *Capital in the Twenty-First Century*. However, Saez has hardly
gone unnoticed, especially in 2010, which was a big year for him.
He became the director of the Center for Equitable Growth at the
University of California at Berkeley, won the Best Young French
Economist prize, and was awarded a lucrative MacArthur "genius" fellowship and the generous $500,000 over five years that
comes with it.[48]

While Saez has contributed in other areas, he is most renowned
for his use of tax data to track income distribution, especially at the
top end. His general conclusion is that incomes have grown very
little for the vast majority, while the already well off have enjoyed
spectacular gains, resulting in rising inequality in the United States,
already one of the least equal among the wealthy nations. In their
most famous article on the subject, Saez and Piketty calculated that

between 1973 and 2000 the average income of the bottom 90 percent of American taxpayers fell by 7 percent. Incomes of the top
1% rose by 148%, the top 0.1% by 343%, and extremely well off in
the top 0.01% by an amazing 599%.[49]

More than the rest of his JBC counterparts, Saez focuses his work
on issues of broad social and economic importance by analyzing
the growing concentration of income and wealth. He is also a JBC
outlier in explicitly placing income distribution in a historical and
comparative perspective. His careful empirical work, tracing the
long-term fall and rise in US inequality has done a great deal to
actually put the debate about inequality and the fairness (or lack
thereof) of income distribution on the economic policy map.[50] He
has also provided valuable international comparisons that demonstrate that several nations have managed to buck the trend to
increased inequality, which suggests that global factors, like technical change or globalization, cannot be responsible for its rise.[51]

When Saez turns from chronicling inequality to explaining it,
he lands on more uncertain ground. He attributes the remarkable
decline in inequality in the 1930s and 1940s to the decrease in top
incomes from the combined shocks of the destruction of capital
values during the wars and the Great Depression.[52] He is less certain about the cause of the increase in inequality in the decades
after 1980. Having said that, he is more certain about what has not
caused it, dismissing Acemoglu's theory of skill-biased technical
change because the real changes in income distribution have come
within the college-educated population, not between those with
differing skill levels.[53] Saez's most definitive claim is that the rise in
the top income shares was caused by an increase in top-end wages.[54]
This creates the impression that it is somehow well-compensated
workers who are the big winners in the income sweepstakes, but
this is not really the case. According to Saez, the growth in wages is
really the growth in executive pay, part of which is due to the fact
that stock options are reported as wages when they are exercised.[55]
While it may be true that the evolution of top incomes since the
1980s includes more people who are actually working, compared
to the rentiers living off previously accumulated wealth who used
to populate the top income group, they are not necessarily workers

in the usual sense of the word, since they are almost exclusively working from the executive suite.

Setting aside the debate about whether the very richest are living in luxury courtesy of wage or capital income, Saez still must explain why top-end compensation has increased so dramatically. While he tries on a large number of explanations, he fails to find one that he thinks fits completely comfortably. In a *Journal of Economic Literature* article, he acknowledges a variety of other authors' possible explanations, from Cornell economist Robert Frank's winner-take-all society to superstar theory, without really championing any of them.[56] In an article two years later, he is a bit more definitive, highlighting four factors that he feels are the likely culprits: changes in tax policy favoring the rich; the increased ability of, and incentive for, executives to bargain for increases in their compensation; the return of inherited wealth – although this is much more true in Europe than the United States; and the growing correlation between earnings and capital incomes – the increasing trend for people at the high end of the earned-income spectrum to also be at the top end of capital-income distribution.[57] Of these explanations, the final appears to be a restatement of his claim that the wage incomes of those high up the income spectrum have increased. The third does not particularly apply to the United States thus far. This leaves the tax-cut explanation, which operates through the obvious impact of increasing after-tax incomes and the secondary impact of creating a greater incentive for executives to dedicate time and effort to bargaining higher rewards for themselves.

Saez has not quite ignored the factors that we argue caused the gap between productivity and compensation that we highlighted earlier in the chapter, but they are in no way centerpieces of his analysis. He claims that it may be "naturally tempting" to argue that "political variables" explain the changes in income inequality, since the trend started during the Reagan administration (and that of Thatcher in the United Kingdom). However, while political differences may be useful for explaining differences across countries – between the more unequal Anglo nations and the more egalitarian social democratic countries, for example – they have not been found to explain the changes over time within nations.[58] Yet, in a more popularly aimed article, far from the prestige of the top mainstream journals, Saez does suggest that the growth in inequality may be caused by the withdrawal of equality-creating policies and institutions in place during the post-war era like progressive taxation, strong unions, and corporate health benefits.[59]

Perhaps predictably for someone who has dedicated so much effort to demonstrating the growth in inequality, Saez is a strong advocate of government intervention to equalize incomes. He points out that the US federal tax system, while still progressive in 2004, has become much less so since 1960, mostly due to changes in corporate and estate taxes. While there has been a dramatic reduction in top income tax rates in this period (the top marginal income tax rate in 1960 was 91 percent), this is less responsible for the declining progressivity because the large number of deductions in 1960 meant that the actual tax paid from top incomes was much lower.[60] Tracking the decline in progressivity is important for Saez, who argued explicitly that top US rates (just over 42 percent) were too low in 2011and should perhaps be as high as 80 percent on a broadly defined income base.[61]

Saez's research suggests that the oft-leveled criticisms of progressive taxation – that it will slow growth and cause people to change their behavior in undesirable ways – are flawed. Perhaps the most damaging criticism of high-end taxation is that it slows economic growth, reducing the income available for all over time. If this were the case, as the top tax rates in the United States have fallen over the last few decades, there should be an impact on economic growth. Yet, Saez finds that although the tax cuts increased the income shares of the top 1 percent of earners, there was no positive effect on economic growth.[62]

This is not to say that there are no impacts of increasing top rates according to Saez. People do change their behavior in response to tax policy. Saez finds that people will use both timing and avoidance strategies to reduce their tax burden. Yet, despite these actions, Saez suggests that the appropriate response is not to decrease tax rates to reduce avoidance, but to broaden the base on which the tax is levied.[63] He also found that high-income earners in Europe (especially soccer players) migrate in response to tax incentives, suggesting both that nations can attract skilled labor using preferential tax policy and that mobility is an important constraint on progressive taxes. However, unlike many who argue that mobility makes high income taxation unwise policy, Saez is careful to point out that these "beggar thy neighbor" policies are not desirable from a global perspective.[64] Saez is a strong advocate of progressive income taxes, using both modelling and empirical work to argue that increasing progressivity of the tax system can be justified on both efficiency grounds, in the sense that this would generate more revenue, and in terms of society's social-welfare preferences.

Saez completes his Robin Hood act by not only taking from the rich but also giving to the poor, although unlike Robin Hood's fairly undiscriminating largesse, Saez wants to be more targeted. In an analysis of European welfare programs, he argued that income transfers have a large impact on recipients' choices about whether to work, but result in only small changes to decisions by the employed about how many hours to work. As a result, additional transfers to all low-income people from the already generous European welfare systems would come with a substantial efficiency cost as people would choose not to work. However, transfers restricted to the working poor would come with a much smaller efficiency cost.[65] In keeping with his advocacy of increased incomes for workers, like Chetty and Acemoglu, Saez makes a case for the minimum wage. He argues that despite the undesirable unemployment-creating effects of the minimum wage, it can still be a wise policy for governments that want to transfer income to low-wage workers. Saez further argues that a modest minimum wage should be augmented by transfers to low-skilled workers funded by taxes on higher earners.[66]

An Evaluation of Saez

Saez focuses his work on issues of broad social and economic importance by analyzing the growing concentration of income and wealth. He is also a JBC outlier (along with Acemoglu) in explicitly placing income distribution in a historical and comparative perspective. While he has certainly put in some time collecting data, his work on inequality does not rely particularly heavily on the old mainstream pillars of mathematical modeling or econometrics. His work justifying welfare for the working poor and progressive taxation, by contrast, does use these techniques. Perhaps it is a confirmation of the critique of the limits of these methods by people like Lawson and Dow, seen in the first chapter, that Saez's more groundbreaking work on inequality does not use these methods, but his less adventurous work on progressive taxation and welfare does.

More importantly, Saez lacks a convincing explanation of what caused the growing income inequality, which would require a political-economy analysis of how those at the upper end of the income distribution range have been able to turn economic policy to their advantage. His most commonly asserted causes of inequality are tax policy and changes to executive bargaining power. Logically, his preferred solution is to increase the progressivity of the tax system by increasing rates on the very rich, which would be both an important improvement to the current political economy in the United States and is, to put it mildly, politically ambitious. Yet, a more complete explanation of the causes of growing inequality would examine the "political variables," which Saez hints at occasionally but are not the focal point of his analysis, and the efforts of firms to restore their profitability after the 1970s. Only by focusing on these changes can one adequately explain the tremendous changes to before-tax income inequality that is driven by the increasing gap between workers' productivity and their compensation.

Further, Saez's claim that high income growth is due to wage increases is misleading (although less misleading than Acemoglu's). It makes it appear that changes in income distribution are due to changes within the wage-earning class. Yet, although a Goldman Sachs executive making $20 million a year might earn this in salary and stock options, this does not make the executive a wage earner in the same sense that a Walmart greeter or even an accountant are workers. The former controls the firm, while the latter two do not. A more accurate conceptualization of the income of the top 1 or 0.1 percent would be to view it as the income of a class that has benefited from the gap that has been created between wages and productivity as well as the growing financialization of the economy. Stressing wage inequality rather than class inequality hides the real reasons for the growth of top incomes, which lie in their power to alter the political and economic rules in their favor.

Conclusion

Given the centrality of income and labor markets in the economy, it should come as no surprise that a number of JBC winners have weighed in on this topic. Their areas of investigation, and therefore their conclusions, vary, from Rabin's individualistic and incomplete concerns for fairness to Saez's much broader evidence on inequality that has provided much of the ammunition for the recent debate over the fairness of US income distribution.

Despite these differences there are some significant common threads between a few of these researchers. Chetty, Acemoglu, and Saez are not free market or right wing economists. Their research often champions interventions, like UI and minimum wages, which would be anathema to the right wing and would improve the bargaining power of workers in the labor market. Saez is even something of an academic Robin Hood, creating an intellectual case for taking from the rich and giving to the poor. Yet, by abstracting from the economic system itself, especially the changes to the power relationships between workers and their employers, all these economists fail to acknowledge the fundamental causes of the changes in incomes since 1980 that Krugman claims has created an "oligarchy" of the rich in the United States.[67]

chapter four

Health, Healthcare, and the Individual

"At least I've got my health" is more than a mere platitude. Few things have a more detrimental impact on quality of life than poor health and, of course, dying makes life difficult to enjoy. When people think about improving their health and prolonging their lives, they probably think about doctors, nurses, scientists, and perhaps for the well-to-do, personal trainers and Pilates instructors. Yet economics plays a massive, and for most people, underappreciated role. Economics has a profound impact on the healthcare system, from how people are insured to what services they can access. More broadly, economics has a crucial role in determining the conditions under which people work and live, which have a substantial impact on health.

The JBC economist most associated with the healthcare system is Amy Finkelstein of MIT. In fact, she researches little else. Within this field, she has dedicated the vast majority of her research to insurance, which she describes as her "first love."[1] Her single-mindedness of purpose and attention to detail has garnered considerable acclaim. According to her former PhD advisor at MIT, James Poterba, "She is one of the leading health economists in North America, in the world."[2] This chapter will also address the work of other JBC economists, like Stanford's Levin, who have weighed in on health insurance, although not with quite the single-issue dedication of Finkelstein.

JBC economists have also done work on what makes people healthy outside the healthcare system. In keeping with his research in the labor market that uses insights from psychology to create a more realistic view of human behavior, Matthew Rabin drops the assumption that people can successfully maximize. In its place he assumes that people prefer immediate rewards to future ones, even if it makes them worse off, which we have seen in Duflo's work. As was the case with Duflo, Rabin uses this alternative assumption about human behavior to explain how people make decisions about their health.

This chapter will be divided into two broad sections. The first will deal with the healthcare system and will evaluate the work of Finkelstein. The second will look at health as an outcome of an individual's lifestyle choices using Rabin's research.

Power and Health Insurance: The Exceptional US Context

The United States has by far the most expensive healthcare system in the world and the worst health indicators among wealthy industrialized nations. In 2012 US life expectancy at birth was 78.7 years. According to the 2013 United Nations Human Development Index, this places it behind 38 other countries, including Cuba, Chile, and Costa Rica. In terms of mortality rates for children under five, it ranks a worrying 47th tied with Bosnia and Herzegovina and St Kitts and Nevis.[3]

These results are not due to underfunding of the healthcare system, which is in a class by itself in terms of spending. The United States spends more in absolute and relative terms than any other industrial economy. In 2011, it spent 18 percent of its GDP on healthcare. This is the highest of the 34 countries in the Organisation for Economic Cooperation and Development (OECD) by a considerable margin. The second-ranked country, the Netherlands, spent 12 percent, while the OECD average was a much more modest 9 percent. The combined level of public and private healthcare spending per person is also much higher in the United States than in any other country. It spent $8500 per person, while the second-highest nation, Norway, spent only $5700 and the OECD average was $3300.[4] The disparity between healthcare spending and health outcomes suggests that the United States has a particularly inefficient healthcare system (although this divergence is also driven by social and economic conditions, examined later in the chapter, that create a less healthy population).

Because of the high cost of many healthcare procedures, access is generally determined by insurance. In terms of health insurance, the United States is an outlier compared to other wealthy nations. Although the United States does offer public insurance to the poor through Medicaid and the elderly through Medicare, until very recently it was alone in the developed world in eschewing a government-led or regulated plan of universal insurance coverage. The United States was the only affluent country that would not ensure that, no matter how the rest of the healthcare system is owned and organized, its citizens would have complete coverage for necessary physician and hospital services. All other wealthy nations have deliberately removed access to healthcare from the realm of the market. Even after the passage of the Affordable Care Act (ACA) in 2010, the United States relied much more heavily on the private, for-profit sector to deliver its health insurance. Although the details of the ACA are byzantine in their complexity, the main thrust of the legislation is to ensure (some might use the word force) that all those who do not qualify for either Medicaid or Medicare purchase private insurance, either through their employer or as individuals. Regulation in other countries limits the use of co-payments or user fees that can hinder people's access to medical care, where in the US these are much more prevalent.

Evidence suggests that public insurance is superior to private in terms of both access and efficiency. This is not to say that public insurance necessarily guarantees full access to all health services. In countries that have public insurance, often not all types of services are covered. In addition, nations like Canada with public insurance often have debates about the wait time that patients face for more specialized services. This is what critics of public insurance refer to as "rationing," and they argue that those with private plans have better access to healthcare. However, private insurance has its own methods of rationing. In health maintenance organizations (HMOs), sick patients have more difficulty in seeking needed care than do healthy patients.[5] In one study, people with histories of illnesses like stroke or cancer had twice as much difficulty accessing medical care, even when they were insured.[6] Some managed-care companies also have a policy requiring preapproval of services, even in the case of emergencies, which can restrict access to suddenly needed care.

Private insurers can also deny coverage for certain services. There are very different levels of private insurance. People often have to pay out of pocket for things like deductibles. As firms have attempted to reduce their share of rising health costs, these kinds of gaps in insurance have increased. One study defined a person as underinsured if they met one of three criteria: self-financed medical expenses were over 10 percent of income, for low-income adults medical expenses were over 5 percent of income, or deductibles equaled 5 percent of income. According to this measure, approximately 25 million people in the United States were underinsured in 2007, up 60 percent from 2003.[7]

This might be excused if the private system was at least delivering efficient services to those who were insured. This is the claim of proponents of the private system, who argue that competition between firms creates an efficient market, providing the best benefits at the lowest costs. But this does not appear to be the case. Although many different US administrations have attempted to unleash the efficiency of the for-profit sector, savings have stubbornly refused to follow. In 1980, Medicare attempted to create cost savings by encouraging people to sign up with private HMOs. It set the payment rate to the HMOs at 95 percent of the average costs in the public Medicare program. The assumption was that private-sector efficiency would generate a 5 percent saving. It soon became clear that the HMOs were "skimming" more healthy patients and rejecting those more prone to illnesses, who were forced back into the public program. Despite a more inherently profitable client base, the HMOs could not compete with the public plan, mostly because their administrative costs ran at 15 percent compared with Medicare's 3 percent. Patients in the HMO program cost Medicare 12 percent more than those in the traditional program.[8]

The overhead cost of administrating a multi-payer system, for both reimbursing agencies and providers, is generally much larger than for a single-payer public system. In the United States, this waste has been estimated at around $400 billion, or about 15 percent of total spending. It is important to stress that although some of this (a healthy $10 to 15 billion) is insurance-industry profit, and another portion goes into the pockets of very well-compensated chief executives, the vast majority comes from simply running the bureaucracy of private, for-profit insurance firms.[9] It is not only US employers who are paying the bill for this expensive insurance system. The cost of an employer-based insurance plan for a typical family of four was $19,393 in 2011, double the $9235 in 2002.[10]

In addition to the higher bureaucratic costs of the private system, there are two other reasons that the costs of a single state insurance program would be lower despite the rhetoric of the benefits of competition. First, a single payer can put more pressure on suppliers to reduce costs. Second, private insurance companies are not cost minimizers, but profit maximizers. As a result, actions that increase costs but also increase profits will be undertaken. Private insurers can increase profits by spending money on things like marketing and risk estimation to set differential premiums. Neither of these costs needs to be incurred in a public system.[11]

Although there has been much fearmongering about the ability of government-funded Medicare to survive, its costs have been better controlled than those in the private sector. Inflation-adjusted costs have escalated by 400 percent per beneficiary under Medicare between 1969 and 2009, but private health insurance premiums have increased by 700 percent during the same period.[12] According to the Congressional Budget Office, the strictly government version of Medicare is 11 percent less expensive than private insurance.[13]

The question, then, is why the United States persists with inefficient and inaccessible private insurance. Part of the reason is the intellectual sway of the logic of consumer choice. Advocates of private insurance (and provision) argue that consumers should be able to choose the level of insurance, type of coverage, and medical procedures that they want rather than a government system that relies on compulsory taxation as the primary means of financing services. This argument resonates with the established common sense in an economy in which many of the goods and services on which we depend, from food to housing, come from the private market. The problem with this seemingly common-sense justification for consumer choice in medical insurance is that choosing healthcare is very different from other purchasing decisions. Most importantly, consumers are not in a great position to effectively evaluate their healthcare needs. While it is relatively easy for car purchasers to conduct a bit of research on the automobile market to reduce the information asymmetry between buyers and sellers, it is more difficult for medical consumers to read up on the latest medical techniques or scientific advances. This problem is exacerbated because medical interventions often can have different impacts on different individuals.

As a result of consumer naivety, decisions on healthcare options are not made primarily by patients but on the advice of their doctor. For most patients this advice has a strong enough weight that "doctor's orders" actually has some meaning. Doctors also act as gatekeepers into medical care, which restricts consumers' ability to act independently from their physicians. If the doctor could somehow fully understand the condition of the patient – their preferences, their desires, and their life circumstances – then it might be possible to claim that the advice of the doctor is the same as the wishes of the patient, but this symbiosis is difficult to achieve. Even if it were possible, a doctor's advice might not represent their patient's desires if they have differing interests, which is often the case. The fact that physicians are both expert advisers on what is necessary and suppliers of those services gives rise to the possibility of supply-induced demand (SID).

SID occurs when the physicians or other suppliers of medical services can influence demand. Intuitively, this would appear to be the case in healthcare, and empirical evidence suggests that it is common. This is the most plausible reason for the fact that high-cost and high-utilization medical systems like that in the United States have failed to produce superior healthcare results. When doctors own medical facilities, like labs, or technology like magnetic resonance imaging (MRI) machines, they prescribe their own services more often than doctors who do not have an ownership stake.[14] Studies have also found that an increase in physicians in a region results in an increase in per capita utilization and an increase in prices, which is consistent with the presence of SID. Some surgeries, like heart bypasses, are particularly susceptible to SID, since it is difficult for patients to determine whether the procedure is necessary. The research on this subject has consistently shown a relationship between the type of physician payment and the number of surgeries performed. In one study, the rate of surgery was 78 percent higher when doctors were paid through fee-for-service rather than by capitation (fee per patient), despite similar patient characteristics.[15]

As gatekeepers doctors also control patient use of much of the rest of the medical system, including technology, pharmaceuticals, specialists, nursing, and hospital visits. According to health economist Robert Evans, patient-initiated "first visits" (as opposed to referrals and other physician-initiated expenses) only make up about 6 or 7 percent of all spending. Since only a small portion of these are in any way unnecessary, patient-initiated waste only accounts for around 1 to 2 percent of total spending.[16] In the less regulated and more profit-oriented US healthcare system the effects of SID can be substantial. A survey of hospital chief financial officers by the Healthcare Financial Management Association found that each physician generated an average of $1.54 million per year in revenue for their hospitals. The most lucrative specialization for the hospital was neurosurgery, in which doctors generated an average of $2.8 million. Invasive cardiologists ($2.2 million a year), orthopedic surgeons ($2.1 million a year), and general surgeons ($2.1 million a year) also ranked above the average. Surgeons are not the only big revenue generators. General internists generate $1.7 million a year, and family physicians $1.6 million each year.[17]

The limits of applying the logic of consumer sovereignty to medical insurance was famously exposed in a RAND study in the 1970s, which randomly assigned US families to health plans that required them to pay zero, 25, 50, or 95 percent of their medical expenses. If consumers could correctly evaluate the value of different healthcare treatments, those that paid 95 percent of their medical expenses should reject treatments for which the cost exceeded the medical benefit and take those whose benefits were greater than their costs. The study found that, predictably, those who paid a greater proportion of their expenses used fewer health services, and so consumers were cutting back on health usage. However, they used less of all kinds of services, even those that would have been extremely valuable. Further, poorer families, predictably, were more negatively impacted by higher payments and cut back more than the wealthy on medical care that could have led to substantial health benefits. For example, people on lower incomes with high blood pressure showed a greater treatment take-up in the free plan, resulting in a mortality improvement of 10 percent.[18]

A second plausible reason for the US persistence with private health insurance is that the firms profiting from this system have invested heavily in political lobbying to maintain it. As early as 1920, the American Medical Association (AMA) issued a declaration opposed to any "system of compulsory contribution insurance" that was "provided, controlled or regulated" by the government.[19] When public health insurance was considered as part of the New Deal, the AMA levied a $25 fee on its members for an unprecedented multi-million-dollar campaign in the late 1940s, portraying public insurance as a Communist plot to bring "socialism" to the United States that would result in "low-grade assembly line medicine."[20]

In an effort to maintain the current private, for-profit system, the insurance industry has spent considerable sums on political activity. The most direct way in which this occurs is through lobbying and donating to politicians. For example, in the 2010 elections, the insurance industry made $44 million in campaign contributions.[21] There is also considerable overlap between government and private industry. In 2009, 350 former members of Congress and government staff were under contract to lobby for insurance, hospital, or medical groups.[22] The health insurance industry has also dedicated considerable time and effort to influencing public opinion. It does so in a wide variety of ways, from direct advertising to funding think tanks and academic positions. The former chief of public relations for health insurance company Cigna, Wendell Potter, offers an insider's view of the industry's efforts to influence the debate around public insurance.[23] When the Clintons were proposing healthcare reform in 1994 the insurance industry funded a $14 million advertising campaign in which "Harry and Louise," two burdened everyday suburbanites, lamented the state of a hypothetical future government health program run by bureaucrats, with the tagline "When they choose we lose."[24] These are not isolated examples. One healthcare expert summarized: "There have been five well-motivated and serious attempts to enact a system of universal coverage in the United States over the last 100 years. On each occasion, health care stakeholders have pulled no punches in using disinformation and obfuscation to confuse and mislead the public."[25]

The private health insurance system in the United States compares poorly with the public model used in the rest of the world. It is kept in place because of a mistaken insistence that consumer choice will lead to desirable outcomes, a belief that both benefits, and is reinforced by, a for-profit insurance industry that has spent lavishly to maintain the private status quo. As we turn to Finkelstein's work, we will evaluate the extent to which her research reflects or abstracts from these health insurance realities.

Health Insurance: Finkelstein

Finkelstein first became interested in insurance because it appeared to be "an area where private markets might not work well, where there might be scope for welfare-improving public policy."[26] According to Finkelstein, and many others in the economic mainstream, the primary problems in health insurance are moral hazard and adverse selection.

Moral hazard occurs when people who are insured change their behavior, taking fewer precautions, which makes them more likely to use their insurance.[27] In the last chapter, this general idea was applied to the labor market by economists who argued that offering workers UI benefits would prolong their unemployment since the insured would not search for new jobs as diligently as the uninsured. In healthcare this concept occurs if those who are insured use more healthcare than the uninsured both because they will take fewer actions to prevent themselves from having to use healthcare and because the costs of healthcare are not fully borne by the patients, so they will consume services whose benefit to them is less than the cost of provision. Theorists in the moral hazard tradition argue that insurance creates risky and wasteful behavior that will increase the use of healthcare.[28] If this theory is correct, universal public insurance should lead to an overwhelming increase in demand for healthcare. It also implies that the problem with any kind of health insurance is that consumers do not directly pay for the costs that they incur. The lower the "out of pocket" costs the greater the moral hazard. This theory implies that the healthcare system will be more efficient when patients are responsible for a greater proportion of the medical bill, which has euphemistically been termed the "consumer-directed" approach.[29]

The other "textbook" problem is known as adverse selection. The idea behind adverse selection is that insurance attracts customers who are more likely to claim. If insurance companies set fees according to the amount that they are likely to spend on healthcare for the average person, then individuals in good health and unlikely to require medical care will not purchase insurance. Those more prone to illness, by contrast, will find insurance an attractive proposition. Insurance companies will then be burdened with high-cost customers and an unprofitable business. This becomes a vicious cycle if the insurance companies raise their rates since, as a result, they will only then be attractive to an even less healthy customer base, and so on.[30] The most obvious solution to the adverse selection problem is to ensure that everyone takes out insurance. This is part of the logic behind universal public systems. The United States has attempted to replicate at least the universal aspect of this in Obama's ACA by forcing everyone not insured with one of the government programs to purchase private insurance.

Both of these problems imply that healthcare is driven by consumer choice and that the primary problem revolves around insurance companies' lack of information about the people they insure. If insurance firms could accurately tell who was not eating their vegetables and who was busy clogging their arteries, they could charge each of their clients appropriately and the problems of both moral hazard and adverse selection would be solved.

Finkelstein's work is very much in this tradition. In her review of the famous RAND health insurance experiment, she argues that the take-home lesson is that people will economize on their healthcare as the price increases. So, traditional health insurance, in which people do not have to pay directly, will create moral hazard.[31] Fellow JBC winner Levin comes to similar conclusions about the problems created for the insurance industry by private information held by consumers. He argues that insurance markets would be efficient if people's premiums reflected their costs. However, Levin argues this is often not the case (to some extent because private information is difficult to obtain but also because of government regulations that prohibit firms from charging different premiums based on the state of their clients' health), which results in a welfare loss.[32]

Finkelstein's major contribution is to develop models with more than one source of private information in insurance markets. For example, if moral hazard exists, it logically follows that increasing the amount that individuals pay, through cost sharing or high deductibles for example, will reduce healthcare spending as people have a greater incentive to take actions that will reduce their use of medical services. However, if people can choose different types of insurance, with different levels of deductible or cost sharing, it is possible that they will select the type of insurance based on their expected level of moral hazard. In plain language this would mean that people with a higher propensity for moral hazard will avoid high-deductible or cost-sharing plans. The implication of this is that providing a high cost-sharing option may not create the desired spending reduction.[33]

Finkelstein also applies the idea of multiple sources of unobservable private information to the problem of adverse selection. If adverse selection is present, then high-risk individuals will be more likely to purchase insurance. Yet, empirical studies have found mixed support for the presence of adverse selection. Finkelstein attempts to resolve this empirical inconsistency by inserting another source of private information – the level of risk aversion. People that are risk averse are more likely to purchase insurance. If risk averse people are more likely to take actions, like using seat belts, which make them low risk, then there are two types of people that purchase insurance: high risk, in which adverse selection is present, and risk averse, which creates "advantageous selection," because those who purchase insurance are less likely to claim. This means that the standard conclusion of adverse selection inevitably creating under-insurance no longer holds. From a public policy standpoint, advantageous selection creates too much insurance, creating a case for a tax or even a more draconian policy of banning coverage.[34]

Finkelstein has also studied whether public insurance crowds out private. She examined how the provision of Medicare (public insurance for the elderly)influenced the demand for private drug insurance. Medicare offers partial insurance, meaning that some medical costs, like prescription drugs, are uncovered. People who want to top up their Medicare coverage can purchase private insurance. If adverse selection results in more low-risk people opting out of private coverage as a result of the partial public program, it is possible that the demand for private insurance might be reduced, even for services not covered by Medicare. So, it remains an open question whether the introduction of partial public insurance like Medicare will increase overall levels of insurance coverage. Finkelstein found no real evidence of crowding out in this case, with no decline in private prescription drug insurance for those over sixty-five.[35] By contrast, Medicaid (public insurance for the poor), does crowd out private insurance for long-term care. The long-term care insurance market in the United States is very small. Only about 10 percent of the elderly purchase private long-term care insurance, which only covers about 4 percent of long-term care costs. Finkelstein argues that the means testing and secondary payer provisions (if any alternative coverage is available, that coverage is used first) in Medicaid create an implicit tax that creates a disincentive to purchase private long-term insurance because purchasing private insurance merely replaces coverage already provided by Medicaid.[36] It is important to note the default assumption in this study. Rather than considering an expansion of Medicare and Medicaid so that they are more comprehensive or, even more radically, universal public coverage, as is the case in Canada,

Finkelstein argues for restructuring Medicaid to eliminate the implicit tax as a necessary condition for expanding private insurance.

Finally, Finkelstein has examined the impact of public insurance on healthcare. She has been applauded for her careful empirical work on Medicare and her use of the Oregon "experiment" as a test of Medicaid.[37] Her work on Medicare covers two different aspects of a change from private to public insurance: health expenditures and health impacts. She finds that in the first five years after the introduction of Medicare, public insurance was responsible for over half of the 63 percent growth of hospital expenditures.[38] This relationship is further demonstrated by the fact that in the areas of the United States where the introduction of Medicare resulted in the greatest expansion of insurance coverage, costs also increased the most. At least part of this increased spending was due to the adoption, as a result of Medicare, of new technologies that were then used to also treat non-elderly patients. In an article published a year later, she found that in its first ten years Medicare had no discernible impact on elderly mortality, although in her typically careful way, she does concede that a very small reduction in mortality, of the range that her study cannot statistically rule out, is possible. More positively, Medicare did play an important role in reducing the risk associated with high medical bills for the elderly. The benefit of decreased risk must be weighed against the cost of Medicare, which in Finkelstein's ledger, includes the moral hazard of increased medical use caused by the decreased out-of-pocket price and the costs of raising revenue through the tax system. The conclusion of her cost-benefit analysis is that the social benefits were less than the social costs, although, as always, this is very carefully qualified as subject to "considerable uncertainty."[39]

Finkelstein is also part of a larger team that uses Oregon's expansion of Medicaid as a natural testing ground for the impact of public insurance. In 2008, the state expanded Medicaid by holding a lottery that drew 30,000 names out of a pool of 90,000. Contrasting those who were admitted with the lottery "losers" provided a handy natural experiment on the benefits of the program. Although at the time of writing this research was in its very early stages, Finkelstein (and the many others on this team) suggests that it does reduce out-of-pocket medical expenses for enrollees, who are 40 percent less likely to have to borrow money or miss paying other bills and 25 percent less likely to have medical bills sent to a collection agency than non-enrollees. They also have better self-reported health outcomes, with enrollees more likely to claim they are in good health and less likely to be depressed.[40] However, these positive self-diagnoses do not seem to translate into objective improvements. Although enrollees had greater access to healthcare, they had no measurable health improvements (at least in terms of blood pressure, cholesterol, or glycated hemoglobin).[41]

What has Finkelstein discovered with her studious empirical testing? Neither Medicare nor Medicaid has had any noticeable impact on measurable health outcomes, although at least under Medicaid people feel they are healthier. Medicare has driven expenditure increases in healthcare. The major benefit of public insurance programs has been the reduced exposure to risk and financial uncertainty, but at least with Medicare, this benefit is outweighed by the social costs caused by moral hazard and tax collection. This accounting does not reflect particularly positively on public insurance. Yet, Finkelstein's research, thus far, has not made the obvious comparison between the privately oriented system in the United States and the more public systems used in other comparable nations, despite an acknowledgment that her conclusions linking Medicare to health spending increases raise "the natural question of whether a similar mechanism can explain why most other OECD countries have also experienced sustained growth in the healthcare sector over the last half-century."[42]

An Evaluation of Finkelstein: Consumer Sovereignty versus SID

Finkelstein's work is true to what we have termed the old mainstream in economics. It is based on formal mathematical modeling, rational maximizing individual self-interest, and econometric testing. It also takes a very particular view of the source of the market failure in healthcare. For Finkelstein, like many of her economic predecessors, the asymmetry of information revolves around insurance companies being unable to accurately perceive the health and lifestyles of their customers. Moral hazard stems from consumers changing their behavior once they are insured. Adverse selection is caused by more risky consumers purchasing more complete coverage. If this asymmetry did not exist the health insurance market would function smoothly, with companies being able to charge efficient premiums based on risk.

Finkelstein uses a consumer-driven analysis of the healthcare industry, which has been the dominant model, at least in the United States. The general thrust of this tradition is that consumers will obtain healthcare if the marginal benefit of improved health exceeds the marginal cost of obtaining that care. An "efficient" level of care is provided and consumed that reflects the preferences of consumers and the cost of healthcare. If insurance provides free healthcare, this model would conclude that reducing the cost of a visit to the doctor (it would not fall to zero because there is still a cost for people's time) will lead to people overusing medical care, since they will demand care for which they have a lower marginal benefit. Historically, this kind of model has had more academic influence in the United States than elsewhere. A WHO international comparison of textbooks of health economics pointed out that the three dominant US textbooks used a market-oriented approach in which individual utility maximization was the principal behavioral assumption. This is remarkably different from a text by preeminent Canadian health economist Robert Evans that is a "clear critique" of the consumer-led model.[43]

Yet, an analysis that places the consumer at the center of the decision making process badly misrepresents healthcare reality. Health is characterized by information asymmetry, but it is not insurance companies' ignorance of their customers that is the major issue but profound uncertainty for consumers about what sort of treatments would be best for them. While Finkelstein's take-home lesson from the famous RAND study is that consumers respond to price incentives in healthcare, as we showed earlier in the chapter, because consumers often couldn't accurately evaluate the benefit of procedures, they used less of all kinds of services, even those that would have been extremely valuable. The problem with a consumer-led model is that people are largely incapable of distinguishing valuable treatments from those that are less important or even modern-day snake oil.

Finkelstein's concern about public programs crowding out private is a particularly American take on health insurance. Other wealthy nations have deliberately allowed the public sector much more scope to correct for the inherent problems of private insurance than in the United States. At its most fundamental level, the argument for less private and more public rests on the egalitarian idea that access to healthcare should not be dependent on income. This sentiment is enshrined in article 25 of the UN's Universal Declaration of Human Rights, which states that everyone "has the right to a standard of living adequate for the health and well-being of himself ... including medical care." President Obama's 2010 ACA demonstrated that it is possible to provide something approaching universal insurance coverage under a private system, but it also demonstrated that the US commitment to a private system required particularly complex and tortured legislation when a single payer, public system is more egalitarian and efficient.[44]

Finkelstein does acknowledge that insurance companies can have "loading factors," which might include the administrative costs of marketing or verifying claims. However, these costs are not treated as unnecessary waste in the system (as she does with raising government revenue), rather they are the regular costs of doing business. According to Finkelstein, the presence of these loading factors in an insurance industry characterized by adverse selection leads to the conclusion that it may be socially inefficient to insure everyone since the additional loading costs will mean that there are people for whom the additional costs of insurance are greater than their willingness to pay.[45] A more obvious conclusion might be to switch to a system that avoids these costs in an effort to ensure that the whole population has insurance.

Finkelstein's conclusion about Medicare's lack of impact on mortality has also been questioned by recent research. There seems to be little doubt that as people move into Medicare at sixty-five they use more medical services, indicating that they were restricting their medical usage in previous years, but as we have seen, access to medical services does not always translate into better health outcomes.[46] A 2009 study attempted to isolate the impact of Medicare on health outcomes by looking at the differences in mortality for people admitted to hospital with severe illnesses just before and after their sixty-fifth birthday. The authors argue that these people are more likely to have their mortality impacted by differences in insurance coverage. They find that the over-65 group had a 20 percent reduction in mortality that persisted for nine months after the date of admission.[47]

Finkelstein's consumer-driven approach to health insurance, in which people can accurately assess the costs and benefits of their treatments, does not take into account SID, in which health providers can determine healthcare demand. The idea that the health sector, like development and the labor market, is not a level playing field but subject to power relationships is not taken into account in Finkelstein's research, as it has been by non-mainstream economists like Robert Evans. Finkelstein also fails to treat the US health insurance system as the inefficient and inaccessible outlier that it is. Among the industrialized countries it is only the United States, to this point, that relies so heavily on a relatively unregulated private, for profit, insurance delivery. It also has the least accessible and most costly healthcare system. Yet this exceptionalism is treated as the norm in Finkelstein's research.

Power and Context: The Social Determinants of Health

When thinking about what influences the state of their health, most people probably think of the healthcare system, but the most important factor is undoubtedly the condition in which they live. The pioneering work arguing that income (and the health-improving things that income can buy, like better nutrition) is more important than healthcare intervention was done in Thomas McKeown's research on the decline of infectious disease.[48] His work was supported by Nobel Prize–winning economic historian Robert Fogel, who examined the historical records on diet and height – on the assumption that people with better nutrition are larger – and concluded that almost the entire reduction in mortality during the 1800s was due to improved nutrition.[49] Living conditions are also heavily influenced by the uses to which income increases are put. As noted in chapter 2, infrastructure projects such as sewage systems, fresh drinking water, and draining swamps, which are what most people associate with public health, as well as broader social measures to improve the general public's working and living conditions – from a social welfare system to rules on occupational safety and health – were also crucial in improving people's health as nations developed.[50]

This general idea can be highlighted by an interesting natural experiment that took place between 1955 and 1960. The Navaho-Cornell Field Health Research Project attempted to correct for the below-average health of residents of the Navaho native American reservation by bringing in modern medical services. This ambitious project provided a well-equipped ambulatory care facility, physicians, nurses, trained Navaho health aides, and transportation for hospital care. However, it did not change the impoverished social and economic conditions of the residents, who were living in windowless, one-room log-and-mud dwellings with dirt floors, with alarming rates of illiteracy and endemic poverty. By objective criteria the project had some successes to report – some common problems among the Navahos, like ear infections among children, were sharply reduced. However, at the end of five years there was virtually no change in the overall disease pattern, and little, if any, change in the death rates, including a shockingly high infant mortality rate which persisted at three times the national average. The investigators concluded that the disease and mortality patterns of the Navaho were a result of the way they lived and could not be changed until basic changes took place in the tribe's way of life.[51]

Given the importance of living conditions for health outcomes, an important debate has emerged – which will by now be a familiar refrain to the reader – about whether it is the individual or broader social forces that are primarily responsible for these conditions. In 1977 John Knowles, the president of the Rockefeller Foundation, argued that the responsibility lay with the individual. Similarly, Marc

Lalonde, Canada's minister of national health, argued that our nar-
cissistic society was undoing progress towards better health through
"indolence, the abuse of alcohol, tobacco and drugs, and eating hab-
its that put the pleasing of the senses above the needs of the human
body."[52] In this view, personal choices about smoking lead to lung
cancer, lack of exercise leads to obesity, and dietary choices contribute to heart disease. In a simplified form, this approach argues that
the increase in heart attacks is caused by over-consumption of unhealthy foods, and the solution is to cut down on the intake of ba-
con McCheeseburgers. A more academic wording of the argument
would be that "human behavior is the single, most important deter-
minant in variations in health outcomes."[53] This emphasis is often
called the behavioral or lifestyle approach to health.

A competing claim, often associated with what is called the social
determinants of health (SDOH) is that, while individual choices are
obviously important, much of what influences health is beyond the
scope of individual decisions and is determined by our environment, our working conditions, even our social stratification.[54] To
paraphrase a leading international health text, economic, political,
and social systems play an important role in determining both the
environment in which people live and their ability to access the
resources (things like food, shelter, and medical care) necessary to
enjoy a healthy life.[55]

If we take smoking as one obvious, harmful behavioral choice,
it might help to illustrate the social nature of what appears at first
glance to be individual decisions. Tobacco is not only toxic but also
addictive, and addiction commonly commences around the age of
fourteen. Consequently, the presumption that users rationally and
voluntarily choose smoking as a lifestyle is not wholly appropriate.
Further, smoking behavior is very sharply graded by socio-economic
class (the lower the class the more likely people are to be addicted
to tobacco), undercutting the argument that smoking represents an
individual choice, and suggesting instead that it is at least in part the
product of social position. In other words, people make individual
lifestyle decisions within a social context. Finally, even those in the
higher social and occupational grades who do choose to smoke have

fewer of the adverse effects of tobacco.[56] With a qualification for the addiction part of the story, a virtually identical tale could be told of the supposedly lifestyle impacts of diet and exercise. Working long hours, not being able to afford childcare, and lack of access to recreational facilities make people much less likely to choose exercise as part of their lifestyle. The SDOH theory argues that choice, and the health consequence of that choice, is heavily influenced by social and economic factors.

The economic circumstances that influence our health are ubiquitous, but in the following section we have included a few of the most important examples in the areas of food, the environment, work, and inequality to demonstrate that restricting the discussion of health to individual decision making is dangerously limited.[57]

No one refutes the importance of eating right. Yet, the economics of modern food production and consumption in the United States have contributed to some major health problems.[58] To take just one example, the increase in consumption of saturated fat that boosts cholesterol is much more a result of the economics of industrial agriculture than of individual choice. It is less expensive to keep cattle in a stall, away from exercise, making it easier to feed and fatten them, than to allow cattle to roam the range. Instead of eating grass and slowly growing into marketable animals, cattle are fed grains (mostly corn, which is even fed to fish, thanks to generous US government subsidies to corn farmers) spiked with chemicals. This results in marbled steak, which affects the quality of the meat. Not only does marbled steak have a higher fat content, this process of "producing cattle" changes the partially unsaturated fats into hard, white, much more saturated fat.[59] So, the food industry has transformed the old type of animal fats into a new type, which is remarkably efficient at increasing the cholesterol in our blood.

Health is also impacted by environmental factors, which are beyond the direct effect of individual choice. In a telling illustration of the ubiquitous nature of chemicals in our environment, when Andrea Martin was forty-two years old she was diagnosed with an advanced case of breast cancer. After aggressive treatment, cancer was found in her other breast, and later still, she was found to have a large malignant brain tumor from which she died. Martin was a volunteer subject in a study that measured the "body burden" of chemicals in people. Biomonitoring by the Centers for Disease Control (CDC), led by researchers from the Mt Sinai School of Medicine in 2003, revealed that she had at least 95 toxic chemicals in her system, 59 of which were cancer causing. Her group had an average of 91 compounds in their bodies, most of which did not even exist 75 years ago. More worryingly, on average, 53 of the chemicals were linked to cancer in humans or animals.[60]

The environment in which we live is being altered by the chemical-laden processes of modern production. Worse, not only are these changes poorly understood, but little effort is being made to understand them. To provide just one example, a 2010 report by the President's Cancer Panel expressed concern over the influence of chemicals on cancer rates. Both the number of new chemicals and the extent to which these have been tested for safety are worrying. Every year between one and two thousand new chemicals are created and introduced into industrial processes. "Only a few hundred of the more than 80,000 chemicals in use in the United States have been tested for safety." The panel also criticized US regulatory oversight of chemicals, claiming that is was ineffective due to, among other reasons, inadequate funding, weak laws and "undue industry influence."[61] Given the limited understanding of the chemicals that are in our environment and how they influence human health, lifestyle decisions alone are unlikely to be adequate protection.

Given the centrality of work in people's lives, it is unsurprising that it has a profound impact on health, beyond even its role in determining income. Negative health results appear more frequently for those at the lower end of the work hierarchy. Evidence suggests that those who can make decisions actually have less stress, while those who have less autonomy over their work life generate increased adrenal hormones and fat energy.[62] In the now famous Whitehall study of British civil servants, those in higher positions had significantly better health results than those lower down the hierarchy. What makes this study particularly interesting is that none of the people in the study could be considered "poor" in any absolute sense of the word. Yet the coronary mortality of those in the lower ranks (clerical and manual) was three and a half times that of those in the top levels. This difference in mortality persists even when obvious differences in risk, like smoking, body mass index, and cholesterol, are accounted for. As a very interesting rebuttal to the behavioral school, the study found that those at lower pay grades smoked more than those at top grades (which in itself calls for an explanation), and that those in the higher echelons who did smoke were much less likely to contract smoking-related diseases than those lower down.[63]

It is not only one's place on the job ladder (or lack thereof) that impacts health. So too does one's place on the income spectrum, although, obviously, the two are often related. Part of the reason for the connection between income and health is that it is most often the less affluent members of the working class who live in hazardous proximity to environmental dangers. This result has been found in many different countries.[64] In the United Kingdom, communities were ranked from poorest to richest and assessed for the number of unfavorable environmental conditions in each area. Over 20 percent of the poorest communities contained three or more problematic conditions and only 28 percent had none. In contrast, 71 percent of the richest areas had no adverse environmental conditions and none had three or more.[65] Another study ranked the environmental hazards from a wide variety of industrial sources in 368 communities in Massachusetts. All but one of the fifteen most "intensively burdened towns" has an average household income of under $40,000.[66]

In general, the poor live shorter, less healthy lives. A study examining health indicators, such as mortality, health status, and activity limitation, of both children and adults found a clear health gradient between the wealthiest, middle, and lowest income groups.[67] In the United States, once people reach twenty-five, college graduates live five years longer than those who do not finish high school. If every person in the United States were to have the mortality rate of those who attended (even if they did not graduate from) university, it would save seven times as many lives as all biomedical advances.[68] The incidence of cardiac arrest in the poorest 25 percent of neighbourhoods in four big US cities is almost double that in the richest quartile.[69] In the United Kingdom, people in the poorest neighborhoods die, on average, seven years earlier than those from the wealthiest. They are also sick for much longer while they are alive. The difference between richest and poorest areas measured in disability-free life expectancy is seventeen years.[70] The general conclusions of this research are nicely summarized by Michael Marmot, who claimed, "Social inequalities in health arise because of inequalities in the conditions of daily life and the fundamental drivers that give rise to them: inequities in power, money and resources."[71]

Matthew Rabin: Problem Behavior

The assumption that people's health is determined by behavioral choices fits nicely with the individualistic bent of mainstream economics. One of the early, and most influential, studies modeling how individual choice influences health was Michael Grossman's article that borrowed from the economics of human capital formation to argue that people invest in their own health in much the same way that people invest in education. People start off with a stock of health that deteriorates, at an increasing rate, over time. Investments in health (doctor's appointments or trips to the gym) are both a consumption good and an investment that improves people's future health to reduce the number of days spent in unproductive sickness. People make optimizing decisions on how much to invest in health based on the costs and benefits. The Grossman model predicts that the amount people are willing to spend on their health will be impacted by a number of factors, like the prices of health-improving goods and changes in income. For example, investments in health are more expensive for people with higher incomes because of the wages foregone during the time spent on health. On the other hand, "the higher a person's wage rate the greater value to him of an increase in healthy time."[72] Overall, the second impact should outweigh the first, leading to an increased demand for health as wages rise. This theory is a classic example of the old mainstream's use of the rational self-interested maximizing individual in mathematical modeling.

Rabin is most famous for incorporating insights from psychology to modify the much criticized assumption of rational maximization. In different works, Rabin has altered this assumption in a variety of ways (which are covered in other chapters, as we have already seen in chapter 3 on the labor market), but the one that is the most relevant to health research is his adoption of the time inconsistency problem that we encountered in Duflo's work using RCTs to improve the behavior of the poor. Rather than making rational maximizing decisions over the long term, Rabin argues that people prefer immediate to future well-being. This present-time bias can manifest itself in either doing currently desirable things when you should wait or avoiding currently undesirable things when they should be done. He further refines this insight to divide time-inconsistent people into two personality types. Sophisticated people are aware of their self-control problems and so are less likely to wait to undertake any activity whether fun but harmful or painful but beneficial. They will avoid procrastination of undesirable but beneficial activities, but are overeager to undertake immediate rewards that are harmful. Naive people are under the impression that they are not time inconsistent and erroneously think they will make the right decisions for their long-term selves in the future. They will inadvisably procrastinate when faced with immediate costs.[73]

According to Rabin, the time inconsistency problem has implications for how to interpret actions that impact health. If someone packs on a few pounds as a result of delaying their visits to the local gym, time-consistent rational maximizing would interpret this as the sweaty costs of working out outweighing the flab-decreasing benefits and is, therefore, welfare improving. In a naive time-inconsistent person, this same action would be caused by a welfare-decreasing self-control problem.[74] Similar conclusions can be arrived at for any behavior in which present costs yield future benefits – from stopping smoking to looking for a job. The implication of self-control problems is that not all individual choices can be assumed to be welfare improving.

An Evaluation of Rabin:
The Limits of Individual Choice

While health is influenced by individual decisions, and no one is suggesting that eating a large portion of lard each day is a wise dietary course of action, research in the Rabin vein completely ignores the economic context in which these decisions occur. In keeping with many of the JBC winners, Rabin has dropped the strong assumption of self-interested maximizing rationality. Relaxing this assumption does open up room for the possibility that individual choices might not be welfare improving for those in society who suffer from time inconsistency.

However, he has retained the focus on individual choice, without digging particularly deeply into what creates preferences beyond the tendency of people to immediate gratification. People's enjoyment of potato chips and cigarettes is taken as a given, so that if naive time consistency is not present, consumption is welfare improving. This analysis is in stark contrast to a perspective that might inquire about the social context of these activities: how preferences are manipulated by marketing, the addictiveness of the ingredients, and the breakdown of consumption by social status.

Further, his division of society into naive and sophisticated is very different from the distinctions between different social and economic classes that we argued were important in explaining health outcomes. Rabin's framing of health problems as the outcome of individuals' inability to maximize their welfare leans very heavily on the lifestyle or behavioral model in that poor health is caused by bad individual decisions (although, like Duflo, Rabin has framed these choices as understandable human characteristics rather than individual personality failures). Rabin's problems of self-awareness hide the fact that people's latitude for decision making is crucially influenced by their socio-economic position. Eating healthy foods is far easier on a high income than low, yet Rabin attributes this choice to individual self-awareness. Further, many health outcomes are the result of conditions over which people have little choice, such as exposure to environmental hazards. While Rabin divides society into sophisticated and naive, much more meaningful distinctions could be drawn by dividing society into high and low income, position on the job ladder, and neighborhood exposure to environmental hazards.

Interestingly, Finkelstein does acknowledge that a person's neighborhood can reveal a great deal about their health. She used postal codes as "unobserved observables," correctly deducing that where someone lives is an indicator of socio-economic status, which has an impact on health. However, she does not use this insight to point out the disparities in health among economic groups in society, but to argue that since people from more affluent neighborhoods live longer and healthier lives, insurance companies should be using this data to more accurately assess the riskiness of their clients. She speculates that the probable reason this straightforward improvement was not undertaken by insurance companies in the United Kingdom during the 1990s was fear of negative public reaction that might lead to government regulation.[75]

Focusing on the individual, while ignoring the broader economic circumstances in which the individual exists, provides the misleading impression that we are responsible for our own health. To a certain extent, this is, of course, true. No one is recommending a lifestyle of sloth and gluttony. However, as one study concluded, "Health inequalities result from the differential accumulation of exposures and experiences that have their sources in the material world ... The effect of income inequality on health reflects a combination of negative exposures and lack of resources held by individuals, along with systematic under investment across a wide range of human, physical, health, and social infrastructure."[76]

Conclusion

The United States has uniquely poor health outcomes. This is, in part, the result of its healthcare system, which is the most expensive, inefficient, and inaccessible of the industrialized nations. It is also the system that relies most heavily on private, for-profit, corporations. Providing the intellectual justification for the unique US system, the health economics literature in the United States is also very different from that in the rest of the world. The US literature is dominated by consumer sovereignty, influenced by the problems of moral hazard (consumers will overuse the health system if they don't have to pay directly for treatment), and adverse selection (only those most likely to use insurance will buy it). Finkelstein and Levin's work is very much in this tradition. The problem with this interpretation, and Finkelstein and Levin's work, is that the assumption of consumer sovereignty is untenable. In the healthcare market, producers profit from the asymmetric information that they hold over their desperate patients, creating SID. This framework leads to a very different analysis about the causes of, and solution to, market imperfections in healthcare. A theoretical framework based on SID supports universal public coverage and a public system of controls for efficiency and effectiveness, precisely the system that is favored in other industrial countries, and which delivers superior results to those in the United States. Finkelstein and Levin's research does not delve into the power structures in the health market dominated by large insurance companies. Nor do they do the kind of cross-country comparisons that would reveal that more efficient, effective, and accessible healthcare options are practised in other industrialized countries. Nor do they engage with the academics, domestic and foreign, who emphasize that for-profit healthcare delivery and insurance is bad medicine.

Poor US health outcomes are also the result of how people live. Rabin analyzes this in terms of individual choice. He argues that people prefer immediate rewards to future ones, but prefer future costs to current ones, a condition dubbed time inconsistency. Rational maximization may have been dropped as an assumption, but methodological individualism remains. This interpretation ignores the myriad health-altering factors that are part of the economic system, and a person's place in it. It fails to acknowledge that so much of what impacts health, from our position at work to the environment in which we live, is beyond individual choice.

chapter five

Crime

Crime has a particularly prominent place in the public consciousness. It is possible that this is merely due to the dramatic stories churned out by media outlets working under the famous maxim, "If it bleeds, it leads." Yet crime is a genuine cause of concern for many people in countries with high crime rates like the United States. People are rightly frightened about the shocking violence of homicides, and the popular imagination is fueled by high-profile gun rampages. According to the US Department of Justice, there were 15,000 homicides – 4.7 per 100,000 people – in the United States in 2012, which at 41 a day is fairly alarming.[1] In a less deadly vein, muggings, burglary, and Bonnie and Clyde–style bank heists also add up to considerable losses for the victims. The FBI estimated the total value of property stolen in the United States in 2012 at the not inconsiderable sum of $13 billion.[2] Given the prevalence of crime, especially violent crime in the United States, and its hold on the populace, it is not surprising that economists have moved into this area of enquiry, previously the purview of sociologists and criminologists.

Despite the hold crime has over the popular imagination, the United States witnessed a significant, long-lived, and completely unexpected decline in crime rates starting in about 1991. This understandably caught many commentators, who had been predicting "chaos" in US cities,[3] by surprise, since crime rates, especially for violent crime, had been increasing at an alarming rate in the

1980s. Although the 2012 statistics on crime make for sobering reading, compared to the 25,000 murders in 1991 (a rate of 9.5 per 100,000), things have improved remarkably.

Among the JBC winners, Steven Levitt is most closely associated with work on crime, which, along with cheating and corruption, is his self-declared favorite area of inquiry.[4] He has looked into the income distribution within criminal gangs.[5] He has attempted to analyze the impact on crime of policing strategies,[6] incarceration,[7] and capital punishment.[8] He has also found that crime is a significant contributor to urban flight.[9] In this chapter, we will be focusing on this kind of more traditional crime, but Levitt has also written on areas that might be considered on the fringes of criminal activity, like schoolteachers helping their classes cheat on standardized tests,[10] sumo wrestlers throwing matches to improve their rankings,[11] whether white-collar workers would obey the honor system in paying for their lunch-room bagels,[12] and the systematic, though entirely legal, fleecing of their clients by real estate agents.[13]

Although Levitt is best known for his work on crime and corruption, his publication list spans a wide variety of other social sciences. In the realm of politics he has looked at the impact of interest groups on political decisions and dismissed the importance of campaign spending on election results. On the subject of race, he has examined the differences in test scores, used "black" names to test for discrimination, and looked at the economic lives of blacks in public housing.

If success is measured in terms of name recognition and book sales, Levitt has succeeded far beyond the wildest dreams of any social scientist. He is best known to the broader public for the bestseller *Freakonomics* (over 3 million copies sold), or perhaps now the slightly less successful sequel, *Superfreakonomics*, but he has also garnered considerable recognition within the discipline. Since 1997 he has been at the University of Chicago, where he earned tenure in only two years.[14] Levitt's success has made his method something of a trendsetter in the discipline. *The Economist*'s survey of economics' rising stars claims they are "recognisably the intellectual heirs of Mr. Levitt."[15]

The Context for Crime

Outside of the upper echelons of large criminal organizations, crime is usually seen as undesirable. Most analysis of crime usually attempts to understand who commits crimes, why they do it, and how to reduce the propensity to break the law. In terms of the causes of, and reductions in, violent crime, any analysis must examine the context that makes the United States such a violent-crime outlier compared to other nations.

Perhaps the most well-known of the authors who place crime in its social and economic context is Loïc Wacquant, who argued that the booming US economy of the 1990s was the largest factor in the reduction in the crime rate, accounting for as much as 30 percent of the decrease. According to Wacquant, while economic growth did not lift many youths from the urban ghetto since many of the jobs were temporary and low wage, the Latino population especially benefited from the upturn in the unskilled labor market. The young black population also responded to the improved economy by attending post-secondary education in much greater numbers, reducing their involvement in street crime.[16]

In addition to examining the economic context that leads to crime, Wacquant pays more attention to the social conditions in high crime areas. He argues that the increase in female immigration with greater opportunity in ethnic labor market niches helped reduce the crime rate, at least on the borders of the ghettos. In addition, younger siblings actually took to heart the cautionary tale that was their older brothers' life of crime. The violence associated with drug dealing also declined as oligopolistic gangs signed peace treaties. Finally, Wacquant argues that some credit should be given to the social pressures of those who organized to rid their neighborhoods of crime.[17]

It is also important to note that the violent crime rate in the United States is much higher than in any other wealthy nation, which suggests that there is something particular about the context in the United States that encourages crime. Wacquant points out that after the big decline in the 1990s, crime in the United States was high by 2000, but not abnormally so. In the 2000 International

Crime Victimization Survey (ICVS) the United States tied for seventh highest of the seventeen countries in the study in terms of crime incidence (the number of crimes per 100 inhabitants). It actually had a lower incidence rate than Sweden and the Netherlands, was about equal to Canada, but was considerably worse than Japan and Switzerland.[18] The big difference is that the United States had more violent crime. In 1991, when US crime rates were at their height, the US murder rate for males aged 15–24 (24.4 per 100,000) was approximately *ten times higher* than in Canada (2.6), Sweden (2.3), and the United Kingdom (2.0), *twenty-five times* higher than in Germany (0.9), and *fifty times higher* than in Japan (0.5).[19] Even after the significant decline in crime rates during the 1990s, the United States still had much higher murder rates. Between 1999 and 2001 the United States averaged 5.5 homicides each year per 100,000 people. In Canada this number was 1.77, while the EU average was 1.59.[20] This homicide rate is for the whole population rather than the high-crime cohort of youth. In 1998, after much of the fall in homicide rates, US youth (aged 10–29) had a homicide rate of 11 per 100,000. This is over six times the Canadian rate (1.7), 12 times the rate in the United Kingdom (0.9), 18 times the French rate (0.6), and 27 times the Japanese rate (0.4).[21] It is not just murder that was high in the United States, even after the 1990s decline. In 2000 the rate of violent crime in the United States was more than double that of Canada (500 per 100,000 people vs. 220). The United States had 324 aggravated assaults for every 100,000 population, while the Canadian rate was less than half of that at 143.[22]

Some countries in Europe, with very different attitudes towards crime and punishment, are enjoying considerable savings on their law and order spending. Sweden and the Netherlands are shutting down jails because of under-crowding. In the Netherlands, which has more prison staff than prisoners, almost half of all prison capacity is empty. The number of prisoners has fallen by 10 percent over the last decade in Sweden, and by 20 percent since 2005 in Germany.[23] In the Netherlands, community service has replaced prison terms for short-term jail sentences and electronic tagging has become more widespread. In Sweden, a "broadly humane approach to sentencing" has reduced the dependence on incarceration. Rather than locking people up, rehabilitation programs for drug addiction and violent behavior are recommended. There are even provisions for post-prison support including members of the public who "volunteer to befriend and support offenders under supervision."[24]

Canada might be a better comparison for the United States since it is closer to home and has a more similar economic context. Canada managed a similar crime-rate reduction between 1991 and 2001, while the number of police per person fell 9 percent and the ratio of those in jail to the total population decreased 7 percent (in the United States these increased by 10 percent and 47 percent respectively).[25] Uniformed police in New York City increased from 27,000 to 41,000 from 1993 to 2001, a remarkable upsurge in enforcement. By 2001 NYC (population 8 million) had half as many uniformed police as the whole of France (population 60 million), heavily concentrated in particular "problem" urban areas.[26]

A discussion of crime in the United States should include an understanding of the context in which crime occurs. The decline in crime in the 1990s must surely be influenced by a changing economic and social context in the United States. Similarly, the fact that the United States remains such an exceptional outlier in terms of violent crime must be influenced by different contexts and approaches to crime in the United States and in nations with lower violent-crime rates. In terms of omission, it is also perhaps worth pointing out that despite Levitt's numerous forays into different areas of crime, he has yet to investigate the statistically much more damaging arena of corporate crime, which occurs in the context of profit-maximizing firms operating in a competitive capitalist economic system.

Levitt: More Abortion Less Crime

What is common in all of Levitt's work, and is nicely captured in his work on crime, is a particular method: "stripping a layer or two from the surface of modern life and seeing what is happening underneath" to uncover unpredictable, often "distant, even subtle" explanatory factors.[27] A second component of Levitt's method is that the answers to these questions will "come from the data." He makes some very strong claims in this regard, arguing that economics represents how the world "actually does work" because its measurement tools can "reliably assess a thicket of information to determine the effect of any one factor."[28] Finally, when searching for these subtle, often distant, causes of life's seemingly perplexing enigmas, understanding how incentives are aligned is the key to the solution.

This is very revealing about Levitt's economic world view. In terms of technique, he is viewed as an unconventional economist because of his partial commitment to the centerpieces of old mainstream theory. He eschews intricate mathematical modeling, an offence sufficiently grave that it inspired one critic of *Freakonomics* to comment, "I could detect very little in the research that depended on economic theory in anything but the most superficial way."[29] He relies heavily on econometrics, but does not feel that this requires using anything but fairly basic techniques. He has not been a strict devotee of *homo economicus*, allowing people to have motivations besides individual self-interest, yet incentives remain central to his explanations. He remains most firmly wedded to the pillar of methodological individualism – placing individual choice at the center of inquiry. If Levitt is an unconventional economist in using a more intuitive approach to problem solving than the "old" mainstream and their mathematical modelling would favor, in other, crucial, ways he has not wandered too far from the rest of the flock.

Levitt has also ignored the traditional subject areas of the economy – interest rates, stock markets, unemployment, economic growth, and corporate behavior – in favor of areas that have normally been the purview of other disciplines like sociology and politics. In this he is following in the path of Chicago mainstay Gary Becker, although Becker was much more a champion of the rational, maximizing individual than Levitt. For Levitt, economics is basically a toolkit – a set of data-finding techniques that is bound by neither theory nor subject matter. Levitt argues that this particular set of tools can be usefully applied to almost any area of social enquiry, since "no subject, however, offbeat, need be beyond its reach."[30] Levitt places great confidence in the truth-revealing properties of data. "I'd like to put together a set of tools that lets us catch terrorists. I mean that's the goal. I don't necessarily know yet how I'd go about it. But given the right data, I have little doubt that I could figure out the answer."[31]

Levitt's work on the causes of the fall in crime in the United States is an excellent example of this. It is outside the traditional economic subject areas. It involves a clever natural experiment in its empirical work and it arrives at a counterintuitive, "surprising" result. There are three versions of Levitt's famous abortion and crime study that move chronologically from the most empirical and academic to the most popular. The first (with John Donohue) appeared in the *Quarterly Journal of Economics* (*QJE*) in 2001, the second in the *Journal of Economic Perspectives* (*JEP*) in 2004, and finally it was popularized in a chapter in *Freakonomics* entitled "Where have all the criminals gone?" Since the *Freakonomics* chapter contributes little in the way of new analysis this chapter will focus on the first two studies.

Levitt's major contribution to the debate on falling crime rates, which was completely consistent with his desire to find surprising or unexpected causes, linked declining criminal activity to the legalization of abortion with *Roe v. Wade* in 1973. The logic behind Levitt's hypothesized connection rests on two assumptions. First, aborted babies are unwanted, which would seem relatively uncontroversial. Second, unwanted babies are more likely than average to grow up to be criminals. It is certainly true that the birth rates of groups that Levitt considered "at risk" for future criminal activity dropped more than the average as a result of the legalization of abortion. The decrease in birth rates was twice as great for teenage and non-white mothers as it was for the non-teen, white population. Levitt also noted the same trend comparing black and white women.[32] Parents with unwanted children were less nurturing and more likely to resent their children. Children of mothers who were denied an abortion were more likely to be involved in crime and have poorer life prospects even when controlling for the income, age, education, and health of the mother.[33] In his own "back of the envelope" calculations Levitt argues that since "at risk" groups (blacks, teens, and unwed mothers) are both more likely to commit crimes and more likely to have decreasing birth rates due to legalized abortion, the crime rate should fall. To take just the black population as an example, Levitt argues that since homicide by black youths is nine times that of whites and the drop in fertility of black women three times as great as for whites (12 percent to 4 percent), the homicide rate will drop by more than just the cohort effect (the impact of having fewer high-crime 18–24 year olds as a result of the legalization of abortion). In a *New York Times Magazine* article, the connection was summarized as follows: "Unwantedness leads to high crime; abortion leads to less unwantedness; abortion leads to less crime."[34]

In support of this hypothesis he produced four pieces of evidence in his *QJE* article. Most obviously, the timing works out. The crime rate (Levitt uses three types of crime to calculate the crime rate in this article: property crime, violent crime, and murder) dropped dramatically starting in 1991, eighteen years after the 1973 legalization. Since most criminals' peak crime years are between 18 and 24 the increased number of abortions should start to show up exactly in 1991 and should have a cumulatively larger impact over time. Second, five states were early movers, legalizing abortion in 1970, three years before the rest of the nation. Crime rates in these five states started to drop three years before the rest of the country. Third, Levitt uses panel data to estimate that states with higher abortion levels in the 1970s and early 1980s had lower crime rates from 1985 to 1997. This connection remains significant even when other factors such as the level of incarceration, the number of police, lagged state welfare generosity, the presence of concealed-handgun laws, per capita beer consumption, and measures of the state's economic well-being (the unemployment rate, income per capita, and poverty rate) are factored into the model.[35] In this regression Levitt also finds that incarceration rates and more police lead to fewer murders, while a higher state unemployment rate is associated with significant increases in property crime, but not violent crime.[36] Fourth, Levitt finds that crime rates drop much more rapidly among the cohorts after abortion is legalized than among those born prior to legalized abortion.[37]

The estimated magnitude of the impact of legalized abortion on crime is large. Levitt finds that it is responsible for up to 50 percent of the total drop in crime rates, making it much more important than any of the other, more popular explanations for the decrease in crime.[38] He even makes a rough calculation that societal saving resulting from legalized abortion's effect on crime may be as much as $30 billion annually.[39] In his conclusion, Levitt does write something of a disclaimer, claiming that these reductions could have been achieved through other methods like providing better environments for children or other forms of contraception.[40]

The *JEP* article was not an original empirical contribution as was the *QJE* piece. Rather, it combined some of his previous research with a review of other quantitative work to distinguish between the factors that did and did not cause the crime rate to fall in the 1990s. His reading of the literature is that innovative, New York City–style police tactics,[41] a strong economy,[42] gun control laws,[43] changing demographics,[44] increased use of capital punishment,[45] and laws that permit carrying concealed weapons[46] had very little or no impact. By contrast, the increased number of police, rising prison population, dwindling use of crack, and, obviously, legalized abortion all had a significant impact.

Further, Levitt attempts to roughly quantify the magnitude of each of the significant factors in reducing homicide, violent crime, and property crime (see table 5.1), as well as speculate about the cost-effectiveness of a few of the measures. Increasing numbers of police have a strong effect on crime reduction according to Levitt,[47] although one of his studies uses the curious proxy of the number of firefighters to estimate this connection.[48] The number of police increased by 14 percent during the nineties and Levitt estimates this was responsible for a 5 to 6 percent reduction in all three types of crime. This created around $20 billion in benefits for an $8.4 billion outlay on police. The dramatic increase in incarceration from the mid-1970s to 2000 also reduced crime by locking up existing criminals and deterring future ones.[49] Further, the reductions in crime are larger when prison conditions are worse.[50] He estimated that the $50 billion spent on incarceration are also outweighed by the benefits of an estimated 8 percent drop in property crime and 12 percent fall in homicide and violent crime, although Levitt does warn that imprisoning large numbers of people may result in declining marginal benefits and have undesirable social consequences.[51] It is worth mentioning here that Levitt's *Freakonomics* explanation for the increase in crime in the 1980s was the decrease in monitoring and penalties in the criminal justice system. "America was getting softer on crime 'for fear of sounding racist,' as the economist Gary Becker has written, since African-American and Hispanics commit a disproportionate share of felonies. So, if you were the kind of person who might want to commit a crime, the incentives were lining up in your favor: a slimmer likelihood of being convicted and if convicted a shorter prison term."[52] The decline in crack and its associated violence had a more modest effect, decreasing homicide by 6 percent and property crime by little or nothing, although Levitt admits that the evidence on this score is very limited.[53] He estimates a more modest impact for abortion in the *JEP* article compared to the original *QJE* piece, claiming it accounts for a ten percent decline in homicide, violent crime and property crime (one third of the total).

An Evaluation of Levitt Part 1: Data Needs a Context

It should hardly come as a surprise that a paper arguing that safer streets have been caused by abortion should spark considerable controversy. Considering the faith that Levitt places in the truth-revealing properties of creative natural experiments, his research has attracted considerable criticism on empirical grounds. Critics have taken him to task on a number of fronts, from the inappropriateness of his data to his poor choice of tests.[54] Although, in the best spirit of empirical endeavor, Levitt has attempted to address and rebut these claims,[55] the uncertainty created by these criticisms reveals that his claim about well-defined research and careful selection of data revealing the undisputed "truth" of an issue, especially one as controversial and difficult to demonstrate as the link between legalizing abortion and crime, is overly simplistic. Interestingly, there is a parallel "surprising" explanation for the

Table 5.1 Levitt's causes of decline in US crime (% decrease in the crime rate)

	Homicide	Violent	Property
Total decline	43	34	29
Contribution of individual factors			
Increased police	5–6	5–6	5–6
Increased prison population	12	12	8
Decline in crack	6	3	0
Abortion	10	10	10

Adapted from Levitt, "Understanding Why Crime Fell in the 1990s" (2004): 184.

drop in US crime during the 1990s – the reduction in lead used in gasoline.[56] Apparently, trends in violent and property crime track the trends in vehicle lead emissions with about a twenty-year lag, indicating that childhood exposure to lead might be a better explanation for crime rates than *Roe v. Wade*. It is possible that Levitt may not have succeeded even on his own, very narrow terms. Further, in the absence of both theory and broader context, the very basic assumption undergirding Levitt's work is the unstable foundation of the objective truth of the data.

Levitt's focus on legalized abortion as the main factor in the reduction in US crime in the 1990s is particularly revealing about the way he views the economic world. Crucially, he is very dismissive of broader macroeconomic factors, or the social context in the reduction in crime, while focusing on a "surprising" explanation. In his *QJE* article the broader context is treated as a control variable, while in the *JEP* article economic factors are more explicitly considered but only in a very rudimentary way.

The only two exceptions to Levitt's downplaying of a broader social context are an article examining juvenile crime and a study of Chicago's Black Kings gang. In the first of these articles, he argues that high levels of poverty and local income inequality are related to increased illegal activity, although he also finds that increased penalties have a strong effect in reducing juvenile crime, which is more in keeping with his other research.[57] The second article examines the evolution of Chicago's gangs from a "family," with a radical political critique of discrimination and oppression, to a business. This transformation is explained by the growing "free market ideology" in the context of a need to at least partially satisfy the income requirements of an "unemployed and alienated youth" given the shift in state relationships with urban youth from social support to incarceration.[58] It is difficult to reconcile this article with Levitt's other work. Perhaps Levitt's second author status is revealing. Alternatively, this article relies on qualitative data from interviews with gang members in contrast with Levitt's preferred investigative technique of data sleuthing, which may perhaps lend itself to less "surprising" explanations. Whatever the explanation, this article is an outlier from the rest of Levitt's work, which largely dismisses or ignores societal explanations for US crime.

There are both theoretical and empirical problems with this dismissal. As was mentioned in the introduction to this chapter, Levitt does not view or publically present himself as much of a theoretician. While moving away from old mainstream economics' complicated mathematical models with their implausibly narrow and unrealistic assumptions has its advantages, jettisoning all economic theory might not. This is nicely highlighted in Levitt's discussion about the relationship between the economy and crime. The most famous old mainstream theory of the economics of crime is that of fellow University of Chicago economist Becker, who uses the assumptions of a rational, self-interested, maximizing individual to argue that the decision to commit a crime is simply the result of a calculation of the costs and benefits. Crime will be reduced when the costs are increased (through increased policing or jail times) or benefits decreased. According to Becker's model, higher non-crime income should reduce the incentive for criminal activity. Levitt argues that while this might be true for crimes with financial gain, it is likely to be less important for more violent crimes. Further, he argues that even theoretically there is an uncertain connection between the economy and crime because increased incomes might lead to a greater number of activities that are related to crime, like "alcohol consumption, frequenting nightclubs and owning a car."[59] As evidence for the lack of importance of economic factors Levitt cites a number of other studies that find only a small, although statistically significant, connection between property crime and the unemployment rate (or other economic measures like the income of low-wage workers) and no relationship at all between economic measures and violent crime. He concludes that the only mechanism through which the economy is likely to impact crime is by providing the necessary tax revenue to pay for police and jails.[60]

Theoretically, it is not clear why Levitt would dismiss the link between violent crime and a strong economy. In keeping with Becker's rational model, people with higher incomes and steady jobs have much more to lose from long-term incarceration than those living an unrewarding life outside of the penal system. Less in keeping with Becker's model, life in desperate economic conditions contains far more pressure and tension, which can often lead to violence. Finally, Levitt appears to be ignoring the strong connection between violent crime and economic crime in many situations. This is especially curious since Levitt does make this connection later in his *JEP* article when he argues that the decline in crack sales (a crime for financial gain) has reduced homicide rates.[61] One problem with Levitt's analysis of the link between the economy and crime is that it lacks a theoretical underpinning, even one as crude and individualistic as Becker's, which leads to some problematic inconsistencies.

Given the lack of theoretical underpinnings, it is very difficult to criticize the assumptions on which Levitt's analysis is based. However, his dismissal of the economy as a factor in the reduction in crime is based on a fairly selective review of the empirical literature. Levitt argues that "empirical estimates of the impact of macroeconomic variables on crime have been generally consistent across studies."[62] Yet, this is not really a consensus opinion. Using an economic model similar to that of Becker, Jeffrey Grogger argues that in the 1980s poor job prospects created an incentive towards the illegal drug trade and away from the legitimate job market. He estimated the impact of young people's wages on youth crime and found that, holding other factors constant, a 1 percent decline in wages would lead to a 1 percent increase in crime. Given that real wages for youth declined by 22 percent in the 1980s, this factor would be responsible for a substantial increase in crime during this decade.[63] After surveying the literature, Joel Wallman and Alfred Blumstein have no difficulty finding empirical support for a connection between an improving economy and decreasing crime in the 1990s. In fact, every study cited by Wallman and Blumstein suggests a strong link between the decrease in crime and an improving economy. This may have been because the studies cited by these authors focus more specifically on youth unemployment and wages as opposed to the general unemployment rate. Their conclusion is a more nuanced acknowledgment that in the debate between Levitt and others on the connection between the economy and crime, the jury is still out.[64]

Although here we are most concerned with the evidence connecting the broader economic context to crime, it is worth noting that the evidence on one of Levitt's "other factors" is also more controversial than he lets on in the *JEP* or *Freakonomics*. He argues that increasing the number of police had an important (and cost-effective) impact. Yet others are not as convinced. Justin McCrary of the University of California, Berkeley, found an important error in Levitt's original 1997 study connecting police numbers to crime.[65] When McCrary tried to replicate Levitt's finding after the error had been corrected, he found that increasing police had no significant impact on crime. Wallman and Blumstein are equally skeptical of Levitt's alternative estimate[66] that was supposed to correct for McCrary's discovery, arguing that "findings that don't make sense should at least raise questions."[67] They are particularly concerned with Levitt's finding that increased police numbers were related to a decrease in homicide but an increase in serious assault. Wallman and Blumstein argue that common sense would suggest that since murder is less likely to be deterred by police presence than violent crime, Levitt's incongruous findings should be viewed with considerable suspicion.[68] Again, the point here is not to say that Levitt is unequivocally incorrect in stating that more police reduce crime. Rather, given the very mixed existing literature on both policing and the economic context, his dismissal of the economy and acceptance of policing seems, at best, somewhat selective.

Levitt's dismissal of the broad macro-economic context, and failure to even address distributional issues or the social context in which US crime occurs, is in sharp contrast to other efforts at explaining crime, like those of Wacquant outlined earlier in the chapter. With the exception of the article on Chicago gangs, Levitt either dismisses or pays little attention to the economic context in which crime occurs. Part of his lack of attention to the social and economic conditions that give rise to crime in the United States is rooted in his failure to contrast the unique situation in the United States with other nations. While Levitt is exploring the decline in crime in the United States rather than the difference in crime between nations, focusing on the former while ignoring the latter downplays the extent to which US violent crime is exceptional in the industrialized world, a fact that would encourage an analysis contrasting the broader social and economic context in the United States compared to other, less violent nations.

Other scholars have attempted, with some success, to do just this. Wacquant places the high US rate of violent crime firmly in the unique US social and economic context, arguing that it is due to the prevalence of handguns, a deep-rooted illegal street economy in the impoverished districts of urban areas, a lack of a social welfare system, and racial segregation.[69] Other authors have also established a link between violent crime and the differing economic contexts. To provide one example, Hsieh and Pugh used a meta-study to demonstrate consistent correlations between income inequality and homicide among nations and US states.[70]

Levitt's one comparison with the European Union is to demonstrate that the US drop in crime (rather than its abnormally high level) was exceptional by showing that US crime rates decreased by far more than those in the EU. For example, EU homicide rates fell by 4 percent between 1995 and 1999, while they dropped 28 percent in the United States.[71] However, even if one were to focus on merely the reduction in crime, as opposed to its level, between nations, Levitt does not capture the different contexts. Most obviously, it is much more unlikely that a country with a very low homicide rate, like most of the EU nations, would be able to achieve the same reductions as one with a high rate. It is also worth remarking that, as Wacquant argues about France, these were not particularly good economic times in much of Europe compared to the United States, so if the economy were a factor it should lead to improved crime statistics in the United States compared to the EU.

An international comparison would also suggest a slightly different cost-benefit analysis than Levitt produced in the *JEP*. If France can achieve a similar crime rate and a much lower rate for violent crime with a fraction of the number of police officers used in the United States, and Canada can achieve similar crime reductions while imprisonment and police numbers decline, are these not better costs and benefits? Societal and economic changes that would create lower crime with fewer police, as is the case in Canada and France, are surely more desirable than less crime with more police. Again, we see that Levitt's focus on the decline in US crime rather than the fact that the United States has a much higher violent crime rate than elsewhere ignores the unique magnitude of US violent crime and prevents questioning just what it is about the United States that creates so many violent individuals. This problem is exacerbated by Levitt's focus on a "surprising" but policy-empty explanation of abortion as the principal cause for the fall in crime in the United States.

An Evaluation of Levitt Part 2: What Is Ignored

Although theft and murder are certainly the regular fare of the nightly news, about which a veritable procession of dangerous thugs and police tape are trotted across the nation's TV screens, this sort of conventional street crime is only one type of illegal activity. Occupational crime, which Levitt does study, occurs when the law is broken in the activity of a legitimate occupation. Because it is often committed by more affluent business people or professionals, it is commonly referred to as "white-collar" crime. An example of this kind of crime would be when executives embezzle money from their corporation or a lawyer defrauds a client.

Organizational crime, as the name implies, is carried out within a large organization. This makes it difficult to pin on a single criminal, since the offence is often not carried out by one individual, but by an entire group of people, from boards of directors to a large number of executives. Although unions and other organizations can commit this type of illegal activity, it has become synonymous with corporate crime. This third type of crime has thus far escaped the notice of Levitt and the other JBC economists.

While Levitt focuses on conventional and, to a lesser extent, occupational crime, evidence suggests that corporate crime does far more societal harm. Compared to the 32,000 to 78,000 annual deaths traced to workplace disease and injury, the murder rate seems relatively minor.[72] The corporate death toll would mount if we added to this the number of people killed or harmed at the consumption end of the production process. In his testimony before the United States Senate Committee on Finance, Dr David Graham of the FDA estimated that the drug Vioxx had led to an "excess" of heart attacks in somewhere between "88,000 to 139,000 Americans. Of these, 30–40 percent probably died." Worse, the maker of Vioxx, Merck, and management at the FDA knew about these potential dangers and attempted to cover up the scientific evidence that eventually led to it being pulled from the market in 2004.[73] Finally, pollution erodes people's health, sometimes fatally. Two economists estimated the gross annual damages to human health in 2002 from air pollution alone at somewhere between $71 and $277 billion in the United States.[74]

Corporations steal as well as kill. Their methods may be less dramatic than a cunning second-storey job, but price fixing, issuing false accounting reports, unfair labor practices that reduce workers' wages, restraint of trade, and false or misleading advertising, all, in one way or another, steal money from households. To provide a few examples, in 1999, F. Hoffmann–La Roche was fined $500 million and BASF $225 million when they pled guilty to price fixing vitamins.[75] In 1996, the Daiwa Bank paid a $340 million fine when it pled guilty to defrauding bank regulators and covering up heavy securities losses. When Enron went bankrupt after massive accounting fraud, it wiped $63 billion off the stock market, including $800 million that was invested from its own employees' pensions. More recently, in one year, 2013, JP Morgan was forced to pay over $20 billion in penalties to federal authorities, much of it for its role in misleading investors prior to the financial crash of

2008.[76] This sort of fraud is not limited to the financial sector. In 2015 Whole Foods was charged by the New York Department of Consumer Affairs for overcharging its high-end customers by overstating the weights of its pre-packaged products.[77] The US Justice Department joined a lawsuit against health insurer Health Management Associates for pressuring doctors to admit patients for unneeded medical care in order to inflate billing from Medicare and Medicaid. This is not an isolated practice by one rogue firm, but rather standard procedure in the private insurance industry. According to the *New York Times*, "Federal regulators have multiple investigations into questionable hospital admissions, procedures and billings at many hospital systems, including the country's largest, HCA."[78]

Death and theft are not the only means through which corporations harm society with illegal activity. Pollution also imposes massive costs even when it has no direct impact on human health. Although the Exxon Valdez oil spill did not actually kill anyone or lift money from people's wallets, it did cause tremendous damage. The cost of cleanup and damage compensation was $3.8 billion (although in 1998 the US Supreme Court slashed the punitive damages on the company from $2.5 billion to $500 million). Despite this disaster, in 2008 Exxon was still using the more spill-prone single-hulled tankers for many of its shipments rather than the safer double-hulled ships because they were about 20 percent cheaper, resulting in a savings of around $18 million in 2008.[79]

We have so far documented a few high-profile, big-money crimes. But these are not isolated events. Rather it is habitual behavior. Marshall Clinard and Peter Yeager conducted a survey of 582 of the largest publicly owned companies in the United States to determine whether or not they had violated the laws of the land. Only counting those violations for which official government action was taken (which the authors argue is "the tip of the iceberg" since most violations were addressed without formal action), 60 percent of the firms had at least one violation, and 42 percent had multiple charges.[80] This is especially remarkable since the survey only accounted for a two-year period between 1975 and 1976. To put these numbers in perspective, imagine how busy the police would be if 60 percent of the general population were arrested and charged at least once every two years.

This is not due to the pathology of a few criminally negligent villains, but is the inevitable result of the normal functioning of the economic system. According to Jeffrey Sachs, "The world is drowning in corporate fraud … There is, however, scant accountability. Two years after the biggest financial crisis in history … not a single financial leader has faced jail … The fines are always a tiny fraction of the ill-gotten gains, implying to Wall Street that corrupt practices have a solid rate of return."[81]

Conclusion

Levitt's neglect of international comparisons and failure to acknowledge the economic context within which the extraordinary US murder rates occur is in sharp contrast to other efforts at explaining crime. Questions about the broad social and economic structures of society that create so much violent crime in the United States compared to other nations would also require an investigation into the power relationships that create those structures and a conversation about how they might be changed. This is not to say that Levitt completely ignores all social influences in his analysis of crime. He does test to see if economic conditions like unemployment have an impact. Yet, compared to Wacquant, his attention to social context, even within the United States, is superficial. Further, the extent to which the United States is an outlier compared to other nations in terms of violent crime is never explored. Although in a later article on the connection between unemployment and crime Levitt does call for more international comparisons,[82] the difference between national social and economic contexts is not the subject of enquiry, as it has been for other researchers like Wacquant. His choice to focus on the US decline exclusively, while ignoring the much lower levels of violent crime in other countries, black boxes the unique social and economic factors that make the United States such an exceptional case. Levitt also has a firm belief in the ability of his creative testing to reveal the truth. The difficulty with this dependence in his study of abortion and crime is that the truth has been very elusive, with other researchers able to cast doubt on his results. Further, Levitt's interpretation of empirical support for what did and did not decrease crime in the United States seems to be a little selective, and results in conclusions that downplayed the broad economic context while stressing the criminal-justice factors like increased policing.

Chapter 3 detailed the uniquely high levels of inequality and poverty in the United States that are a result of a political economy that particularly favors the business class. These conditions are the economic determinants of crime in the United States. Levitt also chooses to focus much more on street crime than that which originates in corporate boardrooms. Just as examining the economic conditions that create the context for crime would require an analysis of the unique political economy and power relationships in the United States, so too would an analysis of why corporate crime was so prevalent and what measures should be undertaken to rectify this crime spree.

chapter six

Two Kinds of Crises

The economy does not sail along on smooth seas. Rather, its often turbulent voyage is interrupted by periodic storms in which investment crashes, asset values plummet, growth sinks, and unemployment rises. The last, and therefore most easily remembered, economic collapse occurred in the wake of the 2008 mortgage market meltdown in the United States, which rapidly spread to become an economic crisis across the wealthy nations of North America and Europe. Unemployment in the United States shot up from just over 4 percent in 2007 to 10 percent in 2010. In Europe, the effects have been more persistent. Unemployment increased from 8 percent in 2007 to 14 percent in 2014. Even this shockingly high rate hides the truly disastrous impacts in the worst-hit nations. For example, Spain's unemployment rate went from around 8 percent in 2007 to over 25 percent by 2014. The massive economic and personal costs of crises, and their annoyingly stubborn propensity to reappear, might suggest that the discipline in charge of studying the economy would dedicate considerable effort into predicting, explaining, and, in an ideal world, avoiding these sorts of economic failures. Yet, as we noted in chapter 1, the queen of England could legitimately question how the vast majority of mainstream economists failed to notice the looming crisis coming.

In addition to these significant periodic economic setbacks, there is mounting evidence that an ecological crisis may compromise the environment on which the economy depends. The scientific consensus that climate change is, in fact, occurring and caused by human activity is only one element of a growing catalogue of environmental troubles, from the depletion of marine life, to species extinction, to deforestation. All these environmental issues are, at their core, economic issues in the sense that it is economic activity, and the economic system that drives and directs that activity in more or less ecologically harmful ways, that is responsible for these problems.

This chapter will investigate the explanations that JBC economists have put forward to explain economic and environmental crises, although the word "crisis" is seldom used explicitly in their work, a fact, that, in and of itself, might be considered revealing. In doing so, we will first provide a contrast to their work using the research of academics that put forward an explanation of crises that revolves around the functioning of the economic system.

Crises: Economic

Unlike the vast majority of economists who so disappointed the queen with their failure to read the writing on the economic wall, economics professor Nouriel Roubini of New York University was one of the very few who predicted the economic crisis that began in 2008. For his prescience he has been christened "Dr Doom" and his perspective on the economy is a regular feature of the serious news. In a remarkable interview, in the *Wall Street Journal* of all places, Roubini declared that "Karl Marx had it right" when he claimed that massive redistribution of income from wages to profits and the resulting inequality could create a problem of inadequate demand sufficiently grave that capitalism could "destroy itself."[1]

In general, what is striking about this analysis is how rare it is to hear an established economist invoking the idea that there is something inherent in capitalist economies that pushes them towards periodic crisis. It is possible to describe two basic mainstream approaches in the history of economic thought, neither of which suggests that instability is caused by anything internal to the functioning of the economy.[2] Rather, the distinction revolves around the speed at which the economy can adjust to unexplainable instability.

The first, the conservative approach, which has been the most popular in the last thirty-five years or so, asserts that the capitalist system is capable of smooth and efficient growth with minimal intervention by the state. In this approach unemployment is voluntary. Business cycles are brief, shallow, and often healthy for the economy. Inequality is more a desirable result of merit-based differences between people than a social problem.

The second mainstream approach is the New Keynesian version of macroeconomics, which acknowledges that the economic system can be erratic and wasteful because, as we explained in chapter 3, left to its own market devices the economy can face periods of prolonged recession. During these periods, the government stabilization repair shop is needed to keep the economic car on the road. Overall, as long as the economy gets the government fine-tuning it needs, the system should be capable of a smooth ride.

Historically, in terms of actual policy, the conservative version gave way to the Keynesian most dramatically when the system was threatened by collapse, as was the case in 1929 and 2008. To provide one recent example, in 2008 the US Department of the Treasury's Troubled Asset Relief Program (TARP) provided hundreds of billions of dollars to private-sector banks to prevent another 1930s-style Great Depression, and subsequently poured trillions more into the private banks in order to stimulate investment and consumption. In addition to this monetary policy, President Obama used deficit spending to generate a general fiscal stimulus and bailed out specific companies like General Motors and Chrysler. This is not to suggest that the 1930s and 2008 were the only periods in which government intervention was used to bail out a troubled economy. The period between 1929 and 2008 required numerous public interventions to keep the private sector afloat.

Despite an active and often acrimonious debate about the tendency of the economy to recovery rapidly from adverse circumstances and the extent to which the government is needed to speed this recovery, most mainstream economists have in common a failure to look at the economic system itself for the source of the instability. Most mainstream macroeconomics attributes downturns to "shocks," by which they mean unpredictable, random events outside their explanatory power. These negative external shocks can take a variety of forms: sunspots, crop failures, psychological cycles of optimism and despair, wars, revolutions, and political blunders, but what they all have in common is that they originate outside the normal smooth working of the economic system. The severity of the crisis then depends on how quickly the economy can recover from these externally imposed disasters.

There are a few problems with this approach. First, external shocks occur all the time, but only at certain times do they set off a general crisis. When the system is healthy, it rapidly revives from all sorts of setbacks, but when it is unhealthy, practically anything can set off a crisis. Second, ascribing crises to shocks creates the impression that there is nothing inherent and internal to the capitalist economy that might lead to downturns. A more careful analysis of the economic system would reveal that this is not the case.

The position taken by what might be called "radical" economists is that the economic system generates internal contradictions that will cause repeated crises. There are several interpretations by different authors about the precise mechanisms through which this might occur, but in fairly general terms there are two candidates.

One is the idea of underconsumption, which is the general expression of Roubini's claim that if the capitalist class increases its share of the income between workers and owners, it will result in a crisis of demand because those that can spend won't and those who would buy products can't. The business class may drop $10,000 on dinner in a Manhattan bistro or buy an $80 million private submarine, but the rich do not, as a rule, spend as high a proportion of their incomes on consumption as do those with more modest means. Workers have a higher propensity to spend their income, but because their wages have been squeezed, they don't have money to spend.[3]

Broadly speaking, the 2008 economic crisis can be seen in this light, although the precise details vary depending on the specific analysis of the individual researcher. As we detailed in chapter 3, there was a profound restructuring of many national economies, including that of the United States, Canada, and the United Kingdom after 1980. In an effort to restore profitability, the structure of the economy was transformed through a variety of policies from monetary policy to deregulation and free trade. These changes resulted in a scaling back of workers' wages and of social income, and regulatory constraints on firms. Chapter 3 looked at how these changes created an increasingly unequal distribution of income between workers and business, but they, also created economic instability.

US workers facing stagnant real wages and the longest work week in the industrialized world resorted to borrowing to maintain their consumption. Business found it profitable to extend extraordinary levels of credit as a complement to increasing profitability in the sphere of production. The result was a dramatic increase in worker indebtedness. The problem with an economic structure in which profitability is based on increasing financialization and family debt is that it creates a precarious future for household consumption.

The common view of the crisis beginning in 2008 was that it was essentially a financial crisis centered in the US mortgage market, but this simple explanation is belied by the facts. The first sign of the impending crisis was triggered by highly indebted households contracting their spending. The resulting reduction in sales created excess fixed-capital capacity for business, which responded with a rapid decline in investment. The financial crisis that erupted in September of 2008 contributed to the decline in investment as expectations for future profitability collapsed and credit contracted.[4]

It might be worth a brief reminder of just how the US mortgage market became the flash point for a world-wide economic crisis. Despite the limited income of many US families, the housing market enjoyed spectacular growth because of a combination of a long period of low interest rates and an increasingly creative menu of tantalizing loans that tempted people into large mortgages with early periods of low monthly payments. Increasingly large loans were being made to increasingly risky customers, on increasingly speculative terms. As families started to default on what they thought was going to be their dream home, the banks and investment firms that had purchased mortgage-backed securities found themselves holding badly overvalued assets. The resulting collapse of the banking system contracted credit, exacerbating the decline in consumption and investment.[5]

We might draw two lessons from the role of credit in sparking this crisis. The first is that this was not some external "shock" to the economic system, but a result of the profit-seeking behavior of private firms in the context of stagnant household incomes. Second, the credit industry lured homeowners into dangerous waters with the siren song of temporarily low monthly charges only to crash them on the rocks of backloaded payments. This was done not only for higher-risk clients, but even for those who should have qualified for regular mortgages in order to increase lender profits.[6] This is not the only example of financial profits coming at the expense of households in this industry. Those of us who have squinted at the fine print of our credit-card agreements might find the interest rates bordering on what a long time ago would have been called usurious. Yet these are nothing compared to the gauging done to those unfortunate enough to have to rely on short-term payday loans to tide them over. Any analysis of the credit industry should take into account the crucial relationship between debtor and creditor as well as the broader context in which the credit industry operates, such as the desperate position of many borrowers. The result of this financialization was extraordinary bank profits and bankers' bonuses accompanying an unsustainably debt-ridden and fragile economy.

The underlying weakness in US household income prolonged the crisis despite the Keynesian efforts of the US federal government. Private banks were provided with an estimated $14 trillion in government grants, loans, investments, and guarantees, but were unwilling to extend credit to already indebted families or non-financial firms with stagnating sales. During the first year of the crisis, global output and trade declined more than it had during the first twelve months of the Great Depression. In the United States, the capacity utilization rate fell to its lowest level since the Great Depression, while unemployment doubled to 10 percent.[7] For those who see the crisis in this light, the portents for an imminent recovery do not look good. As of 2014, US non-financial corporations are sitting on over $5 trillion of idle balances,[8] an amount nearly one-third the size of the entire US economy. The crisis has also had negative impacts on the income of most households. Between 2007 and 2012 the real family income of all but the richest 5 percent of the population declined. For the poorest 20 percent it declined by 2.7 percent a year.[9] Declining incomes are an unwelcome development if debt-free consumption is going to contribute to economic recovery. The problem is that the underlying structural problem has not been fixed. High profits continue to depend on low wages and corporate taxes, the banks are still speculating, and investment on which growth depends has not recovered in spite of high profits.[10] The 2008 crisis is a specific example of a general type of crisis in which capital is "too strong."

The second broad reason for crisis is that capital is "too weak." Workers and the so-called middle class did not require access to credit to fuel their consumption when their wages were growing in the 1950s and 1960s. The flip-side internal crisis mechanism takes effect when the labor force gets a larger share of the income and firms respond to this squeeze on their profits by reducing their investment, causing economic crisis. Although rising worker compensation in a period of low unemployment is the most obvious threat to profitability, it is also possible that societal demands, such as citizens demanding taxes to fund health and education, environmentalists demanding regulations to curb pollution, and consumer organizations demanding safer products, can also increase costs. Bowles, Gordon, and Weisskopf suggest that the 1960s and 1970s were such a period.[11] Like the deficient demand crisis, these supply-side tendencies are not shocks from outside the system, but are driven by the inevitable conflict over how income is distributed in the economy. A period of high unemployment and demands for lower taxes and deregulation (neoliberalism) can restore profits by reducing costs, but it also leads back to the underconsumption hypothesis. And so the system swings from one kind of crisis to another, albeit with decades in between of more or less tension filled transition.

Radical economists agree, in general, about the system's tendencies, conflicts, and contradictions, but differ over the proximate cause. For example, economic historian Robert Brenner of UCLA claimed that overproduction (too many factories in too many countries producing the same products) has resulted in falling prices and profits.[12] A contrasting explanation was put forward by the New School's Anwar Shaikh, who argued that firms' tendency to increase their fixed capital costs in order to keep ahead of the competition and undermine the demands of labor for higher wages will also lead to long-term declines in the rate of profit.[13] Despite the differences between scholars in this tradition, they all look inside the system to explain crises rather than resorting to external shocks.[14]

This chapter will analyze how those few JBC-winning economists who do study economic fluctuations frame their research. Do they fall into either of the two mainstream camps by emphasizing external causes or do they argue that the system itself creates tendencies towards instability?

Crises: Environmental

No doubt, there are pedants or corporate spokespersons who might dispute whether current environmental trends warrant the term crisis. Yet, few would deny that the adverse effects of human beings on the environment are growing at an alarming rate. Indeed, it is a telling indicator of just how profound those impacts are that remarkably few people even balk at the mention of an environmental crisis. Although most people currently think of this crisis in terms of the rising temperature and unpredictably extreme weather that will accompany global warming, the decline in marine life, deforestation, and reduction of biodiversity are all widely known problems.

What is less widely agreed on is the cause of these problems. Popular would-be culprits include energy inefficiency, dependence on fossil fuels, overpopulation, and industrialization, although this list is hardly the complete who's who of villains. Although mainstream economists do not disagree with the role that these factors play in environmental problems, they tend to argue that these are more symptoms than causes. The real cause, they argue, is incorrect prices. If fossil fuels are causing global warming, for example, it is because the true cost of global warming is not reflected in the costs to firms and the price that consumers pay. If the environment is being negatively impacted, then the cost of that impact should be factored in along with other, privately incurred, costs. In the example of global warming, this would increase the price of fossil fuels, decreasing consumption and encouraging alternative energy sources.

Other scholars take great issue with the "prices are not right" analysis of the environmental problem. Of the many criticisms, the one that is most relevant to the perspective of this book is that it neglects to include the logic of the economic system in its analysis, which creates two broad problems. First, the economic system makes it very unlikely that the policies required to "get prices right" will actually be implemented. Second, even if environmental costs were fully incorporated, it would not solve the problem.

According to James O'Connor, profit-seeking firms will always attempt to get access to environmental inputs on as favorable a basis as possible. In pursuit of this objective, corporations use their economic and political power to influence the state in its role as environmental regulator. Like all other conflicts in the realm of the government, the state will not inevitably grant businesses their wishes, and citizen groups will inevitably organize, with more or less cohesion and effectiveness, in opposition. Yet, because of the centrality of private investment in the economy, firms are likely to triumph.

However, inexpensive access to the environment will create overuse and degradation, which in turn creates increased costs for firms. For example, as soil deteriorates, farms have to pay for increased inputs to maintain their productivity. As the globe warms, expensive forms of remediation and adaptation become necessary. O'Connor explains the tendency to increasing costs associated with environmental deterioration through the concept of "underproduction." He argues that the competitive dynamics of capitalism incentivize firms to "underproduce" (or fail to reproduce) the ecological systems upon which they depend, thus resulting in decline over time and increased costs as a result. O'Connor was principally concerned with demonstrating that the revenge of nature would create economic crises – what he termed the "second contradiction of capitalism."[15]

According to the University of Oregon's John Bellamy Foster, the deterioration of the environment is an intrinsic issue, not merely an instrumental one that causes economic crisis. According to Foster, this distinction is important because much environmental damage is unlikely to "rebound" on the economy in the form of higher costs. Just to take one example, the decline in biodiversity caused by habitat loss is unlikely to result in cost increases for firms, yet this is a genuine problem for the natural world. More generally, capitalism's tendency to use the earth as a free gift from nature will result not only in deterioration of those elements of the natural world that have value for firms, like natural resources, but also those elements that have no instrumental value (or those whose instrumental value is not yet understood or discovered).

Capitalism is an expansionary system. Firms want to increase revenue. They are continually on the lookout for new profitable opportunities. The result has been an economic system in which production and income increase over time. Of course, this is the source of the remarkable growth in income and living standards in capitalism. Yet, that same economic growth has, at least thus far, also required increasing use of environmental resources both in terms of the throughput of resources required in the production system and those expelled by that system in the form of waste. It is this increasing impact on the environment that has called into question whether there are environmental limits to economic growth. If economic growth is to continue in perpetuity, the rate at which resource inputs and waste grow must be limited to the rate at which these environmental services can be replenished. This implies not only a move from non-renewable to renewable resources, but also limiting the draw on renewable resources to their rate of renewal. Similarly, the rate of waste expulsion cannot indefinitely exceed the rate at which it can be absorbed by the environment. According to Foster, even with "correct" prices, the desire of firms to grow will likely result in the economic system exceeding these limits, leading to environmental crisis.[16]

O'Connor and Foster are just two examples of the numerous researchers who have connected the economic system to environmental issues. For these authors, any discussion of the environment that fails to incorporate the central role played by the nature of the economic system that dominates production in our world is woefully incomplete. Although mainstream economists have certainly weighed in on environmental issues, the nature of the system is rarely a part of the discussion. Further, when it comes to handing out the JBC award, researchers on environmental issues seem to have been snubbed.

JBC Winners and Economic Crisis (or Lack Thereof)

As we mentioned in the introduction to this chapter, crisis is not a word found in the mainstream-economics dictionary and the JBC winners have continued this trend. This is true in terms of both formulating a general theory of crisis and turning their attention to the specific crisis that erupted in 2007–8. This is not because the crisis is too recent for JBC winners to constructively turn their attention to this topic. One obvious consequence of the 2008 crisis was the weighing down of bookstore shelves with popular and academic analysis of the causes of, and solutions to, the economic meltdown. Yet, this was not a topic to which the JBC winners turned their attention. Therefore, it is difficult to analyze their work on crisis. Rather, we will focus on the work of three authors who are related in different ways to the concept of economic crisis discussed in the previous section. The first is Levin, whose relational contract between workers and employers was introduced in chapter 3, on labor and income. We will examine his work on credit because that industry had such a prominent role in the run-up to the 2008 meltdown. Second, Acemoglu and Saez will be studied. Recall that Acemoglu's work on the labor market incorporated the possibility of unemployment. Saez's work on income inequality and justifications for a higher tax rate on the rich also figured prominently in the chapter on labor and income. Both authors explain the original cause of a downturn that causes unemployment through "shocks" to the system, which can cause long-term downturns, a tradition very much in line with the mainstream New Keynesian explanation of an economic slump.

Levin on Credit

Levin's studies on credit focus on the subprime market for auto loans, which is characterized by low-income borrowers, high defaults, and high interest rates. The stated goal is to discover how, in a competitive credit market, certain borrowers might have difficulty getting loans. He (and his co-authors) argues that this problem can be traced to the now familiar problems created by information asymmetry in the credit market. Moral hazard occurs when the likelihood of default increases with loan size, since borrowers can take actions (or as the authors are careful to point out – face circumstances) that will make them less able to pay back the loan. Adverse selection happens because risky borrowers, who are less likely to repay a loan, will want large loans precisely because they are likely to default.

In an empirical study of one large auto sales company, the authors find evidence that both of these problems are present and substantial. They find that because of moral hazard, for any given borrower the default rate increases by 16 percent for a $1000 increase in the size of the loan. Adverse selection results in buyers in the worst credit category asking to borrow $180 more than those in the best category when other variables are controlled for. The solution to the adverse selection problem is risk-based pricing, where higher-risk borrowers are asked to pay large down payments, resulting in them taking out smaller loans.[17]

In a later paper Levin examines a second solution: automated credit scoring, which uses a "centralized risk-based pricing regime" to determine minimum down payments. The authors conclude that the switch from more informal mechanisms of credit screening, like interviews, to the automated system increased profits by about $1000 per loan, quite the leap when the average principal was only $9000. They also found that the firm loaned money to fewer applicants (by 15 percent), increased its required down payments, reduced its default rate, and sold better (more expensive) vehicles. Interestingly, despite observing that interest rates push up against the legal limits of state usury laws, and that relatively good credit scores result in larger loans rather than lower interest rates, this article examines the credit rating system very much from its benefits to the firm, rather than from how the subprime market impacts borrowers.[18]

An Evaluation of Levin on Credit

Levin's work in this area is true to the pillars of the old mainstream. It includes mathematical modeling, statistical analysis, and individual rational maximization. It also abstracts from the context in which the credit market operates, especially the subprime market. Other authors studying the subprime market have been critical of how lenders took advantage of the dreams of low-income households to coerce them into large, expensive loans.[19] This is true of both cars and the housing market that touched off the 2008 crisis. Yet Levin argues that the real problem with the subprime credit market is the lack of information that lenders have on borrowers, which makes them unable to properly serve the credit-worthy. As has so often been the case with the JBC winners, Levin's market transactions are modeled mostly as negotiations between equals, although some might have a little more information that others, rather than as situations in which power relationships are present within a broader social context. Most importantly, Levin's argument rests on the assumption that consumers may have an information advantage over the seller. The FBI, by contrast, was warning of a mortgage fraud epidemic as early as 2004, noting that lenders initiated 80 percent of the frauds.[20] Levin's microeconomic analysis of the world of finance does not take into account the advantages (often ones that were illegal) that lenders hold over borrowers, the effect of which is to misunderstand who holds the power in the credit market.

Acemoglu and Saez on Recessions

In addition to his many works in other areas, Acemoglu has also weighed in on what creates economic fluctuations. Or, more precisely, in the New Keynesian tradition, he has investigated the factors that might make the negative consequences of a shock more profound. In chapter 3, on income and inequality, we examined Acemoglu's explanation for lasting unemployment in which employers and employees have differing information on the extent of an economic shock that negatively affects workers' productivity and, therefore, the wages that firms are willing to offer them. The cost of ignorance is unemployment when workers are unwilling to accept firms' reduced wage offer.[21] Another paper offers a slightly different take on how an initial downturn (or upswing) can persist. Acemoglu argues that if fixed capital (long-lasting capital that is not used up in the creation of the product, like an assembly line) yields increasing returns to scale over time, then firms' investment decisions can lead to more persistent economic cycles. As an example, if a firm has recently invested in technology and its workers have recently received the latest training, then its cost of adopting new technology in the future is reduced. As a result, firms will find it more profitable to invest if they have recently done so. The dependence of investment decisions on past investment behavior creates more persistent economic upswings and downturns in response to economic shocks.[22]

Like Acemoglu, Saez (with co-author Michaillat) created a model of the economy to explain prolonged high periods of unemployment. In Saez's macro-model, in the *Quarterly Journal of Economics*, aggregate-demand shocks can create unemployment because of frictions in an economy with price and wage rigidity. In this case, frictions are the costs of "matching" for both sellers and buyers. The friction for sellers is that they might be unable to sell all their products, modeled by the degree of "tightness" in the product and labor markets. If the sellers are workers, this means that there are not jobs for all, so there will be a cost to finding a job. The friction for buyers is the extra costs of finding the thing they wish to buy. If the firm is "buying" workers, this is the extra recruiting cost of finding a worker to hire. In what the authors describe as the most realistic version of their model, using rigid prices and wages (as opposed to those that are more flexible), a decline in aggregate demand (from a decrease in consumption, for example) will increase firms' difficulty in selling their products. This will reduce firms' sales and increases the amount of time their workers spend idle (meaning there is extra productive capacity). Since idle workers are not very profitable, firms will decrease their demand for labor, which decreases tightness in the labor market and increases unemployment. In contrast to many other macro-models, like that of Acemoglu, Saez and Michaillat argue that it is aggregate-demand fluctuations that influence unemployment, not changes to labor supply or technology.[23]

In an earlier, pre–*Quarterly Journal of Economics*, version of this paper, the two authors examine a variety of interventions designed to pull the economy out of periods of high unemployment. Predictably, given the emphasis on aggregate demand in the Saez model, increasing aggregate demand can help reduce unemployment. For example, redistributing income from savers to spenders or from firms to workers will increase consumption and aggregate demand, and thus reduce unemployment. So, too, can increasing government purchases.[24]

It is interesting that when this earlier paper was amended for the prestigious *Quarterly Journal of Economics*, many of these policy issues had been jettisoned. The earlier version of Saez's model is more policy rich than that of Acemoglu (and even that of Saez's in the *Quarterly Journal of Economics*) in the sense that he has created room to analyze a variety of different government interventions – from the minimum wage to employment insurance. It also permits a discussion of income distribution between profits and wages. Saez is also quite redistribution friendly in that his model often suggests that transferring income from rich to poor, or firms to workers, can reduce unemployment.

An Evaluation of Acemoglu and Saez on Recessions

Acemoglu's and Saez's analysis of instability fits largely within the old mainstream pillars. Both of them build their mathematical modeling around the assumption that economic outcomes are the result of individual decisions (methodological individualism). The use of microfoundations that are consistent with the assumptions used in the rest of the discipline, such as profit-maximizing firms and maximizing individuals, to create the Keynesian result of business cycles is a hallmark of New Keynesian macro-analysis.

In these types of models some sort of friction (incorrect information or increasing returns to fixed capital for Acemoglu, matching frictions for Saez) creates economic fluctuations after a shock hits in the absence of government intervention. So, for example, for Acemoglu, under certain conditions when workers refuse to lower their wages unemployment might be the result because firms would be unwilling to hire workers at the wage they seek. This opens up room for government intervention to stimulate the economy out of its downturn.

As we saw in chapter 3, neither Acemoglu nor Saez could be thought of as a free market, conservative economist. Yet, even while advocating for government intervention, Acemoglu and Saez's use of methodological individualism involves a crucial obfuscation. Subsumed in the mathematics and statistical analysis of both authors' research in this area is the assumption that there is no power differential between firms and their workers or, as we saw in chapter 3, acknowledgment of the importance of unemployment in creating this power. Their use of methodological individualism actually assumes away power. An unemployed worker and Goldman Sachs are treated as equals in most models in a way that is unrealistic under the economic laws that govern capitalist economies. In reality, firms (especially large ones) and the business organizations to which they belong (see ALEC in chapter 1 by way of example) have considerable influence over economic policy that affects not only wage levels and profitability, as we have discussed in chapter 3, but also the conditions that can lead to economic instability that were covered at the beginning of this chapter. While it may not be inevitable for mathematical modeling to abstract from power, thus far JBC winners have done so.

Further, although Acemoglu's and Saez's research on economic fluctuations obviously examines what we have termed the macroeconomic context in the sense that it attempts to provide an explanation of how recessions and unemployment can persist, in another sense, by using shocks as the source of economic instability their macroeconomic analysis ignores an important source of instability – the context of the economic system itself. Acemoglu argues that his deficient-worker information model could apply to any kind of shock from productivity to a decline in aggregate demand.[25] Saez does distinguish between aggregate demand and aggregate supply shocks, arguing that each of these will have differing effects on economic fluctuations and on what policies might be necessary or helpful in dealing with each type of shock. Yet, in contrast to the authors, like Roubini, at the beginning of this chapter, who suggest that capitalist power and success can breed economic crisis, Acemoglu and Saez fail to acknowledge that instability can stem from the internal or class-based working of the economic system. For example, although Saez's model finds that income redistribution can stimulate aggregate demand and reduce unemployment, it does not locate the cause of the unequal distribution in the structure of a labor market in which firms have power over their workers. This is not to say that Saez has no interest in what causes income inequality. This is clearly not the case, although as we pointed out in chapter 3, his success in this area was fairly limited compared to his ability to track inequality because of his failure to incorporate the economic transition in the labor market since the 1980s.

For both Acemoglu and Saez the source of the shock comes from outside the economic system and, as a random and unforeseeable event, is impossible to predict and investigate. The question, then, becomes how quickly the system will respond once this unpredictable shock hits. For Acemoglu, the adjustment to the shock depends on information problems or investment persistence and does not require an analysis of the structure of the economic system or of the particular problems that caused this shock in the first place. As an example of why this is important, we can look at the crisis of 2008, which we have traced to the unequal distribution of income and rising household debt because of the changes to the economic structure since 1980. The strength and nature of the economic recovery will depend on how and whether firm profits are restored given this economic weakness. Acemoglu's analysis focuses on neither the specific source of the downturn nor how recovery is dependent on correcting the problem.

Finally, although Acemoglu's and Saez's models often contain policies, from an emphasis on Keynesian full employment policy to income redistribution, which might actually improve economic efficiency and equity, the structural impediments to their implementation are not the subjects of investigation. For example, while it might be beneficial in certain circumstances to transfer incomes from firms to workers through rising wages, as Saez advocates, this is likely to have an impact on profitability and be strongly resisted by the business community. This New Keynesian treatment of government is incomplete because although it can often identify situations in which intervention might improve economic results, it has no political economy analysis. This renders it incapable of predicting the likelihood of its recommended improvements actually being undertaken or of analyzing problems that might arise should they actually get implemented.

JBC Winners and Environmental Crisis (or Lack Thereof)

If there were gala events reuniting past JBC winners, environmental issues would not be a popular topic of conversation. The research that comes closest to touching on an environmental theme is Susan Athey's work (with Levin) on timber auctions.

Susan Athey

Athey has been largely ignored thus far in this book. This is not due to her lack of influence, but more a result of her subject matter, which has little overlap with the topics we have chosen to discuss. Like her sometime co-author, Levin, Athey is fond of the economics of information, especially as it pertains to auction markets and dynamic games.[26] She has also done work on the economics of organizations: in one paper showing that social hierarchies, like seniority, provide trust in situations when there is weak contract enforcement,[27] and, in another paper, demonstrating that firms might use affirmative action programs to increase their diversity.[28] She is, perhaps, best known for her ground-breaking work in econometrics, developing nonlinear techniques for difference in difference models.[29]

In keeping with Athey's research interests, her work on timber is more about auctions than about the environment. When the US Forest Service decides to put a tract of land up for harvesting, it auctions off the rights to the highest bidder. However, the nature of the auction provides an opportunity for firms to skew their bids to profit from any superior information that they can glean on the mix of tree species in the tract. The first stage in the auction process is for the Forest Service to estimate the quantity of different species on a tract. Timber companies then make their own assessment of the species mix. Firms are then asked to bid on a price for each of the species. The winner of the bid is the firm that bids the highest based on the Forest Service estimates of species and the per unit price submitted by the timber firm. The winning firm earns the right to harvest the entire lot and pays the actual amount of each species removed at their bid price for each species. When there is a difference between the actual harvest and the Forest Service estimate, there is an opportunity for timber firms to profit by skewing their high bids towards species the Forest Service has overestimated. This is not an infrequent occurrence. The Forest Service's estimate was accurate within 5 percent only 50 percent of the time. Athey and Levin create and test a model that captures the main details of this auction process and find that winning bids are skewed towards overestimated species, indicating private information on species mix is better than that of the Forest Service. However, although winning bids are higher when the Forest Service estimates are less accurate, the actual Forest Service revenues from the harvest do not decline, suggesting that the auction process forces firms to bid away the profits that they might otherwise gain from their ability to more correctly value the species mix compared to the Forest Service.[30]

An Evaluation of Athey

Athey only deviates from the much-criticized four pillars of the "old" mainstream by dropping the strong assumption of perfect information. The rest of the analysis, with its focus on modelling, individual analysis, and econometrics is very much in the mainstream tradition. Athey and Levin's research demonstrates the important point that government has not left money on the table in awarding its timber contracts. However, it is not, nor was it intended to be, a broader analysis of whether the payments from the timber companies, or the amount of land put up for auction, represent anything that might represent an ideal from an environmental perspective. For example, the bids from the timber companies will reflect their private costs, yet any reasonable consideration of the true cost of deforestation must take into account the environmental costs associated with decreased habitat, biodiversity loss, and the costs of climate change. Further, the powerful position of the timber industry and its ability to influence forest policy make it less likely that environmental costs will be fully incorporated. The Forest Service has long been a venue of conflict between competing interests, but the overwhelming driver of policy has often been the desires of the timber industry.[31] Yet this, too, is not an important subject of enquiry.

This is not to say that economists do not study the environment. This is patently not the case. Nor is it to say that when they do study the environment, they always follow an Athey-like research agenda. The entire field of ecological economics has made major contributions to how the economy impacts the environment and makes a strong case for taking a much broader, more holistic approach to environmental issues that moves beyond the "getting prices right" recommendation of much of the discipline. But none of these researchers have won the JBC award.

Conclusion

The mainstream of the discipline has historically focused on individual choice, rather than the powerful social and economic institutions that shape those choices. Our twenty-first-century JBC winners have reinforced that tradition. In fact, their preoccupation with microfoundations neglects the macrofoundations that actually drive the system, in turn offering little in the way of a systemic analysis on the two big crises of our times.

Economic fluctuations (although not particularly the 2008 economic crisis) are the subject of inquiry, but JBC winners have limited their analysis to explaining the duration or severity of a shock. Acemoglu focuses on how imperfect information can increase the duration of a downturn, while Saez argues for redistribution or Keynesian policy to move the economy out of a recession. Neither of these authors can explain how these shocks happen, preferring instead to treat them as unexplainable phenomena from outside the economy. Nor do they examine how the economic system itself can create both these shocks and the underlying weakness that turns shocks into crises.

Reading the work of JBC economists would leave one under the impression that environmental issues, let alone anything that might be termed a looming crisis, were not a particularly interesting topic of study. The only work on the environment was conducted by Athey and Levin, whose analysis of timber auctions uses forests as a convenient data mine for their main interest on information and auctions, rather than as a source of inquiry for environmental issues.

chapter seven

Conclusion

Arguably more than any other discipline, economics has a profound influence on the public policy that shapes people's lives. Unfortunately, many economic ideas, like the theories that justified the wage stagnation in the United States since the 1980s or the failed Washington Consensus approach to developing countries, have had a negative impact on the vast majority while benefiting business.

The winners of the JBC award make up the leading edge of mainstream economics research. They are the best of the new generation of American economists as defined by those inside the discipline itself. Their influence inside the profession, as measured by citations or emulation, is undeniable. Even outside economics they have had a tremendous impact on the policy debate in their areas of expertise. Some, like Levitt, have even achieved a modicum of actual celebrity. As the most capable descendants of the evolution of economic ideas, the JBC winners make ideal candidates for determining the current state of the discipline.

The question that we set out at the very beginning of this book, long before the reader was dragged through the minutiae of individual economists' assumptions and conclusions, was the extent to which the JBC economists fell afoul of what we have termed the Dow-Heilbroner-Milberg critique that was leveled at the old mainstream, which highlighted four quite specific problematic pillars that added up to a more overarching limitation. The four pillars were (1) modeling human behavior using the assumption of rational, self-interested maximization; (2) the individual, and in

particular individual choice, as the subject of inquiry; (3) a preoccupation with formal mathematical modeling disconnected from
the actual economy; and (4) the use of econometric statistical techniques lacking relevant institutional and historical context for empirical verification of hypotheses.

Critics of the old mainstream, including Dow-Heilbroner and
Milberg but certainly not limited to them, argued that, taken together, these four pillars created a discipline that lacked attention
to the effects of broader social forces on the individual. According
to these critics, people do make choices, but only do so within powerful social and economic institutions that shape those choices.
Ignoring those broader forces shrouds what actually determines
economic reality in the illusion of voluntary, individual, welfare
improving, individual decisions. The most important of these ignored social forces that were overlooked was the functioning of the
economic system that shapes people's behavior and creates power
relationships in society. The economic system creates a structure in
which power is not distributed equally. It creates differing rights
and privileges for different members of society. A crucial component of this broad social context, and the economic system that does
so much to create it, is the specific policy environment in different
capitalist economies. Failing to acknowledge the different policy
environments in different nations results in the unique system in
the United States being treated as the rule rather than the exception. Yet the underlying social order created by the political and
economic system is not, generally, a subject of enquiry for JBC winners any more than it was a topic of concern for the old mainstream.

On the crucial question of how to improve the lives of people who
live in poor nations Duflo and Acemoglu take very different approaches. Duflo's RCT studies focus on nudging the poor towards
better decisions that, she claims, can have a transformative impact
on their lives. Duflo makes a deliberate choice to avoid large-scale
issues, which she views as irresolvable, but this decision leaves
the larger structures, which we have argued are so important in
constraining the development of poor nations, unquestioned and
unchallenged. Further, the currently wealthy countries solved the
problems studied by Duflo using the type of big-picture policies

that Duflo ignores, like the public health movement. Acemoglu paints with a much broader and ambitious brush. However, his focus on the legacy of colonialism hides current developed-country influence on the developing world. Crucially, it ignores the most powerful contemporary determinants of the economic trajectories of developing nations. Multinational corporations, international institutions, and modern foreign governments all have a substantial influence on the development of many poor countries. Yet these post-colonial external factors are completely ignored by both Duflo and Acemoglu.

Given the centrality of work and income in both economics and people's actual lives, more JBC medalists have weighed in on this subject than our other areas. Their work is undeniably diverse, ranging from those who largely follow the old mainstream to Saez's work on income inequality that abandons many of the old linchpins. The work closest to the old mainstream is Levin's idea of the relational contract that incorporates mathematical models, maximizing behavior, and individual-level analysis. Rabin drops the assumption about maximizing behavior in order to incorporate the idea that people also care about fairness in exchanges. Yet, methodological individualism and mathematical modeling leads him to conceptualize fairness in a strangely naive manner (hurt me, I'll hurt you; help me, I'll help you) that cannot explain why people's ideas of fairness vary over time, across cultures, and even between different groups in any given society. It also neglects the fact that most other nations would define fairness in a much more inclusive manner that incorporates how others in society are treated, a concern that is the foundation for social welfare policies in these nations.

Chetty, Acemoglu, and Saez all conduct research that champions social welfare policies like UI benefits and minimum wages. Saez even advocates steeply progressive tax rates that would take from the rich. Yet, their work in these areas ignores the power relationships between workers and their employers that are inevitable in the economic system. Perhaps worst of all these omissions is Chetty's assumption of full employment when unemployment is a persistent problem for workers in capitalist nations. In general, all these researchers ignore the impact that business decisions have over employment and state policies. Neither do they acknowledge the effect of unemployment on workers. Their research treats the labor market as an arena in which equals arrange a mutually acceptable contract, ignoring the role of unemployment in tilting the power in this negotiation in the employer's favor.

In the area of income and the labor market, Saez's work on income distribution comes the closest to transcending the critique of the old mainstream. His work on inequality has brought a broad issue of massive importance into the public eye. Further, by placing income distribution in a historical and comparative perspective he has highlighted the fact that current US inequality is high compared to both its own past and that in other nations. Yet despite an accurate dismissal of Acemoglu's skill-biased explanation of income inequality, Saez cannot explain the causes of the inequality he so successfully documents. In fact, none of the JBC winners acknowledge the fundamental causes of the changes in incomes since 1980 that Krugman claims has created an "oligarchy" of the rich in the United States.

The US healthcare system is extraordinary in the worst sense of the word. It spends more on health than any other nation while boasting some of the worst overall indicators of any wealthy country. It is also alone in offering more for-profit service delivery than other nations and relying more heavily on unregulated private insurance to provide access. The US economic healthcare literature is similarly an outlier. Like many of the JBC economists in other specializations, Finkelstein's work is dominated by the assumption that healthcare and health insurance is demand driven. For Finkelstein, health insurance is an unconventional industry because of the problems of moral hazard and adverse selection, but, as in other markets, consumers are capable of choosing the level of healthcare and health insurance appropriate for them. The problem with this assertion is that it is not accurate. Consumers are not able to distinguish their healthcare needs independent of medical advice, creating an industry subject to Supply Induced Demand (SID). It is physicians and other medical professionals who determine demand in this industry, not patients. An analysis that incorporates SID justifies universal public coverage, as well as quality and cost controls, precisely the system that is favored in other industrial countries, and which delivers superior results to those in the United States. Finkelstein has not made this comparison in her work thus far.

Health is not only about healthcare. It is also about the conditions in which we live and the decisions we make. Rabin's analysis of people's health deals with the latter but ignores the former. His work drops the old assumption of rational maximization in favor of time inconsistency. In the health context this means that decisions, like eating delicious yet dangerous snacks, revolve around whether people are self-aware in their propensity to pleasure their current selves at the expense of their future well-being. His focus on individual choice, no matter how self-deluded, fails to acknowledge the broader social context that creates preferences. People's enjoyment of cigarettes is taken as a given, not subject to questions about the social gradient in both smoking incidence and the differing health impacts that smoking has on different classes. Any analysis that fails to incorporate the crucial social context that influences people's decisions – the influence of class and gender-based patterns of consumption – is dangerously misleading. How would Rabin's approach address the fact that smoking among working-class women has increased over time while smoking among higher-income males has declined dramatically? Perhaps they have different time-inconsistency tendencies.

Crime also has an important social component. One might even talk about the social or economic determinants of crime in a manner similar to the social determinants of health. Yet Levitt ignores these broader social factors that contribute to crime in favor of explaining falling crime rates in the United States through the legalization of abortion. Both his subject matter and his method in dealing with that subject matter are revealing. His work focuses on street crime, yet ignores the much more damaging world of organizational or corporate crime, which would require examining the political and economic power wielded by the business community. Further, in dealing with street crime he neglects to compare the uniquely high rates of violent crime in the United States with that in other nations or to examine the factors that might cause this remarkable difference. His method is dependent on a clever use of empirical testing and loose modeling that focuses on individual incentives. His method does deviate from some of the centerpieces of the old mainstream. He discards formal mathematical modeling. Econometrics and testing are at the center of his research, but he relies much more on clever test design than advanced technique. In fact, Levitt makes some strong clams about the ability of his empirical work to uncover the "truth." One might even claim that given his lack of theory or context, he is dependent on the strength of his empirical testing. Yet other researchers have been able to point out important flaws in his empirical work and put forward equally surprising explanations for the drop in US crime, like the regulation of lead. His research is a little unclear on where he stands in terms of rational self-interested maximization. He allows people motivations besides individual self-interest, yet incentives remain central to his explanations. However, he certainly maintains the focus on individual choice as the level of analysis. He has been dubbed a "rogue" economist, in the sense that he pursues unconventional testing on subject areas outside what are normally considered the purview of the field, but in his neglect of the broader social and economic context for crime he is very old school.

To the casual observer, it might appear as though two of the biggest economic issues facing the wealthy nations today are the continuing economic crisis and escalating environmental deterioration. Yet neither of these topics has piqued the interest of JBC award winners. In fact, even the term crisis is difficult to find in their research. Having said that, a few JBC winners do undertake analyzes of economic fluctuations. Saez and Acemoglu fall squarely in the New Keynesian tradition that argues that downturns can persist when some impediment in the market prevents rapid adjustment from adverse economic shocks. Importantly, this type of analysis fails to acknowledge that frequently shocks are not caused by unpredictable external events but by the regular functioning of the economy. An explanation of crises that rests on an examination of the economic system itself does not exist.

The one JBC research topic that touches, however tangentially, on a subject germane to the causes of the 2008 crisis is Levin's work on the credit market. While the specifics of the causes of the 2008 financial meltdown are complicated, at the center was the increasing indebtedness of a cash-strapped US population. Part of this increased debt level was due to some fairly underhanded activities by banks and other lenders. Yet Levin's work (like Finkelstein's on health insurance) treats the credit market as a negotiation between equals, in which information asymmetry creates problems for the lender. His solution is a technological fix that allows credit firms to better determine the credit worthiness of their applicants. His analysis is very much from the perspective of the problems of the firm rather than the difficulties faced by low-income borrowers.

Environmental problems receive even less attention from JBC winners than economic crises. Only a Levin and Athey paper, using timber auctions to analyze imperfect information, could be generously described as taking on environmental issues. With the exception of relaxing the very strong assumption of perfect information, this work, with its focus on modeling, individual analysis, and econometrics is in the old mainstream tradition. It is also not a piece of research that genuinely attempts to probe the environmental issues associated with forestry or the role that timber companies play in setting forestry policy, although, to be fair this was not the purpose of the paper. Yet this is in keeping with the fact that neither the environmental nor the economic crises are topics that have attracted the attention of the JBC awards committee.

Taken as a group, JBC winners have little dedication to the old linchpin of *homo economicus*, which assumes that people have the information, capacity, and narrow motivation to rationally maximize their individual self-interest. Yet the majority of the nine JBC winners do not stray very far from the other pillars named in the critique. While slight tweaks to the assumptions in economic models, like allowing imperfect information and non-maximizing behavior, have been introduced, the focus has predominantly still been on using formal modeling techniques, complex econometrics, and a focus on the individual. Of the nine JBC winners, five would fit into this category. Two other winners, Duflo and Levitt, have also moved away from formal modeling and elaborate econometrics for their testing, but still retain a strong focus on individual analysis and empirical testing. As a group, the analysis of this seven focuses on the choices made by individuals rather than the historical and institutional environment within which those choices occur. A further two, Saez and Acemoglu, do broaden their approach beyond the individual to a consideration of the broader social and economic context in which people operate. Yet even these two, who have moved the furthest from the Dow-Heilbroner-Milberg critique, are still wedded to the old mainstream linchpin of ignoring the main source of the power dynamics inherent in the current economic system. In particular, their approach to those crucial issues that they do examine, from poverty in the developing world to income inequality, neglects any systematic role of the power of for-profit corporations and their impact on the government's role in creating these conditions.

This book is about what is missing from nearly all of their work and why it matters. While these JBC-winning economists have largely disregarded both the economic and environmental crises, arguably the most important subjects at this historic conjuncture, the manner in which they study the topics that they do research is more telling. The work of the new generation of economic superstars, like its predecessors, in the words of Yanis Varoufakis, Joseph Halevi, and Nicholas Theocarakis, "remains innocent of the logic of contemporary capitalism."[1]

The institutions of modern capitalism – from private ownership to business enterprise and the price system – are treated as "natural," and therefore beyond the scope of inquiry. Further, the specific institutions that exist in current capitalism are also ignored. For example, development issues are studied without critically examining the effects of the International Monetary Fund or multinational corporations. What this means is that, with very few exceptions, economics tends to abstract itself from the real world analysis of the how the actual economy operates.

In doing so, the JBC winners ignore the specific institutions that make up the unique version of capitalism that exists in different countries. One consequence of this myopia is a failure to contrast conditions in differently performing economies. This is particularly noticeable in the failure of the JBC-winning economists who focus on the United States to treat it as an exceptional economic structure that stands in stark contrast to more social democratic nations. This exceptionalism is largely caused by the uniquely powerful influence of US businesses in setting its economic policy. Rarely in the works of these economists will you find an analysis of the role of these major influences on economic policy. The economics of health are studied without mentioning the role of the private, for-profit insurance firms. Inequality is studied without examining the power structures in the unique US labor market that have been so harmful to workers and so beneficial to firms. Research on crime fails to acknowledge the particularly high US violent crime rate and the context in which it occurs. As a result, their analysis frequently either downplays or completely ignores the real cause of economic difficulty and, therefore, suggests solutions that are of limited effectiveness, at best, and quite harmful at worst.

Notes

1 Introduction

1 P. Vale, "Queen Visits Bank of England, Asks about 2008 Financial Crisis, Calls FSA 'Complacent,'" *Huffington Post UK*, 12 December 2012. Available at http://www.huffingtonpost.co.uk/2012/12/13/queen-visit-bank-of-england_n_2294771.html. In typically British fashion, a group of economists actually apologized to the queen for their failings. American Press, "British Economists Send Apology to Queen," *Huffington Post*, 26 August 2009. Available at http://www.huffingtonpost.com/2009/07/26/british-economists-send-a_n_244998.html.
2 I. Basen, "Economics Has Met the Enemy, and It Is Economics," *Globe and Mail*, 15 October 2011.
3 T. Leonard, "'A Certain Rude Honesty'": John Bates Clark as a Pioneering Neoclassical Economist," *History of Political Economy* 35(3) (2003): 521–58.
4 J. Clark, *The Distribution of Wealth: A Theory of Wages, Interests and Profits* (New York: Macmillan and Co., 1899).
5 P. Krugman, "Divided over Trade," *New York Times*, 14 May 2007, A19.
6 R. Scott, *The High Price of "Free" Trade* (Washington, DC: Economic Policy Institute, 2003).
7 For an example of this debate see D. Neumark and W. Wascher, "Minimum Wages and Employment: A Case Study of the Fast Food Industry in the New Jersey and Pennsylvania: Comment," *American Economic Review* 90(5) (2000): 1362–96; D. Card and A. Krueger, "Minimum Wages and Employment: A Case Study of the Fast Food Industry in New Jersey and Pennsylvania: Reply," *American Economic Review* 90(5) (2000): 1397–420.

8   A. Krueger, "Report on the Commission on Graduate Education in Economics," *Journal of Economic Literature* 29(3) (1991): 1035–53.

9   T. Lawson, "Mathematical Modelling and Ideology in the Economics Academy," *Economic Thought* 1(1) (2012): 3–22. For other variations on this broad theme see B. Fine and D. Milonakis, *From Political Economy to Economics: Method, the Social and the Historical in the Evolution of Economic Theory* (New York: Routledge, 2008); B. Fine and D. Milonakis, *From Economics Imperialism to Freakonomics: The Shifting Boundaries between Economics and Other Social Sciences* (New York: Routledge, 2009) and Y. Varoufakis, *Modern Political Economics: Making Sense of the Post-2008 World* (New York: Routledge, 2011).

10 J. Sachs, "Can We Save the World Economy? A Conversation with George Soros, Nouriel Roubini, and Jeffrey Sachs" (Columbia University, 20 October 2008).

11 W. Buiter, "The Failure of Academic Economics," *Financial Times*, 4 March 2009: 12. For other examples see D. McCloskey, *The Rhetoric of Economics* (Madison: University of Wisconsin Press, 1985); G. Hodgson, "On the Problem of Formalism in Economics," *Post-Autistic Economics Review* 28 (2004).

12 R. Backhouse, "The Rise of Free Market Economics: Economists and the Role of the State since 1970," *History of Political Economy* 37(1) (2005): 355–92.

13 See, for example, D. Foley, *Adam's Fallacy: A Guide to Economic Theology* (Harvard: Harvard University Press, 2006); P. Mirowski, *Never Let a Serious Crisis Go to Waste: How Neoliberalism Survived the Financial Meltdown* (London: Verso Books, 2013); S. Keen, *Debunking Economics: The Naked Emperor Dethroned?* (London: Zed Books, 2011); J. Quiggin, *Zombie Economics: How Dead Ideas Still Walk among Us* (Princeton: Princeton University Press, 2012).

14 E. Andrews, "Greenspan Concedes Error on Regulation," *New York Times*, 24 October 2008, B1.

15 S. Dow, *Economic Methodology: An Inquiry* (New York: Oxford University Press, 2002).

16 R. Heilbroner and W. Milberg, *The Crisis of Vision in Modern Economic Thought* (Cambridge: Cambridge University Press, 1995).

17 Ibid., 86.

18 A. Smith, *An Inquiry into the Nature and Causes of the Wealth of Nations* (Edinburgh: Thomas Nelson, 1843), 6.

19 P. Mirowski, *Never Let a Serious Crisis Go to Waste: How Neoliberalism Survived the Financial Meltdown* (London: Verso, 2013).

20 If any proof of this statement is required see L. Bartels, *Unequal Democracy: The Political Economy of the New Gilded Age* (Princeton: Princeton University Press, 2010) and M. Gilens, *Affluence and Influence: Economic Inequality and Political Power in America* (Princeton: Princeton University Press, 2012).

21 For an example of comparative systems research see G. Olsen, *Power and Inequality: A Comparative Introduction* (Oxford: Oxford University Press, 2011).

22 S. Dow, *Economic Methodology: An Inquiry* (New York: Oxford University Press, 2002), 24.

23 For an excellent book that examines the history of economic thought from an institutional perspective see J.K. Galbraith, *Economics in Perspective: A Critical History* (Boston: Houghton Mifflin, 1987).

24 A. Shaikh, "The Poverty of Algebra," in I. Steedman et al., *The Value Controversy* (London: Verso, 1979), 266–300. A very similar quote – "The prestige accorded to mathematics in economics has given it rigor, but, alas, also mortis" – can be found in R. Heilbroner, "Modern Economics as a Chapter in the History of Economic Thought," *History of Political Economy* 11(2) (1979): 192–8.

25 Backhouse, "The Rise of Free Market Economics."

26 R. Frank, T. Gilovich, and D. Regan, "Does Studying Economics Inhibit Cooperation?" *Journal of Economic Perspectives* 7(2) (1993): 159–71.

27 M. Thatcher, "Interview for Women's Own," Margaret Thatcher Foundation, 23 September 1987. Available at http://www.margaretthatcher.org/document/106689.

28 Backhouse, "The Rise of Free Market Economics," 384.

29 D. Colander, "The Making of an Economist Redux," *Journal of Economic Perspectives* 19(1) (2005): 175–98.

30 P. Cohen, "Ivory Tower Unswayed by Crashing Economy," *New York Times*, 5 March 2009, C1.

31 M. Gabbert, *Academic Freedom in Conflict: The Struggle over Free Speech Rights in the University* (Toronto: James Lorimer, 2014).

32 Cohen, "Ivory Tower Unswayed."

33 T. Keys and T. Malnight, *Corporate Clout: The Influence of the World's Largest 100 Economic Entities* (Global Trends, 2012).

34 S. Bowles and H. Gintis, *Democracy and Capitalism: Property, Community, and the Contradictions of Modern Social Thought* (New York: Basic Books, 1987).

35 A. Stratton, "Vince Cable and Chris Huhne Clash over Carbon Emissions," *The Guardian*, 10 May 2011, 1.

36 J. Nichols, "ALEC Exposed," *The Nation*, 1–8 August 2011.

37 J. Rogers and L. Dresser, "ALEC Exposed: Business Domination Inc," ibid.

2 Development and Growth

1 D. Acemoglu, S. Johnson, and J. Robinson, "The Colonial Origins of Comparative Development: An Empirical Investigation," *American Economic Review* 91(5) (2001): 1369–1401.
2 N. Farndale, "Esther Duflo: Can This Woman Change the World?" *Telegraph*, 7 August 2011, available at http://www.telegraph.co.uk/culture/books/authorinterviews/8681481/Esther-Duflo-Can-this-woman-change-the-world.html.
3 I. Parker, "The Poverty Lab," *The New Yorker*, 17 May 2010, 78–89.
4 R. Prebisch, *The Economic Development of Latin America and Its Principal Problems* (Lake Success, NY: United Nations, 1950).
5 A.G. Frank, *Capitalism and Underdevelopment* (New York: Monthly Review Press, 1967).
6 I. Wallerstein, *The Modern World-System*, vol. 1: *Capitalist Agriculture and the Origins of the European World-Economy in the Sixteenth Century* (New York: Academic Press, 1974); I. Wallerstein, *The Modern World-System*, vol. 2: *Mercantilism and the Consolidation of the European World-Economy, 1600–1750* (New York: Academic Press, 1980); I. Wallerstein, *The Modern World-System*, vol. 3: *The Second Great Expansion of the Capitalist World-Economy, 1730s–1840s* (San Diego: Academic Press, 1989).
7 For more recent works in this tradition, see J. Loxley, *Interdependence, Disequilibrium and Growth: Reflections on the Political Economy of North–South Relations at the Turn of the Century* (London: Macmillan, 1998) and K. Levitt, *Reclaiming Development: Independent Thought and Caribbean Community* (Kingston: Ian Randle Publishers, 2005).
8 L. Ndikumana and J.K. Boyce, *Africa's Odious Debts: How Foreign Loans and Capital Flight Bled a Continent* (London: Zed, 2011).
9 Ibid., 54.
10 L. Ndikumana and J. Boyce, *Capital Flight from North African Countries* (University of Massachusetts Amherst: Political Economy Research Institute, 2012), 5.
11 Ndikumana and Boyce, *Africa's Odious Debts*, 4. For a more general work on capital flight, tax evasion, and offshore finance see R. Naylor, *Hot Money and the Politics of Debt*, 3rd ed. (Montreal: McGill-Queen's University Press, 2004).
12 W. Blum, *Killing Hope: US Military and CIA Interventions since World War II* (Monroe, ME: Common Courage Press, 2004).
13 S. Zeller, "AID Awards Contract for Iraq Economic Recovery," 25 July 2003, available at http://www.govexec.com/defense/2003/07/aid-awards-contract-for-iraq-economic-recovery/14631/.

14 C. Foote, W. Block, K. Crane, and S. Gray, "Economic Policy and Prospects in Iraq," *Journal of Economic Perspectives* 18(3) (2004): 47–70.

15 N. Klein, "Baghdad Year Zero," *Harper's Magazine*, September 2004, 43–53.

16 J. Sachs, "Corporate Crime Wave Threatens Global Economy," *Taipei Times*, 3 May 2011.

17 D. Kaufmann, "Myths and Realities of Governance and Corruption," in A. Lopez-Carlos et al., *Global Competitiveness Report 2005–2006* (Davos: World Economic Forum, 2006), 81–98.

18 Ibid., 81–98.

19 Sachs, "Corporate Crime Wave."

20 H. Leonard, "Multinational Corporations and Politics in Developing Countries," *World Politics* 32(3) (1980): 454–83.

21 Ibid.

22 J. Williamson, "The Strange History of the Washington Consensus," *Journal of Post Keynesian Economics* 27(2) (2004): 195–206.

23 C. Gore, "The Rise and Fall of the Washington Consensus as a Paradigm for Developing Countries," *World Development,* 28(5)(2000): 798–804.

24 For an evaluation of the IMF's role in the debt crisis of the 1980s see J. Loxley, *Debt and Disorder: External Financing for Development* (Boulder, CO: Westview Press, 1986).

25 J. Stiglitz, *Globalization and Its Discontents* (New York: Norton, 2002), 213.

26 Ibid., 20.

27 World Bank, *World Development Report* (Washington: World Bank, 2005).

28 H-J. Chang, *Kicking Away the Ladder: Development Strategy and Historical Perspective* (London: Anthem Press, 2002).

29 P. Davidson, "A Post Keynesian View of the Washington Consensus and How to Improve It," *Journal of Post Keynesian Economics* 27(2) (2004): 207–27.

30 Stiglitz, *Globalization and Its Discontents*, 209.

31 Ibid., 207.

32 G. Monbiot, "Spin, Lies and Corruption," The Guardian,14 June 2005, available at http://www.monbiot.com/2005/06/14/spin-lies-and-corruption/.

33 Ndikumana and Boyce, *Africa's Odious Debts*, 30.

34 J. Sachs, *The End of Poverty: Economic Possibilities for Our Time* (New York: Penguin Press, 2005).

35 W. Easterly, *The White Man's Burden: Why the West's Efforts to Aid the Rest Have Done So Much Ill and So Little Good* (Oxford: Oxford University Press, 2006).

36 N. Farndale, "Esther Duflo: Can This Woman Change the World?" *Telegraph*, 7 August 2011, available at http://www.telegraph.co.uk/

culture/books/authorinterviews/8681481/Esther-Duflo-Can-this-woman-change-the-world.html.

37 A. Banerjee and E. Duflo, "The Economic Lives of the Poor," *Journal of Economic Perspectives* 21(1) (2007): 141–67.

38 A. Banerjee and E. Duflo, *Poor Economics: A Radical Rethinking of the Way to Fight Global Poverty* (New York: PublicAffairs, 2011), 41–71; A. Banerjee, E. Duflo, R. Glennerster, and D. Kothari, "Improving Immunisation Coverage in Rural India: Clustered Randomised Controlled Evaluation of Immunisation Campaigns with and without Incentives," *British Medical Journal* 340 (2010).

39 Banerjee and Duflo, "Economic Lives of the Poor."

40 Banerjee and Duflo, *Poor Economics*, 23.

41 Ibid., 33.

42 E. Duflo, R. Hanna, and S. Ryan, "Incentives Work: Getting Teachers to Come to School," *American Economic Review* 102(4) (2012): 1241–78.

43 Banerjee and Duflo, *Poor Economics*, 71–97.

44 Ibid., 269.

45 Ibid., 270.

46 Ibid., 3.

47 Ibid., 271.

48 For an example of these criticisms see J. Heckman, "Randomization and Social Policy Evaluation," in C. Manski and I. Garfinkel, eds, *Evaluating Welfare and Training Programs* (Cambridge, MA: Harvard University Press, 1992), 201–30). For Duflo's response see A. Banerjee and E. Duflo, "The Experimental Approach to Development Economics," *Annual Review of Economics* 1 (2009): 151–78.

49 Banerjee, Duflo, Glennerster, and Kothari, "Improving Immunisation Coverage in Rural India."

50 Banerjee and Duflo, *Poor Economics*, 65.

51 Ibid., 62.

52 S. Maxwell, "Poor Economics: A Review," 4 March 2012, available at http://www.simonmaxwell.eu/book-reviews/poor-economics-a-review.html.

53 T. Malthus, *An Essay on the Principle of Population* (1803; Cambridge: Cambridge University Press, 1992), 101.

54 W. Easterly, "Development Experiments: Ethical? Feasible? Useful?" *Aid Watchers*, 16 July 2009, available at http://aidwatchers.com/2009/07/development-experiments-ethical-feasible-useful/.

55 Banerjee and Duflo, *Poor Economics*, 225–6.

56 Ibid., 232–5.

57 Ibid., 42.

58 S. Szreter, "Rethinking McKeown: The Relationship between Public Health and Social Change," *American Journal of Public Health* 92(5) (2002): 722; J. Colgrove, "The McKeown Thesis: A Historical Controversy and Its Enduring Influence," *American Journal of Public Health* 92(5) (2002); H. Brenner, "Commentary: Economic Growth Is the Basis of Mortality Rate Decline in the 20th Century – Experience of the United States 1901–2000," *International Journal of Epidemiology* 35 (2005).

59 Ndikumana and Boyce, *Africa's Odious Debts*, 82–3.

60 S. Reddy, "Randomise This! On Poor Economics," *Review of Agrarian Studies* 2(2) (2012): 63.

61 D. Acemoglu and J. Robinson, *Why Nations Fail: The Origins of Power, Prosperity and Poverty* (London: Profile Books, 2012).

62 Ibid., 74–5.

63 D. Acemoglu and J. Robinson, "Why Is Africa Poor?" *Economic History of Developing Regions* 25(1) (2010): 21–50.

64 Acemoglu and Robinson, *Why Nations Fail*, 79.

65 D. Acemoglu, S. Johnson, and J. Robinson, "The Colonial Origins of Comparative Development: An Empirical Investigation," *American Economic Review* 91(5) (2001): 1369–401; D. Acemoglu, S. Johnson, and J. Robinson, "The Colonial Origins of Comparative Development: An Empirical Investigation. Reply," *American Economic Review* 102(6) (2012): 3077–110.

66 Acemoglu and Robinson, "Why Is Africa Poor?"

67 D. Acemoglu, S. Johnson and J. Robinson, "The Rise of Europe: Atlantic Trade, Institutional Change, and Economic Growth," *American Economic Review* 95(3) (2005): 546–79.

68 Ibid.

69 Acemoglu and Robinson, *Why Nations Fail*, 323.

70 Ibid., 457.

71 D. Acemoglu, J. Robinson, and T. Verdier, "Can't We All Be More Like Scandinavians?" NBER working paper no. 18441, 2012.

72 Acemoglu and Robinson, *Why Nations Fail*, 90.

73 Ndikumana and Boyce, *Africa's Odious Debts*, 1.

74 S. Kelly, *America's Tyrant: The CIA and Mobutu of Zaire* (Washington, DC: American University Press, 1993).

75 Acemoglu and Robinson, *Why Nations Fail*, 447.

76 Ibid.

77 J. Sachs, "Government, Geography, and Growth: The True Drivers of Economic Development," *Foreign Affairs* 91(5) (2012): 142–50.

78 D. Acemoglu and J. Robinson, "Response to Jeffrey Sachs" (review of *Why Nations Fail*), available at http://whynationsfail.com/blog/2012/11/21/response-to-jeffrey-sachs.html.

79 Similarly, Acemoglu and Robinson's *Economic Origins of Dictatorship and Democracy* (Cambridge: Cambridge University Press, 2006) seeks to explain which of these two forms of government will emerge in a nation almost exclusively using economic factors internal to a nation. For example, the discussion of the political history of Guatemala, El Salvador, and Nicaragua makes no meaningful mention of the determining role of US influence.

80 Sachs, "Government, Geography, and Growth.

81 D. Acemoglu and J. Robinson, "Economics versus Politics: Pitfalls of Policy Advice," *Journal of Economic Perspectives* 27(2) (2013): 173–92.

82 Chang, *Kicking Away the Ladder*.

83 M. Mazzucato, *The Entrepreneurial State: Debunking Public vs. Private Sector Myths* (London: Anthem Press, 2013).

84 L. Thurow, *The Future of Capital: How Today's Economic Forces Shape Tomorrow's World* (New York: Penguin Books, 1996).

85 Acemoglu, Robinson, and T. Verdier, "Can't We All Be More Like Scandinavians?"

86 R. Reich, *Aftershock: The Next Economy and America's Future* (New York: Knopf, 2010), 62.

87 K. Schwab, *The Global Competitiveness Report 2013–2014* (Geneva: World Economic Forum, 2013), 22.

88 R. Wilkinson and K. Pickett, *The Spirit Level: Why Equality Is Better for Everyone* (New York: Penguin Books, 2009).

89 PBS, "Inequality Hurts: The Unhealthy Side Effects of Economic Disparity," *PBS*, 11 September 2011, available at http://www.pbs.org/newshour/bb/business-july-dec11-makingsense_09-28/.

3 Labor, Income, and Inequality in the United States

1 B. Stein, "In Class Warfare, Guess Which Class Is Winning," *New York Times*, 26 November 2006.

2 T. Piketty, *Capital in the Twenty-First Century* (Harvard: Belknap Press of Harvard University Press, 2014).

3 J. Galbraith, *Created Unequal: The Crisis in American Pay* (New York: Free Press, 1998); J. Galbraith, *Inequality and Instability: A Study of the World Economy Just before the Great Crisis* (Oxford: Oxford University Press, 2012); J. Stiglitz, *The Great Divide: Unequal Societies and What We Can Do about Them* (New York: W.W. Norton, 2015); P. Krugman, "Graduates vs. Oligarchs," *New York Times*, 1 November 2011.

4 C. Campbell, "Republicans Are Suddenly Talking about Income Inequality," *Business Insider*, 5 February 2015, available at http://www.businessinsider.com/republicans-are-suddenly-talking-about-income-inequality-2015-2; M. Reilly, "Thomas Piketty Calls Out Republican 'Hypocrisy' On Income Inequality," *Huffington Post*, 11 March 2015, available at http://www.huffingtonpost.com/2015/03/11/thomas-piketty-jeb-bush_n_6848718.html.

5 S. Bowles, D. Gordon, and T. Weisskopf, "Power and Profits: The Social Structure of Accumulation and the Profitability of the Postwar U.S. Economy," *Review of Radical Political Economics* 18 (1986).

6 For a much more detailed discussion of the structure of the post-war US economy, see Bowles, Gordon, and Weisskopf, "Power and Profits" and R. Pollin, *Contours of Descent: U.S. Economic Fractures and the Landscape of Global Austerity* (London: Verso, 2003).

7 There is considerable controversy about the precise cause of the fall in profits. See, for example, R. Brenner, *The Economics of Global Turbulence: The Advanced Capitalist Economies from Long Boom to Long Downturn, 1945–2005* (New York: Verso, 2006).

8 R. Gordon, "Recent Developments in the Theory of Inflation and Unemployment," in P. Korliras and R. Thorn, eds, *Modern Macroeconomics: Major Contributions to Contemporary Thought* (New York: Harper & Row, 1979), 259–84; R. Gordon, "The Time Varying NAIRU and Its Implications for Economic Policy," *Journal of Economic Perspectives* 11(1) (1997): 11–32; R. Pollin, "The Natural Rate of Unemployment: It's All about Class Conflict," *Dollars and Sense Magazine*, September/October 1998: 219.

9 D. Trilling, "A 'Nightmare' Experience? The Tories Economic Advisor on the Thatcher Years," *New Statesmen*, 8 March 2010, available at http://www.newstatesman.com/blogs/the-staggers/2010/03/thatcher-economic-budd-dispatches.

10 This broad restructuring of the economy has often been termed neoliberalism. For a more complete discussion of the policies involved and the history of their implementation, see D. Harvey, *A Brief History of Neoliberalism* (Oxford: Oxford University Press, 2007) and P. Mirowski, "Postface: Defining Neoliberalism," in P. Mirowski and D. Plehwe, eds, *The Road from Mont Pelerin: The Making of a Neoliberal Thought Collective* (Cambridge, MA: Harvard University Press, 2009), 417–56.

11 P. Krugman, "Divided over Trade," *New York Times*, 14 May 2007: A19.

12 A. Greenspan, "Performance of the U.S. Economy," testimony of Chairman Alan Greenspan before the Committee on the Budget of the United States Senate, Federal Reserve Board, 21 January 1997, available at http://www.federalreserve.gov/boarddocs/testimony/1997/19970121.htm.

13 D. Kotz, *The Rise and Fall of Neoliberal Capitalism* (Cambridge, MA: Harvard University Press, 2015), 88–97. For an analysis that focuses on the perverse incentive structure arising from paying executives with stock options, see R. Martin, *Fixing the Game: Bubbles, Crashes, and What Capitalism Can Learn from the NFL* (Boston: Harvard Business Review, 2011).

14 Center on Wisconsin Strategy, *The State of Working Wisconsin Update 2005* (Madison, WI: University of Wisconsin, Madison, 2005), 8.

15 R. Reich, *Aftershock: The Next Economy and America's Future* (New York: Knopf, 2010), 62.

16 F. Baragar and R. Chernomas, "Profit without Accumulation," *International Journal of Political Economy* 41(3) (2013).

17 J. Levin, "Relational Incentive Contracts," *American Economic Review* 93(3) (2003).

18 J. Levin, "Multilateral Contracting and the Employment Relationship," *Quarterly Journal of Economics* 117(3) (2002).

19 M. Rabin, "Incorporating Fairness into Game Theory and Economics," *American Economic Review* 83(5) (1993): 1294. An extension to this view pointed out that fairness considerations can even apply in situations of large material consequences: W. Nelson, "Incorporating Fairness into Game Theory and Economics: Comment," *American Economic Review* 91(4) (2001).

20 See J. Jost, S. Blount, J. Pfeffer, and G. Hunyady, "Fair Market Ideology: Its Cognitive-Motivational Underpinnings," *Research in Organizational Behavior* 25 (2003) or, for a more popular version, S. Blount, "Grand Illusion: Contrary to Popular Belief, Free Markets Aren't Really Fair," *Stern Business*, Fall 2002.

21 R. Backhouse, "The Rise of Free Market Economics: Economists and the Role of the State since 1970," *History of Political Economy* 37(1) (2005); J. Jenkins and C. Eckert, "The Corporate Elite, the New Conservative Policy Network, and Reaganomics," *Critical Sociology* 16 (1989); J. Jenkins and C. Eckert, "The Right Turn in Economic Policy: Business Elites and the New Conservative Economics," *Sociological Forum* 15(2) (2000); L. Lapham, "Tentacles of Rage: The Republican Propaganda Mill, A Brief History," *Harpers Magazine*, September 2004; and Mirowski and Plehwe, *The Road from Mont Pelerin*.

22 B. Cronin, "Economist Is Awarded Top Honor in the Field," *Wall Street Journal*, 12 April 2013.

23 R. Chetty and E. Saez, "Dividend Taxes and Corporate Behavior: Evidence from the 2003 Dividend Tax Cut," *Quarterly Journal of Economics* 120 (3) (2005).

24 R. Chetty, J. Friedman, S. Leth-Petersen, T. Nielsen and T. Olsen, "Active vs. Passive Decisions and Crowd-out in Retirement Savings Accounts: Evidence from Denmark," *Quarterly Journal of Economics* 129(3) (2014).

25 R. Chetty, J. Friedman, T. Olsen, and L. Pistaferri, "Adjustment Costs, Firm Responses, and Micro vs. Macro Labor Supply Elasticities: Evidence from Danish Tax Records," *Quarterly Journal of Economics* 126(2) (2011): 758–9.

26 Ibid.

27 D. Card, R. Chetty, and A. Weber, "The Spike at Benefit Exhaustion: Leaving the Unemployment System or Starting a New Job?" *American Economic Review* 97(2) (2007).

28 R. Chetty, "Moral Hazard versus Liquidity and Optimal Unemployment Insurance," *Journal of Political Economy* 116(2) (2008). He works a variation on this theme in R. Chetty and A. Looney, "Consumption Smoothing and the Welfare Consequences of Social Insurance in Developing Economies," *Journal of Public Economics* 90 (2006).

29 R. Chetty, N. Hendren, P. Kline, E. Saez, and N. Turner, "Is the United States Still a Land of Opportunity? Recent Trends in Intergenerational Mobility," *American Economic Review Papers and Proceedings* 104(5) (2014).

30 R. Chetty, N. Hendren, P. Kline, E. Saez, and N. Turner, "Where Is the Land of Opportunity? The Geography of Intergenerational Mobility in the United States," NBER working paper no. 19843 (2014).

31 Ibid., 42.

32 OECD, *Economic Policy Reforms: Going for Growth* (2010), 187, available at http://www.oecd.org/eco/growth/economicpolicyreformsgoingforgrowth2010.htm.

33 M. Corak, "Income Inequality, Equality of Opportunity, and Intergenerational Mobility," *Journal of Economic Perspectives* 27(3) (2013).

34 Chetty, Friedman, Olsen, and Pistaferri, "Adjustment Costs," 771.

35 Statistics Denmark, "Unemployment," available at http://www.dst.dk/en/Statistik/emner/arbejdsloeshed.aspx.

36 D. Acemoglu, "Asymmetric Information, Bargaining, and Unemployment Fluctuations," *International Economic Review* 36(4) (1995). Other articles present variations on this theme. See, for example, D. Acemoglu and R. Shimer, "Holdups and Efficiency with Search Frictions," *International Economic Review* 40(4) (1999); the more empirically oriented D. Acemoglu and A. Scott, "Asymmetries in the Cyclical Behaviour of UK Labour Markets," *Economic Journal* 104(427) (1994); and D. Acemoglu, "Credit Market Imperfections and Persistent Unemployment," *European Economic Review* 45(4–6) (2001), in which the

friction is the poor performance of the big European banks relative to the more flexible US credit market.

37 D. Acemoglu, "Why Do New Technologies Complement Skills? Directed Technical Change and Wage Inequality," *Quarterly Journal of Economics* 113(4) (1998); D. Acemoglu, "Technical Change, Inequality, and the Labor Market," *Journal of Economic Literature* 40(1) (2002).

38 D. Acemoglu, "Changes in Unemployment and Wage Inequality: An Alternative Theory and Some Evidence," *American Economic Review* 89(5) (1999). In a slightly different vein he modelled an economy in which the frictions come in the form of a costly search by employers and employees for a "production partner." One of the implications of this model is that economies, like that of the United States, with a more flexible labor market will have greater inequality. D. Acemoglu, "Matching, Heterogeneity, and the Evolution of Income Distribution," *Journal of Economic Growth* 2 (1997).

39 D. Acemoglu, "Patterns of Skill Premia," *Review of Economic Studies* 70 (2003).

40 D. Acemoglu, P. Aghion, and G. Violante, "Deunionization, Technical Change and Inequality," Carnegie-Rochester Conference Series on Public Policy 55 (2001).

41 D. Acemoglu and J. Robinson, "The Problem with U.S. Inequality," *Huffington Post* Blog, 11 March 2012, available at http://www .huffingtonpost.com/daron-acemoglu/us-inequality_b_1338118.html.

42 D. Acemoglu and R. Shimer, "Efficient Unemployment Insurance," *Journal of Political Economy* 107(5) (1999). In a paper a year later – D. Acemoglu and R. Shimer, "Productivity Gains from Unemployment Insurance," *European Economic Review* 44(7) (2000) – the same two authors provide empirical evidence that the positive impacts of UI is greater than its negative consequences.

43 D. Acemoglu, "Good Jobs versus Bad Jobs," *Journal of Labor Economics* 19(1) (2001). Gary Becker, among others, argued that a minimum wage would reduce training because workers cannot accept jobs at lower wages while they are being trained. Acemoglu found that this hypothesized impact did not exist, in D. Acemoglu and J.-S. Pischke, "Minimum Wages and On-the-job Training," NBER working paper no. 7184 (1999).

44 For an illustrative example, see K. Silverstein, "Labor's Last Stand: The Corporate Campaign to Kill the Employee Free Choice Act," *Harper's Magazine*, July 2009.

45 T. Edsall, "Capitalism vs. Democracy," *New York Times*, 28 January 2014.

46 P. Krugman, "Graduates vs. Oligarchs," *New York Times*, 1 November 2011.

47 Ibid.

48 K. Maclay and S. Yang, "Two Young Faculty Members Named MacArthur 'Genius' Fellows," UC Berkeley News Center, available at http://news.berkeley.edu/2010/09/28/macarthur/.

49 T. Piketty and E. Saez, "Income Inequality in the United States, 1913–1998," *Quarterly Journal of Economics* 118(1) (2003): 1–39. Series updated to 2014 online, available at http://eml.berkeley.edu/~saez/TabFig2014prel.xls. Saez has done similar work, and arrived at similar conclusions, on wealth distribution, in W. Kopczuk and E. Saez, "Top Wealth Shares in the United States, 1916–2000: Evidence from Estate Tax Returns," *National Tax Journal* 57(2), part 2 (2004): 445–87; in Canada in E. Saez and M. Veall, "The Evolution of High Incomes in Northern America: Lessons from Canadian Evidence," *American Economic Review* 95(3) (2005): 831–49; and contributions in the edited volume *Top Incomes over the Twentieth Century: A Contrast between European and English Speaking Countries* (Oxford: Oxford University Press, 2007). Piketty and Saez are not alone in finding that income for much of the population has stagnated during this period while the income distribution has become much more unequal. See also the work of J. Galbraith at the *Inequality Project*, available at http://utip.gov.utexas .edu/; L. Thurow, *The Future of Capitalism: How Today's Economic Forces Shape Tomorrow's World* (New York: Penguin, 1996); and E. Warren, "The Middle Class on the Precipice," *Harvard Magazine*, January/February 2006.

50 A. Atkinson, T. Piketty, and E. Saez, "Top Incomes in the Long Run of History," *Journal of Economic Literature* 49(1) (2011). He also suggested that people who are informed about the degree of inequality are far more likely to find it unpalatable, in I. Kuziemko, M. Norton, E. Saez, and S. Stantcheva, "How Elastic Are Preferences for Redistribution? Evidence from Randomized Survey Experiments," NBER working paper no. 18865 (March 2013).

51 F. Alvaredo, A. Atkinson, T. Piketty, and E. Saez, "The Top 1 Percent in International and Historical Perspective," *Journal of Economic Perspectives* 27(3) (2013).

52 Atkinson, Piketty, and Saez, "Top Incomes in the Long Run of History." This claim is very much front and center in Piketty's *Capital in the Twenty-First Century*.

53 Ibid., 58.

54 Ibid., 62.

55 Piketty and Saez, "Income Inequality in the United States, 1913–1998."

56 Atkinson, Piketty, and Saez, "Top Incomes in the Long Run of History."

57 Alvaredo, Atkinson, Piketty, and Saez, "The Top 1 Percent in International and Historical Perspective," 18.

58 Atkinson, Piketty, and Saez, "Top Incomes in the Long Run of History," 63.
59 E. Saez, "Striking It Richer: The Evolution of Top Incomes in the United States," *Pathways Magazine*, Stanford Center for the Study of Poverty and Inequality, Winter 2008 (updated September 2013).
60 T. Piketty and E. Saez, "How Progressive Is the U.S. Federal Tax System? A Historical and International Perspective," *Journal of Economic Perspectives* 21(1) (2007): 12.
61 P. Diamond and E. Saez, "The Case for a Progressive Tax: From Basic Research to Policy Recommendations," *Journal of Economic Perspectives* 25(4) (2011): 173. He has also argued for progressive taxes on capital in E. Saez, "Optimal Progressive Capital Income Taxes in the Infinite Horizon Model," *Journal of Public Economics* 97 (2013).
62 T. Piketty, E. Saez, and S. Stantcheva, "Optimal Taxation of Top Labor Incomes: A Tale of Three Elasticities," *American Economic Journal: Economic Policy* 6(1) (2014).
63 E. Saez, J. Slemrod, and S. Giertz, "The Elasticity of Taxable Income with Respect to Marginal Tax Rates: A Critical Review," *Journal of Economic Literature* 50(1) (2012).
64 H. Kleven, C. Landais, and E. Saez, "Taxation and International Migration of Superstars: Evidence from the European Football Market," *American Economic Review* 103(5) (2013); H. Kleven, C. Landais, E. Saez, and E. Schultz, "Migration and Wage Effects of Taxing Top Earners: Evidence from the Foreigners' Tax Scheme in Denmark," *Quarterly Journal of Economics* 129(1) (2013).
65 H. Immervoll, H. Kleven, C. Kreiner, and E. Saez, "Welfare Reform in European Countries: A Microsimulation Analysis," *Economic Journal* 117(516) (2007).
66 D. Lee and E. Saez, "Optimal Minimum Wage Policy in Competitive Labor Markets," *Journal of Public Economics* 96(9–10) (2012).
67 Krugman, "Graduates vs. Oligarchs."

4 Health, Healthcare, and the Individual

1 J. Smialek, "MIT Economist Seeks Facts in Health-care Policy Debate," *Bloomberg*, 2 January 2014, available at http://www.bloomberg.com/news/articles/2014-01-03/mit-economist-seeks-facts-in-health-care-policy-debate.
2 Ibid.
3 United Nations, *UN International Human Development Indicators* (2013), available at http://hdr.undp.org/en/data/.

4 OECD, *Health at a Glance 2013: OECD Indicators*, OECD Publishing (2013): 155, 157, available at http://dx.doi.org/10.1787/health_glance-2013-en.

5 Consumer Reports, "Is an HMO for You? Practices of Health Maintenance Organizations," *Consumer Reports* 65(7) (2000).

6 D. Himmelstein and S. Woolhandler, "Care Denied: U.S. Residents Who Are Unable to Obtain Needed Medical Services," *American Journal of Public Health* 85(3) (1995).

7 C. Schoen, S. Collins, and J. Kriss, "How Many Are Underinsured? Trends among U.S. Adults, 2003 and 2007," *Health Affairs*, June 2008.

8 S. Woolhandler and D. Himmelstein, "Competition in a Publicly Funded Healthcare System," *British Medical Journal* 335 (2007).

9 J. Freeman, "A Modest Proposal: Bribe the Insurance Companies," *Medicine and Social Justice*, 23 August 2009, available at http://medicinesocialjustice.blogspot.ca/2009/08/modest-proposal-bribe-insurance.html. See also S. Woolhandler, T. Campbell, and D. Himmelstein, "Costs of Health Care Administration in the United States and Canada," *New England Journal of Medicine* 349(8) (2003): 768–75; R. Evans, "Waste, Economists and American Healthcare," *Healthcare Policy* 9(2) (2013): 14.

10 L. Mayne, C. Girod, and S. Weltz, *2011 Milliman Medical Index* (Milliman Research Report, 2011).

11 For an analysis of the financial viability of the Canadian single-payer pubic insurance system, see A. Sepehri and R. Chernomas, "Is the Canadian Health Care System Fiscally Sustainable?" *International Journal of Health Services* 34(2) (2004): 229–43.

12 P. Krugman, "Medicare Saves Money," *New York Times*, 13 June 2011, A23.

13 CBO, *Long Term Analysis of a Budget Proposal by Chairman Ryan* (Washington, DC: US Government Printing Office, 2011).

14 M. Bernstein, "Propaganda and Prejudice Distort the Health Reform Debate," *Health Affairs*, 22 April 2009, available at http://healthaffairs.org/blog/2009/04/22/proganda-and-prejudice-distort-the-health-reform-debate/.

15 J. Shafrin, "Operating on Commission: Analyzing How Physician Financial Incentives Affect Surgery Rates," *Health Economics* 19(5) (2010). See also D. Hemenway et al., "Physicians' Responses to Financial Incentives – Evidence from a For-Profit Ambulatory Care Center," *New England Journal of Medicine* 322(15) (1990) and A. Hillman, M. Pauly, and J. Kerstein, "How Do Financial Incentives Affect Physicians' Clinical Decisions and the Financial Performance of Health Maintenance Organizations?" *New England Journal of Medicine* 321(2) (1989).

16 Evans quoted in Canadian Health Services Research Foundation, "Myth: User Fees Would Stop Waste and Ensure Better Use of the Healthcare System," *Mythbusters* (2001), available at http://www.cfhi-fcass.ca/ sf-docs/default-source/mythbusters/ Myth_User_Fees_EN.pdf?sfvrsn=0.

17 J. Commins, "Physicians Generate $1.5M Annually for Their Hospitals, Says Survey," *Health Leaders Media*, 17 March 2010, available at http:// healthleadersmedia.com/content.cfm?topic=FIN&content_id=248119 .

18 J. Newhouse, *Free for All? Lessons from the Rand Health Insurance Experiment* (Cambridge, MA: Harvard University Press, 1993), 339.

19 J. Hacker, *The Divided Welfare State: The Battle over Public and Private Social Benefits in the United States* (Cambridge: Cambridge University Press, 2002), 198.

20 J. Quadagno, "Why the United States Has No National Health Insurance: Stakeholder Mobilization against the Welfare State, 1945–1996," *Journal of Health and Social Behavior* 45, extra issue (2004): 30.

21 Center for Responsive Politics, "Top Industries" overview (2010), available at http://www.opensecrets.org/bigpicture/industries .php?cycle=2010.

22 D. Eggan and K. Kindy, "Former Lawmakers and Congressional Staffers Hired to Lobby on Health Care," *Washington Post*, 6 July 2009.

23 W. Potter, *Deadly Spin* (London: Bloomsbury, 2010).

24 N. Singer, "Harry and Louise Return, with a New Message," *New York Times*, 16 July 2009, B3.

25 J. Geyman, "Myths as Barriers to Health Care Reform in the United States," *International Journal of Health Services* 33(2) (2003): 316.

26 Smialek, "MIT Economist Seeks Facts in Health-care Policy Debate."

27 M. Pauly, "The Economics of Moral Hazard: Comment," *American Economic Review* 58(3) (1968): 531–7.

28 M. Gladwell, "The Moral Hazard Myth: The Bad Idea behind Our Failed Healthcare System," *The New Yorker*, 29 August 2005.

29 See, for example, J.R. Cogan, G. Hubbard, and D. Kessler, *Healthy, Wealthy, and Wise: Five Steps to a Better Healthcare System* (Washington, DC: AEI Press, 2005).

30 L. Einav and A. Finkelstein, "Selection in Insurance Markets: Theory and Empirics in Pictures," *Journal of Economic Perspectives* (Winter 2011): 115–38.

31 A. Aron-Dine, L. Einav, and A. Finkelstein, "The RAND Health Insurance Experiment, Three Decades Later," *Journal of Economic Perspectives*, Winter 2013: 197–222.

32 M. Bundorf, J. Levin, and N. Mahoney, "Pricing and Welfare in Health Plan Choice," *American Economic Review* 102(7) (2012): 3214–48. Finkelstein has also conducted empirical studies that demonstrate that even in the presence of information asymmetry, the welfare losses may not be great: L. Einav, A. Finkelstein, and P. Schrimpf, "Optimal Mandates and the Welfare Cost of Asymmetric Information: Evidence from the U.K. Annuity Market," *Econometrica* 78(3) (2010): 1031–92; L. Einav, A. Finkelstein, and M. Cullen, "Estimating Welfare in Insurance Markets Using Variation in Prices," *Quarterly Journal of Economics* 123(3) (2010): 877– 921.

33 L. Einav, A. Finkelstein, S. Ryan, P. Schrimpf, and M. Cullen, "Selection on Moral Hazard in Health Insurance," *American Economic Review* 103(1) (2013): 178–219.

34 A. Finkelstein and K. McGarry, "Multiple Dimensions of Private Information: Evidence from the Long-Term Care Insurance Market," *American Economic Review* 96(4) (2006): 938–58; Einav and Finkelstein, "Selection in Insurance Markets."

35 A. Finkelstein, "The Interaction of Partial Public Insurance Programs and Residual Private Insurance Markets: Evidence from the U.S. Medicare Program," *Journal of Health Economics* 23(1) (2004): 1–24.

36 J. Brown and A. Finkelstein, "The Interaction of Public and Private Insurance: Medicaid and the Long-Term Care Insurance Market," *American Economic Review* 98(3) (2008): 1083–102. Finkelstein finds that asset rules are not a large source of the disincentive, in J. Brown, N. Coe, and A. Finkelstein, "Medicaid Crowd-Out of Private Long-Term Care Insurance Demand: Evidence from the Health and Retirement Survey," *Tax Policy and the Economy* 21 (2007): 1–34.

37 J. Levin and J. Poterba, "Amy Finkelstein: 2012 John Bates Clark Medalist," *Journal of Economic Perspectives*, Fall 2012: 171–84.

38 A. Finkelstein, "The Aggregate Effects of Health Insurance: Evidence from the Introduction of Medicare," *Quarterly Journal of Economics* 122(3) (2007): 22.

39 A. Finkelstein and R. McKnight, "What Did Medicare Do? The Initial Impact of Medicare on Mortality and Out of Pocket Medical Spending," *Journal of Public Economics* 92(7) (2008): 1661.

40 A. Finkelstein et al., "The Oregon Health Insurance Experiment: Evidence from the First Year," *Quarterly Journal of Economics* 127(3) (2012): 1057–106; K. Baicker and A. Finkelstein, "The Effects of Medicaid Coverage – Learning from the Oregon Experiment," *New England Journal of Medicine* 365(8) (2011): 683–5.

41 K. Baicker et al., "The Oregon Experiment – Effects of Medicaid on Clinical Outcomes," *New England Journal of Medicine* 368(18): 1713–22.

42 Finkelstein, "The Aggregate Effects of Health Insurance," 33.

43 M. Hersh-Cochran, *Compendium of English Language Course Syllabi and Textbooks in Health Economics* (Copenhagen: World Health Organization Regional Office for Europe, 1989), 214.

44 For a more complete analysis of the ACA, see M. Buettgens, B. Garrett, and J. Holahan, *America under the Affordable Health Care Act* (Washington, DC: The Urban Institute, 2010); T. Marmor and J. Oberlander, "The Health Bill Explained at Last," *New York Review of Books*, 19 August 2010.

45 Einav and Finkelstein, "Selection in Insurance Markets," 122–3.

46 D. Card, C. Dobkin, and N. Maestas, "The Impact of Nearly Universal Insurance Coverage on Health Care Utilization: Evidence from Medicare," *American Economic Review* 98 (2008): 2242–58.

47 D. Card, C. Dobkin, and N. Maestas, "Does Medicare Save Lives?" *Quarterly Journal of Economics* 124(2) (2009): 597–636.

48 T. McKeown, *The Role of Medicine* (London: Nuffield Provincial Hospitals Trust, 1976); T. McKeown, *The Modern Rise of Population* (London: Edward Arnold, 1976); T. McKeown, *The Role of Medicine: Dream, Mirage or Nemesis?* 2nd ed. (Oxford: Basil Blackwell, 1979).

49 R. Fogel, "New Findings on Secular Trends in Nutrition and Mortality: Some Implications for Population Theory," in M.R. Rosenzweig and O. Stark, eds, *Handbook of Population and Family Economics* (New York: Elsevier Science, North Holland, 1997); R. Fogel, *The Escape from Hunger and Premature Death, 1700–2100* (Cambridge: Cambridge University Press, 2004).

50 S. Szreter, "The Importance of Social Intervention in Britain's Mortality Decline 1850–1914: A Reinterpretation of the Role of Public Health," *Social History of Medicine* 1(1) (1988); S. Szreter, "Rethinking McKeown: The Relationship between Public Health and Social Change," *American Journal of Public Health* 92(5) (2002).

51 E. Cassel, *The Heale's Art* (Philadelphia, PA: J.B. Lippincott, 1976), 71–2.

52 A-E. Birn, Y. Pillay, and T. Holtz, *Textbook of International Health: Global Health in a Dynamic World* (New York: Oxford University Press, 2009), 346.

53 D. Satcher and E. Higgenbotham, "The Public Health Approach to Eliminating Disparities in Health," *American Journal of Public Health* 98(3) (2008), 401.

54 There is a growing literature on SDOH. For excellent examples see D. Raphael, "A Society in Decline: The Social, Economic, and Political

Determinants of Health Inequalities in the USA," in R. Hofrichter, ed., *Health and Social Justice: A Reader on Politics, Ideology, and Inequity in the Distribution of Disease* (San Francisco: Jossey Bass/Wiley 2003); V. Navarro, C. Borrell, J. Benach, C. Muntaner, A. Quiroga, M. Rodríguez-Sanz, et al., "The Importance of the Political and the Social in Explaining Mortality Differentials amongst Countries of the OECD, 1950–1998," *International Journal of Health Services* 33(3) (2003): 419–94; V. Navarro and C. Muntaner, eds, *Political and Economic Determinants of Population Health and Well-Being: Controversies and Developments* (New York: Baywood Publishing, 2004); D. Raphael, "Social Determinants of Health: An Overview of Key Issues and Themes," in L. Fernandez, S. MacKinnon, and J. Silver, eds, *The Social Determinants of Health in Manitoba* (Winnipeg: CCBA-MB, 2010); and N. Krieger, *Epidemiology and People's Health* (Oxford: Oxford University Press, 2011).

55 Birn, Pillay, and Holtz, *Textbook of International Health*, 140.
56 R. Evans, B. Morris, and T. Marmor, eds, *Why Are Some People Healthy and Others Are Not?* (New York: Walter de Gruyer, 1994), 6, 44.
57 For a more complete discussion see R. Chernomas and I. Hudson, *To Live and Die in America: Class, Power, Health and Healthcare* (London: Pluto Press, 2013).
58 For a discussion of the rise of the corporation in agriculture see J. Clapp, *Food* (Cambridge: Polity Press, 2012), 90–124.
59 M. Pollan, "Power Steer," *New York Times Magazine*, 31 March 2002; M. Pollan, *The Omnivore's Dilemma: A Natural History of Four Meals* (New York: Penguin, 2006).
60 J. Houlihan et al., *Body Burden: The Pollution in People* (Washington, DC: Environmental Working Group, 2003), available at http://www.trwnews.net/Documents/Dioxin/BBreport_final.pdf.
61 S. Reuben, *Reducing Environmental Cancer Risk: President's Cancer Panel 2008–2009* (Washington, DC: US Department of Health and Human Services, 2010), ii.
62 R. Karasek and T. Theorell, *Healthy Work, Stress, Productivity and the Reconstruction of Working Life* (New York: Basic Books, 1990).
63 M. Marmot, *Fair Society Healthy Lives: The Marmot Review Executive Summary* (2010), available at http://www.instituteofhealthequity.org/projects/fair-society-healthy-lives-the-marmot-review; M. Marmot, J. Siegrist, and T. Theorell, "Health and the Psychosocial Environment at Work," in M. Marmot and R. Wilkinson, eds, *Social Determinants of Health* (Oxford: Oxford University Press, 2006); G. Rose and M. Marmot, "Social Class and Coronary Heart Disease," *British Heart Journal* 45(1) (1981).

64 In addition, nations with more equal income distributions fare better on a wide variety of social indicators. R. Wilkinson and K. Pickett, *The Spirit Level: Why More Equal Societies Almost Always Do Better* (New York: Bloomsbury, 2009).
65 Marmot, *Fair Society Healthy Lives*, 25.
66 D. Faber and E. Krieg, "Unequal Exposure to Ecological Hazards: Environmental Injustices in the Commonwealth of Massachusetts," *Environmental Health Perspectives* 110(Suppl 2) (2002): 277–88.
67 P. Braverman et al., "Socioeconomic Disparities in Health in the US: What the Patterns Tell Us," *American Journal of Public Health* 100(1) (2010).
68 S. Woolf, "Public Health Implications of Government Spending Reductions," *Journal of the American Medical Association* 305(18) (2011): 1902.
69 K. Reinier et al., "Socioeconomic Status and Incidence of Sudden Cardiac Arrest," *Canadian Medical Association Journal* 183(15) (2011).
70 Marmot, *Fair Society Healthy Lives*, 16.
71 Ibid.
72 M. Grossman, "On the Concept of Health Capital and the Demand for Health," *Journal of Political Economy* 80(2) (1972): 241.
73 T. O'Donoghue and M. Rabin, "Doing It Now or Later," *American Economic Review* 89(1) (1999): 103–24.
74 Ibid., 120.
75 A. Finkelstein and J. Poterba, "Testing for Asymmetric Information Using 'Unused Observables' in Insurance Markets: Evidence from the U.K. Annuity Market," NBER working paper 12112 (2008).
76 J. Lynch et al., "Income Inequality and Mortality: Importance to Health of Individual Income, Psychosocial Environment, or Material Conditions," *British Medical Journal* 320 (2000): 1202.

5 Crime

Portions of this chapter are adapted from R. Chernomas and I. Hudson, "Steven Levitt on Abortion and Crime: Old Economics in New Bottles," *American Journal of Economics and Sociology* 72 (2013): 675–700.

1 US Department of Justice, *Crime in the United States 2012*, table 1, "Crime in the United States," available at https://www.fbi.gov/about-us/cjis/ucr/crime-in-the-u.s/2012/crime-in-the-u.s.-2012/tables/1tabledatadecoverviewpdf/table_1_crime_in_the_united_states_by_volume_and_rate_per_100000_inhabitants_1993-2012.xls.
2 US Department of Justice, *Crime in the United States 2012*, table 24, "Property Stolen and Recovered," available at https://www.fbi.gov/

about-us/cjis/ucr/crime-in-the-u.s/2012/crime-in-the-u.s.-2012/tables/
24tabledatadecoverviewpdfs/table_24_property_stolen_and_recovered_
by_type_and_value_2012.xls.

3   Cited in S. Levitt, "Understanding Why Crime Fell in the 1990s: Four
    Factors That Explain the Decline and Six That Do Not," *Journal of
    Economic Perspectives* 18(1) (2004): 163–90.

4   S. Dubner, "Economist of Odd Questions: Inside the Astonishingly Curious
    Mind of Steven D. Levitt," *New York Times Magazine*, 3 August 2003, 23–8.

5   S. Levitt and S. Venkatesh, "An Economic Analysis of a Drug-Selling
    Gang's Finances," *Quarterly Journal of Economics* 115(3) (2000): 755–89.

6   S. Levitt, "Using Electoral Cycles in Police Hiring to Estimate the Effect
    of Police on Crime," *American Economic Review* 87(3) (1997): 270–90; S.
    Levitt, "Using Electoral Cycles in Police Hiring to Estimate the Effects of
    Police on Crime: Reply," *American Economic Review* 92(4) (2002): 1244–50.

7   S. Levitt, "An Empirical Analysis of Imprisoning Drug Offenders,"
    Journal of Public Economics 88(9–10) (2004), 2043–66

8   L. Katz, S. Levitt, and E. Shustorovich, "Prison Conditions, Capital
    Punishment, and Deterrence," *American Law and Economics Review* 5(2)
    (2003): 318–43.

9   J. Cullen and S. Levitt, "Crime, Urban Flight and the Consequences for
    Cities," *Review of Economics and Statistics* 81(2) (1999):159–69.

10 B. Jacob and S. Levitt, "Rotten Apples: An Investigation of the Prevalence
    and Predictors of Teacher Cheating," *Quarterly Journal of Economics* 118(3)
    (2003): 843–77.

11 M. Duggan and S. Levitt, "Winning Isn't Everything: Corruption in Sumo
    Wrestling," *American Economic Review* 92(5) (2002): 1594–605.

12 S. Levitt, "White-Collar Crime Writ Small: A Case Study of Bagels, Donuts,
    and the Honor System," *American Economic Review* 96(2) (2006). 290–4.

13 S. Levitt and C. Syverson, "Market Distortions When Agents Are Better
    Informed: The Value of Information in Real Estate Transactions," *Review
    of Economics and Statistics* 90(4) (2008): 599–611.

14 Dubner, "Economist of Odd Questions."

15 "International Bright Young Things," *The Economist*, 30 December 2008,
    available at http://www.economist.com/node/12851150?story_
    id=12851150.

16 L. Wacquant, "The 'Scholarly Myths' of the New Law and Order Doxa,"
    in L. Panitch and C. Leys, *Socialist Register 2006* (London: Merlin Press,
    2005), 93–115.

17 Ibid.

18 J. Van Kesteren, P. Mayhew, and P. Nieuwbeerta, *Criminal Victimization in
    Seventeen Industrialized Countries: Key Findings from the 2000 International*

Crime Victimization Survey, United National Interregional Crime and Justice Research Institute, 2000. Available at http://www.unicri.it/services/library_documentation/publications/icvs/publications/index.htm.

19 M. Wolff, P. Rutten, and A. Bayers, *Where We Stand: Can America Make It in the Global Race for Wealth, Health and Happiness* (New York: Bantam Books, 1992), 116.

20 G. Barclay and C. Tavares, *International Comparisons of Criminal Justice Statistics 2001* (London: Home Office, 2003).

21 World Health Organization, *World Report on Violence and Health* (Geneva: World Health Organization, 2002), 28.

22 Statistics Canada, *Juristat: Crime Comparisons between Canada and the United States,* 21(11) (2001), Catalogue no. 85-002-XPE.

23 S. Cessou, "Prisons across Europe: Lessons to Be Learned from UK's Neighbors," *The Guardian,* 29 April 2014, available at http://www.theguardian.com/society/2014/apr/29/prisons-across-europe-lessons-learned-uk-neighbours.

24 E. James, "Why Is Sweden Closing Its Prisons?" *The Guardian,* 1 December 2013, available at http://www.theguardian.com/society/2013/dec/01/why-sweden-closing-prisons.

25 Wacquant, "'Scholarly Myths.'"

26 Ibid.

27 S. Levitt and S. Dubner, *Freakonomics: A Rogue Economist Explores the Hidden Side of Everything* (New York: HarperCollins, 2005), 12.

28 Levitt and Dubner, *Freakonomics,* 13.

29 J. DiNardo, "Interesting Questions in *Freakonomics,*" *Journal of Economic Literature* 45(4) (2007): 973–1000.

30 Levitt and Dubner, *Freakonomics,* 14.

31 Dubner, "Economist of Odd Questions."

32 J. Donohue and S. Levitt, "Legalized Abortion and Crime," *Quarterly Journal of Economics* 116(2) (2001): 379–420.

33 Ibid.

34 Dubner, "Economist of Odd Questions."

35 Donohue and Levitt, "Legalized Abortion and Crime."

36 Ibid.

37 Ibid.

38 Ibid.

39 Ibid.

40 Ibid.

41 Levitt, "Understanding Why Crime Fell in the 1990s."

42 Donohue and Levitt, "Legalized Abortion and Crime."

43 Levitt, "Understanding Why Crime Fell in the 1990s."
44 S. Levitt, "The Exaggerated Role of Changing Age Structure in Explaining Aggregate Crime Changes," *Criminology* 37 (1999): 537–99.
45 Katz, Levitt, and Shustorovich, "Prison Conditions, Capital Punishment, and Deterrence."
46 Levitt, "Understanding Why Crime Fell in the 1990s."
47 Levitt, "Using Electoral Cycles in Police Hiring."
48 Ibid.
49 S. Levitt, "The Effect of Prison Population Size on Crime Rates: Evidence from Prison Overcrowding Litigation," *Quarterly Journal of Economics* 111(2) (1996): 270–90.
50 Katz, Levitt, and Shustorovich, "Prison Conditions, Capital Punishment, and Deterrence."
51 Levitt, "Understanding Why Crime Fell in the 1990s."
52 Levitt and Dubner, *Freakonomics*.
53 Levitt, "Understanding Why Crime Fell in the 1990s."
54 DiNardo, "Interesting Questions in Freakonomics"; J. Lott and J. Whitley, "Abortion and Crime: Unwanted Children and Out of Wedlock Births," *Economic Inquiry* 45(2) (2007): 304–24; C. Foote and C. Goetz, "Testing Economic Hypotheses with State-Level Data: A Comment on Donohue and Levitt," *Quarterly Journal of Economics* 123(1) (2008): 407–23; T. Joyce, "A Simple Test of Abortion and Crime," *Review of Economics and Statistics* 91(1) (2009): 112–23.
55 J. Donohue and S. Levitt, "Further Evidence that Legalized Abortion Lowered Crime: A Reply to Joyce," *Journal of Human Resources* 39(1) (2004): 29–49; J. Donohue and S. Levitt, "Measurement Error, Legalized Abortion, and the Decline in Crime: A Response to Foote and Goetz," *Politics and the Life Sciences* 123(1) (2008): 425–40.
56 H. Mielke and S. Zahran, "The Urban Rise and Fall of Air Lead (Pb) and the Latent Surge and Retreat of Societal Violence," *Environment International* 43 (2012): 48–55; J. Wolpaw Reyes, "Environmental Policy as Social Policy? The Impact of Childhood Lead Exposure on Crime," *B.E. Journal of Economic Analysis & Policy* 7(1) (2007); R. Nevin, "How Lead Exposure Relates to Temporal Changes in IQ, Violent Crime, and Unwed Pregnancy," *Environmental Research* 83(1) (2000): 1–22; P. Stretesky and M. Lynch, "The Relationship between Lead and Crime," *Journal of Health and Social Behavior* 45(2) (2004): 214–29.
57 S. Levitt and L. Lochner, "The Determinants of Juvenile Crime," in J. Gruber, *Risky Behavior among Youths: An Economic Analysis* (Chicago: University of Chicago Press, 2001), 327–73.

58 S. Venkatesh and S. Levitt, "Are We a Family or a Business? History and Disjuncture in the Urban American Street Gang," *Theory and Society* 29(4): 427–62.

59 Levitt, "Understanding Why Crime Fell in the 1990s."

60 Ibid.

61 Ibid.

62 Ibid.

63 J. Grogger, "An Economic Model of Recent Trends in Violence," in A. Blumstein and J. Wallman, *The Crime Drop in America*, rev. ed. (New York: Cambridge University Press, 2006), 266–87.

64 J. Wallman and A. Blumstein, "After the Crime Drop," in Blumstein and Wallman, *The Crime Drop in America*, 319–48.

65 J. McCrary, "Using Electoral Cycles in Police Hiring to Estimate the Effects of Police on Crime: Comment," *American Economic Review* 92 (2002): 1236–43.

66 Levitt used the number of firefighters as a proxy for the number of police in an effort to get away from the endogeneity problem that connects the number of police to the amount of crime.

67 Wallman and Blumstein, "After the Crime Drop."

68 Ibid.

69 Wacquant, "'Scholarly Myths.'"

70 C. Hsieh and M. Pugh, "Poverty, Income Inequality, and Violent Crime: A Meta-Analysis of Recent Aggregate Data Studies," *Criminal Justice Review* 18(2) (1993): 182–202.

71 Levitt, "Understanding Why Crime Fell in the 1990s."

72 K. Steenland, C. Burnett, N. Lalich, E. Ward, and J. Hurrell, "Dying for Work: The Magnitude of US Mortality from Selected Causes of Death Associated with Occupation," *American Journal of Industrial Medicine* 43 (2003): 461–82.

73 "Testimony of David J. Graham, MD, MPH" before United States Senate Committee on Finance, 18 November 2004; available at http://www .finance.senate.gov/imo/media/doc/111804dgtest.pdf.

74 N. Muller and R. Mendelsohn, "Measuring the Damages of Air Pollution in the United States," *Journal of Environmental Economics and Management* 54(1) (2007): 1–14.

75 US Department of Justice, "F. Hoffmann-La Roche and BASF Agree to Pay Record Criminal Fines for Participating in International Vitamin Cartel," press release, US Department of Justice, 20 May 1999, available at http:// www.justice.gov/archive/atr/public/press_releases/1999/2450.htm.

76 J. Silver-Greenberg and S. Craig, "Fined Billions, JP Morgan Chase Will Give Dimon a Raise," *New York Times*, 24 January 2014, A1.

77 J. Moyer, "Whole Foods under Investigation for Overcharging in NYC," *Washington Post*, 25 June 2015, available at http://www.washingtonpost.com/news/morning-mix/wp/2015/06/25/whole-foods-under-investigation-for-overcharging-in-nyc/.

78 J. Creswell and R. Abelson, "Hospital Chain Said to Scheme to Inflate Bills," *New York Times*, 24 January 2014, A1.

79 A. Nightingale and T. Hopfinger, "Valdez Ghost Haunts Exxon with Spill-Prone Ships," *Bloomberg*, 24 March 2009, available at http://www.bloomberg.com/news/articles/2009-03-24/exxon-valdez-ghost-lives-on-as-company-hires-spill-prone-ships.

80 M. Clinard and P. Yeager, *Corporate Crime* (New Brunswick, NJ: Transaction Publishers, 2005).

81 J. Sachs, "The Global Economy's Corporate Crime Wave," Project Syndicate, 30 April 2011, available at http://www.project-syndicate.org/commentary/the-global-economy-s-corporate-crime-wave.

82 S. Levitt, "Alternative Strategies for Identifying the Link between Unemployment and Crime," *Journal of Quantitative Criminology* 17(4) (2001): 377–90.

6 Two Kinds of Crises

1 N. Roubini, "Nouriel Roubini: Karl Marx Was Right," *Wall Street Journal* interview, 12 August 2011, available at http://www.wsj.com/video/nouriel-roubini-karl-marx-was-right/68EE8F89-EC24-42F8-9B9D-47B510E473B0.html.

2 For a discussion of the limits of mainstream macroeconomics and how heterodox and post-Keynesian schools can improve on the mainstream see F. Lee and M. Lavoie, eds, *In Defense of Post-Keynesian Economics and Heterodox Economics: Response to Their Critics* (London: Routledge, 2012).

3 J. Foster and F. Magdoff, "Financial Implosion and Stagnation," *Monthly Review* 60(7) (2008): 1–29; J. Foster and R. McChesney, "Monopoly-Finance Capital and the Paradox of Accumulation," *Monthly Review* 61(5) (2009): 1–20; D. Kotz, "Economic Crisis and Institutional Structures: A Comparison of Regulated and Neoliberal Capitalism in the USA," in J. Goldstein and M. Hillard, eds, *Heterodox Macroeconomics: Keynes, Marx, and Globalization* (New York: Routledge, 2009), 176–88.

4 For a more complete discussion of how the structure of the US economy created the 2008 crisis see D. Kotz, "The Financial and Economic Crisis of 2008: A Systemic Crisis of Neoliberal Capitalism," *Review of Radical Political Economics* 41(3) (2009): 305–17; T. McDonough, M. Reich, and D. Kotz, *Contemporary Capitalism and Its Crises: Social Structure of*

Accumulation Theory for the 21st Century (Cambridge: Cambridge University Press, 2010); D. McNally, *Global Slump: The Economics and Politics of Crisis and Resistance* (Winnipeg: Fernwood, 2010); G. Duménil and D. Lévy, *The Crisis of Neoliberalism* (Cambridge, MA: Harvard University Press, 2011); and Y. Varoufakis, *The Global Minotaur: America, the True Origins of the Financial Crisis and the Future of the World Economy* (London: Zed Books, 2011). For a more general explanation on the role of money and monetary policy on economic stability see M. Lavoie, L.P. Rochon, and M. Seccareccia, *Money and Macroeconomic Issues: Alfred Eichner and Post-Keynesian Economics* (Armonk, NJ: M.E. Sharpe, 2010).

5 For more on the role of finance in the economic crisis, especially the role of the rise of new financial instruments and speculative investments, see H. Minsky, *Stabilizing an Unstable Economy* (New Haven, CT: McGraw-Hill, 1986); B. Spotton Visano, *Financial Crises: Socio-Economic Causes and Institutional Context* (New York: Routledge, 2006); J. Crotty, "Structural Causes of the Global Financial Crisis: A Critical Assessment of the 'New Financial Architecture,'" *Cambridge Journal of Economics* 33(4) (2009): 563–80; R. Martin, *Fixing the Game: Bubbles, Crashes, and What Capitalism Can Learn from the NFL* (Harvard: Harvard Business Review Press, 2011).

6 For a discussion of how deregulation in the US financial sector led to the 2008 financial collapse see the two chapters in J. Guard and W. Antony, eds, *Bankruptcies and Bailouts* (Winnipeg: Fernwood, 2009): I. Hudson, "From Deregulation to Crisis" and J. Loxley, "Hyper-Credit: The Financial Dimension of the Economic Crisis."

7 D. Kotz, *The Rise and Fall of Neoliberal Capitalism* (Cambridge, MA: Harvard University Press, 2015), 151–5.

8 J. Sanchez and E. Yurdagul, "Why Are Corporations Holding So Much Cash?" *The Regional Economist Federal Reserve Bank of St. Louis* (January 2013). Available at https://www.stlouisfed.org/Publications/Regional-Economist/January-2013/Why-Are-Corporations-Holding-So-Much-Cash.

9 E. Gould, "Why America's Workers Need Faster Wage Growth – And What We Can Do about It," *Economic Policy Institute Briefing Paper*, figure C, 27 August 2014; available at http://www.epi.org/publication/why-americas-workers-need-faster-wage-growth/. It might be possible to argue that the economic stimulus could have been much better spent on helping the average citizen rather than bailing out financial institutions. See, for example, G. Albo, S. Gindin, and L. Panitch, *In and Out of Crisis: The Global Financial Meltdown and Left Alternatives* (Oakland, CA: PM Press, 2010); T. Palley, *From Financial Crisis to Stagnation: The*

Destruction of Shared Prosperity and the Role of Economics (Cambridge: Cambridge University Press, 2012).

10 Kotz, *The Rise and Fall of Neoliberal Capitalism*, 175–80. For other accounts of the financial crisis see Kotz, "The Financial and Economic Crisis of 2008."

11 S. Bowles, D. Gordon, and T. Weisskopf, "Power and Profits: The Social Structure of Accumulation and the Profitability of the Postwar U.S. Economy," *Review of Radical Political Economics* 1–2(18) (1986): 132–67. See also T. Weisskopf, "Marxian Crisis Theory and the Rate of Profit in the Postwar U.S. Economy," *Cambridge Journal of Economics* 3(4) (1979): 341–78. For an alternative explanation of the fall in the rate of U.S. profits in the late 1970s based on the rise of unproductive labor, see F. Moseley, "The Rate of Profit and the Future of Capitalism," *Review of Radical Political Economics* 29(4) (1997): 23–41.

12 R. Brenner, *The Economics of Global Turbulence* (London: Verso, 2006).

13 A. Shaikh, "The First Great Depression of the 21st Century," in L. Panitch, G. Albo, and V. Chibber, eds, *Socialist Register 2011: The Crisis This Time* (New York: Monthly Review Press, 2010).

14 For an explanation of crisis that revolves around the need of the US state to resolve profitability problems for US business see S. Gindin and L. Panitch, *The Making of Global Capitalism: The Political Economy of American Empire* (London: Verso, 2013).

15 J. O'Connor, "Capitalism, Nature, Socialism: A Theoretical Introduction," *Capitalism Nature Socialism* 1(1) (1988): 11–38.

16 J.B. Foster, B. Clark, and R. York, *The Ecological Rift: Capitalism's War on the Earth* (New York: Monthly Review Press, 2010). For another analysis on the connection between accumulation and environmental deterioration see A. Schnaiberg, *The Environment: From Surplus to Scarcity* (New York: Oxford University Press, 1980).

17 W. Adams, L. Einav, and J. Levin, "Liquidity Constraints and Imperfect Information in Subprime Lending," *American Economic Review* 99(1) (2009): 49–84.

18 L. Einav, M. Jenkins, and J. Levin, "The Impact of Credit Scoring on Consumer Lending," *RAND Journal of Economics* 44(2) (2013): 249–74.

19 For example, see E. Warren, "Making Credit Safer: The Case for Regulation," *Harvard Magazine*, May–June 2008.

20 W. Black, "The Two Documents Everyone Should Read to Better Understand the Crisis," *Huffington Post*, 28 March 2009, available at http://www.huffingtonpost.com/william-k-black/the-two-documents-everyon_b_169813.html.

21 D. Acemoglu, "Asymmetric Information, Bargaining, and Unemployment Fluctuations," *International Economic Review* 36(4) (1995).

22 D. Acemoglu and A. Scott, "Asymmetric Business Cycles: Theory and Time-Series Evidence," *Journal of Monetary Economics* 40(3) (1997). For an earlier variation on a similar theme, see D. Acemoglu and A. Scott, "Asymmetries in the Cyclical Behaviour of UK Labour Markets," *Economic Journal* 104(427) (1994).

23 P. Michaillat and E. Saez, "Aggregate Demand, Idle Time and Unemployment," *Quarterly Journal of Economics* 130(2) (2015): 507–69.

24 P. Michaillat and E. Saez, "A Model of Aggregate Demand and Unemployment," NBER working paper no. 18826 (July 2013).

25 Acemoglu, "Asymmetric Information."

26 See, for example, S. Athey, J. Levin, and D. Coey, "Subsidies and Set-Asides in Auctions," *American Economic Journals: Microeconomics* 5(1) (2013): 1–27; S. Athey and G. Ellison, "Position Auctions with Consumer Search," *Quarterly Journal of Economics* 126(3) (2011): 1213–70; S. Athey and I. Segal, "Designing Efficient Mechanisms for Dynamic Bilateral Trading Games," *American Economic Review* 97(2) (2007): 131–6; S. Athey and P. Haile, "Identification in Standard Auction Models," Econometrica 70(6) (2002): 2107–40.

27 S. Athey, E. Calvano, and S. Jha, "A Theory of Community Formation and Social Hierarchy," working paper, July 2013, available at http://web .stanford.edu/~saumitra/papers/ACJCommunityFormation.pdf.

28 S. Athey, C. Avery, and P. Zemsky. "Mentoring and Diversity," *American Economic Review* 90(4) (2000): 765–86.

29 S. Athey and G. Imbens, "Identification and Inference in Nonlinear Difference-in-Differences Models," *Econometrica* 74 (2006): 431–97.

30 S. Athey and J. Levin, "Information and Competition in U.S. Forest Service Timber Auctions," *Journal of Political Economy* 109(2) (2001). For a slightly different emphasis see S. Athey, J. Levin, and E. Seira, "Comparing Open and Sealed Bid Auctions: Theory and Evidence from Timber Auctions," *Quarterly Journal of Economics* 126(1) (2011): 207–57.

31 M. Hudson, *Fire Management in the American West: Forest Politics and the Rise of Megafires* (Boulder: University Press of Colorado, 2011).

7 Conclusion

1 Y. Varoufakis, J. Halevi, and N. Theocarakis, *Modern Political Economics* (New York: Routledge, 2011), 288

Index

Note: Page numbers in italics refer to figures and tables.

abortion: crime rates and, 113–14; crime study (Levitt), 112–15; unwanted children, 112–13
ACA. *See* Affordable Care Act
Acemoglu, Daron, 20, 21, 45, 47, 48, 66–9, 70–1, 149; attachment to property rights criticized, 43–5; colonial institutions and failing nations, 36–9, 47; colonial institutions and poverty, 37–8; current extractive institutions, ignoring, 43; economic systems, minimizes role of, 69–70; evaluation of, 40–6, 69–72; evaluation of recessions research, 140–3; fixed capital and investment behavior, 139; government role, ignoring, 43–4; inclusive economic policy, 37, 39; information asymmetry in labor market, 67; methodological individualism, 140, 141; minimum wage, 69; Mobutu and the Congo, 40–1; New Keynesian approach, 140–1; power and unemployment,

ignoring, 72; protection of private property rights from state power, 38; recessions, causes of, 138–40, 146; reduced equality of opportunity, 68; research, 22–3; settler colonies, 38; skill-biased technical change, 67–8, 71–2; time inconsistency, 36–9; unemployment insurance and economic efficiency, 69
advantageous selection (Finkelstein), 87, 88, 89–90
adverse selection: auto loans, 137; credit, 137; healthcare, 87, 88, 89–90, 93, 150; risk-based pricing, 137
Affordable Care Act (ACA) (US), 81, 88, 94
Africa: capital flight and, 24–5; extractive states and, 37, 38; health problems and lack of resources, 36; plundering by predatory states, 37
Africa's Odious Debts (Ndikumana and Boyce), 24

aid: debate over, 30, 33; to developing countries, 27–8, 30; USAID, 27–8; Washington Consensus, 27–8, 147
American Economic Association, 4, 9
American Legislative Exchange Program (ALEC), 18–19
American Medical Association (AMA), 86
Apple, 44
asymmetrical information. *See* information asymmetry
Athey, Susan, 21; areas of research, 143–4; evaluation of, 144–5; timber auctions, 144, 145, 153
automated credit scoring, 137–8
Automatic Income Tax Reduction Act (US), 19

Backhouse, Roger, 14–15
Banerjee, Abhijit, 23, 37
BASF, 122
Bearing Point, 26
Becker, Gary, 111, 115; crime, economics of, 112
beggar thy neighbor policies, 76
behavioral economics: health choices (Grossman), 101–2; Matthew Rabin on, 60–1; Raj Chetty, 62–6; Emmanuel Saez, 75
Belgium, 41
beneficial liquidity effect of unemployment insurance (Chetty), 63–4
birth rates, legalized abortion and, 112
black population: education and crime, 108; homicide rate and abortions, 113

Blum, William, 25
Blumstein, Alfred: economic improvement and crime, 119; police and crime, 119
Bowles, Samuel, 51, 132
Boyce, James, 24–5, 29–30, 36
Brazil, 38; Worker's Party, 39
Bremer, Paul, 25–6
Brenner, Robert, 132–3
bribery, 27
Budd, Alan, 52
Buffett, Warren, 49
Buiter, William, 9
Bush, Jeb, 50
business, common interest and, 18–19
business class, cutthroat capitalism and, 45

Cable, Vince, 18
Calvó-Armengol International Prize in Economics, 62
Canada: crime rate in, 109, 110; crime-rate reduction, 110, healthcare, 81, 96–7, 151
cancer: chemicals and, 98–9; smoking and, 97
capital flight: African leaders and, 25; external debt and, 25; US support for corrupt regimes, 25; Western banks benefiting, 29–30
Capital in the Twenty-First Century (Piketty), 50, 72–3
capitalism: crony, 39, 43; cutthroat vs. cuddly (Acemoglu), 45–6; economic crises and, 127–8; economic growth and, 135; environmental deterioration and, 134, 135; "Golden Age" of in the US, 51–2; laissez-faire (Clark), 5;

income inequality, 49, 50; policy environment, 148; specific institutions, 13

carbon target, 18

Center on Wisconsin Strategy, 54

Centers for Disease Control (CDC), 99

Chang, Ha-Joon, 28

chemicals, cancer and, 98–9

Cheney, Vice-president Dick, 26–7

Chetty, Raj, 20; evaluation of, 64–6; full employment assumption, 66, 149; intergenerational social mobility, 64, 65; taxation and behavior, 62–3, 66; unemployment insurance as welfare enhancing, 63–4, 65, 149

Chicago gang study (Levitt), 116–17

Chile, 27

China, 7

Chrysler, 128

Citigroup, 9, 29–30

Clark, John Bates, 4–5

class, 6–7; free trade and, 7; social, and smoking, 97–8, 151; as unit of analysis, 6

Clinard, Marshall: corporate crime survey (US), 123–4

Coalition Provisional Authority, 25–6

Colonial Origins of Comparative Development, The (Acemoglu, Johnson, and Robinson), 23

colonialism, 40; extractive states, creating, 37–8

common interests, power and, 18–19

comparative advantage theory, 6–7

comparative systems analysis, 13

competition, restricting, 11

Congo: IMF loans to, 41; Mobutu, reign of, 40–1

consumer behavior, 6

consumer choice: healthcare and, 83–4, 85–6, 88, 150. *See also* individual choice

consumer sovereignty, and healthcare, 92–5, 105

consumption: borrowing to sustain, 130; household debt, and, 55–6; while on unemployment insurance (Chetty), 63–4

Coors family, 18

Corak, Miles, 65

corporate crime, 122–3; deaths, causing, 122; pollution, 122, 123; theft, 122–3

corporations: common interest and economic policy, 18–19; influence and ALEC, 18–19; power and, 17–19; revenues, 17; too big to fail, 17. *See also* multinational corporations

credit: adverse selection and, 137; household debt and, in US, 55–7, 130, 131; information asymmetry, 137, 138, 146; profitability and, 130; subprime auto loan market (Levin), 137–8. *See also* debt

credit rating system, 138

crime, 20; at-risk groups (US), 112–13; decline in, 106–7, 109–10; economics of (Becker), 117; incarceration for, 109–10, 113, 114; juvenile (Levitt), 116; police numbers and, 119; policy costs, 109, 110, 114; punishment in Europe, and, 109–10; unwanted children and, 112–13; violent, *see* crime, violent crime, United States, 106, 108; abortion and, 113–14; decline in, 106–7, 108, 110, 112–15; economic and social context, 108–9; reduced during economic boom, 108; social and economic context, 120, 151; violent, 106, 108–9, 114–15; violent crime outlier, 110. *See also* homicide

crime, violent: international comparisons, cost-benefit analysis, 121

crime rates: abortion and, 113–14; lead vehicle emissions and, 116

crony capitalism, 39, 43

cutthroat vs. cuddly capitalism (Acemoglu), 39, 45–6

Daiwa Bank, 122

Danish tax records, Chetty's study of, 62–3, 66

Deadly Sins (Potter), 86–7

debt: types of (US), 56; of workers' families, in US, 55–6. *See also* credit; household debt

deficit spending, as fiscal stimulus, 128

dependency theory, 24

deregulation in US, 10

de-unionization, 68

developed nations: dependency theory, 24; developing nations and, 24; world systems approaches, 24

developing nations: aid to, 27–8, 30; bribery in, 27; colonialism and, 37–8, 40; corrupt regimes, 26; dependency theory and, 24; developed nations and, 24; financial institutions and, 27–8;

international trade and, 27–8; political manipulation, 26–7; state property privatization, 29; Washington Consensus, 27–8; world systems approaches, 24

development economics, 20; Duflo's work, 30–3; formulaic thinking (Duflo), 30; power, importance of, 23–30; random control testing (RCT) and, 23; two questions for, 22

distribution of income. *See* income distribution

Donohue, John, 112

Dow-Heilbroner-Milberg critique: JBC winners and, 12–13, 147; social forces (macrofoundations) analysis and, 12, 16–17

Dow, Sheila, 10, 14

Duflo, Esther, 4, 20, 22, 23, 46–7, 48, 102; behavioral assumptions, 80; development economics and, 30–3; entrepreneurship, 34–5; evaluation of work, 33–6; health and education, 31; large public works, 35–6; macrofoundations of poverty, ignores, 46–7, 148; random control testing, 30–2, 35–6; research, 23, 30–1

Easterly, Richard, 33, 34

econometrics, 8, 9; explanatory variables, 8

economic boom, and reduced crime (US), 108

Economic Commission of Latin America, 24

economic crises, 21; distribution of income and, 127, 142; environmental degradation and, 134–5;

instability and, 127–8, 141;
shocks and, 128–9, 140–1, 152;
societal demands and, 132; "too
strong" capital, 132; "too weak"
capital, 132–3; underconsumption and, 129, 132; unemployment and, 132
economic crisis (2008): as consumption demand crisis, 129–30, 132;
credit, role of, 130, 131–2; effects
of, 127, 131; failure to predict,
3–4, 9; as financial crisis, 130;
JBC winners and, 136; New
Keynesian approach to, 128, 131;
recovery prospects, 131–2, 142;
unemployment and, 126, 127,
131; US household income and,
131–2; US mortgage market and,
130
economic cycles, 21
economic development, as distinct
discipline of economics, 24
*Economic Development of Latin
America and Its Principal Problems,
The* (Prebisch), 24
economic growth: capitalism and,
135; innovation, 43–4; political
institutions, 38; progressive
taxation (Saez), 75, 76, 149
economic inequality: equality of
opportunity (Acemoglu) and, 68;
JBC economists and, 20
economic mainstream. *See* mainstream economics
economic policy: inclusive
(Acemoglu), 39; investment and,
18
Economic Policy Institute, 7
economic system, 10–14; behavior
and, 11; environmental crises,

134–6; financialization of, 131;
four pillars vs. broader social
forces, 10–14, 148; periodic crises,
explanation for, 127–8; "radical"
explanations for crisis in, 129–30,
132–3; restructuring of, international, 129–30; shocks and crises
in, 128–9, 141–2; shocks as source
of instability, 141
economics discipline: criticisms
of, 3–4; of development, 20; free
market bias, 10; health, 20; realism, lack of, 3–4. *See also* mainstream economics
economists: groupthink training,
16; incentives in academic studies, 16; individualistic behavior,
15; Prisoners' Dilemma, 15;
relevance of studies, 15–16; as
technicians, 15; tools and techniques, 15–16; training, 14–16;
worldview, 15
education: limited attainment
(Duflo), 32; teacher attendance
(Duflo), 32
efficient-markets hypothesis, 10
employment: full, in Chetty's
tax study, 66, 149. *See also*
unemployment
Enron, 122
Entrepreneurial State, The
(Mazzucato), 43–4
entrepreneurship, random control
testing and, 34–5
environment: health, affecting, 98–9
environmental crises, 21; economic
system ignored, 134–5; higher
costs and, 134, 135; incorrect
prices and, 133–4; underproduction and (O'Connor), 134

environmental crisis, John Bates
Clark medal winners and, 143
equality of opportunity
(Acemoglu), 68
Evans, Robert, 85, 93, 95
Europe: colonialism, 41; merchant
class, rise of, 38
external debt, capital flight and, 25
external impediments, theory of,
23, 24
extractive institutions, the Congo
and, 40–1
Exxon Valdez oil spill, 123

fairness: income inequality and
(Saez), 73; in labor market (Rabin),
60, 149; social democracies and,
61–2; social mobility and, 64;
variable perceptions of, 61
Fama, Eugene, 10
Federal Bureau of Investigation
(FBI), 138
female immigration, crimes rates
(US) and, 108
F. Hoffmann–LaRoche, 122
financial institutions, developing
nations, 27–8, 150
Finkelstein, Amy, 20; adverse
selection, 87, 88, 89–90, 93, 150;
consumer-driven model, 93–4, 95,
105, 150; cost-benefit analysis of
public insurance, 91; evaluation
of, 92–5; health insurance, 87–92;
health insurance, crowding out,
90–1; international comparison
not made, 92, 105, 151; loading
factors, 94; Medicare, 94–5; moral
hazard, 87–8, 89, 91, 150; power
structure, ignores, 105; private
information, 89–90; RAND study,

89, 93; research, 79; risk aversion,
89–90; social factors and health,
104; supply-induced demand, 95,
105, 150
Finland, innovation ranking of, 46
firms: investment decisions of
large, 17–18; large, and power,
17–19; lobbying, 11; markets and,
11; political activity in foreign
nations, 26–7
Fogel, Robert, 95–6
food: choices made by poor, 31;
production, 98; protection and
health, 98. See also nutrition
Foster, John Bellamy, 135
France, crime rates in, 109
Frank, Robert, 74
fraud, corporate, 122–3, 124
Freakonomics (Levitt), 4, 107, 111,
112, 115
free market: mainstream economics and, 10; power and economic
analysis, 14
free trade, 6–7; China and, 7; class
effect and, 7; developing nations
and Washington Consensus, 28
Fürst, Erhard, 30
Future of Capitalism, The (Thurow),
44

Galbraith, James K., 16, 50
Gates, Bill, 23
General Motors, 128
Gordon, David, 51, 132
government(s): economic policy lim-
ited by investment, 18; innovation
and growth, 43–4; New Keynesian
approach, 128, 143
Graham, Dr David, 122
Great Depression, 128, 131

Greenspan, Alan, 10; "traumatized" worker, 53
Grogger, Jeffrey: youth wages and crime, 118–19
Grossman, Michael, 101
groupthink, 16
growth. *See* economic growth
guaranteed income, labor and, 51–2

Halevi, Joseph, 154
Halliburton, 26–7
health: behavioral (lifestyle) approach, 97, 102–4; choices made by poor (Duflo), 31; economic context of, 98–101, 102–4; environmental factors affecting, 98–9; food production and, 98; income, effects on, 100–1; individual choice vs. social context, 96–9, 103; living conditions and, 96; personal investment in (Grossman), 101–2; smoking, individual vs. social choice, 97–8; social determinants of, 95–101; work factors offsetting, 99–100
healthcare: consumer sovereignty, 92–5, 105; supply-induced demand, 84–5
healthcare decisions: consumer choice, 83–4, 85–6, 88; doctors make most, 84; individual choice vs. social context, 96–9, 103
Healthcare Financial Management Association survey, 85
healthcare system: consumer-directed approach, 88; costs of, 85; doctors as gatekeepers, 85; economics and, 79; rationing, 81; spending comparisons, 80–1;

US, exceptional context for, 80–7, 104–5, 150
healthcare system, United States: costs of, 83, 150; HMOs and inefficiency, 82; poor health outcomes, 104, 105; private insurance, reasons for, 85–6; revenues, 85; spending, 80; supply-induced demand, 84–5, 105, 150
health economics, 20
health insurance: adverse selection (Finkelstein), 87, 88, 89–90, 93, 150; co-payments, 81; moral hazard, 87–8, 89, 91, 150; public vs. private, 81–3; RAND study in US, 85–6, 89; underinsurance, 82; in US, 81–4; user fees, 81. *See also* private health insurance; public health insurance
health insurance, United States, 81–4; Medicaid, 81; Medicare, 81, 82, 83; underinsured, 82. *See also* private health insurance; public health insurance
health maintenance organizations (HMOs), 82
Health Management Associates, 123
Heilbroner, Robert, 10, 11
homicide: income inequality, 120; in US, 106, 109, 114–15
homo economicus, 6, 12, 60,153
household debt: economic crisis (2008), 130, 131–2; in US, 55–6, 56
household income. *See* income
Hsieh, C-C: income inequality and homicide, 120
Hussein, Saddam, 25–6

ideology, methodology and, 14
IMF. *See* International Monetary Fund

incarceration: comparative costs,
109–10; rates and conditions
(US), 114–15

income: determination of, 49;
health/mortality, effects on,
100–1; household, 131–2; productivity and, 51, 54; of US labor
force, 1979–2007, 53–4

income distribution, 142, 150; importance of, 49–50; marginal productivity theory of, 5; unequal,
and economic crises, 127, 142

income inequality: barrier to intergenerational social mobility, 65;
causes of (Saez), 73–4, 150; equality of opportunity (Acemoglu),
68, 70; government intervention
and (Saez), 75; JBC economists
and, 20; Saez's tax study of, 72–3;
skill-biased technical change
(Acemoglu), 67–8, 70, 71–2; 150;
social welfare and, 20; top-end
wages and (Saez), 73–4; US labor
market, 54; US vs. Germany
(Acemoglu), 68

individual(s): power, 16–17; research
and social forces, 10–11, 12–13

individual behavior: social forces
and Dow-Heilbroner-Milberg
critique, 16–17, 154

individual choice, vs. social context
re health, 96–9, 103

individual incentives, limits of, 33–6

individual preferences, 16–17

inequality. See economic inequality;
income inequality

information asymmetry: auto
loans (Levin), 137, 138, 146;
choices made by poor (Duflo),
31; healthcare insurance and

(Finkelstein), 88–9, 93, 94;
labor market (Acemoglu), 67;
— (Levin), 58; timber auctions
(Athey), 144–5

innovation, hours worked and, 45

Inquiry into the Nature and Causes of
the Wealth of Nations, An (Adam
Smith), 22

instability: power differentials
in economic system, 141, 142;
shocks as, 128–9, 141–2

institutional structure: and economic performance (Acemoglu),
37–9; inclusive nature of, 37, 39;
property rights and, 39

intergenerational social mobility
(Chetty), 64, 65; US vs. other
nations, 65

International Crime Victimization
Survey (2000), 108–9

international economy, power and,
23–30

International Monetary Fund (IMF),
154: developing nations and
creditors, 29; loan conditions
for borrowers, 28; loans to the
Congo, 41; stabilization policies,
27–8; Why Nations Fail on, 42–3

International Petroleum Company,
27

international trade: comparative advantage theory, 6–7; developing
nations, 27–8; income inequality
and, 68, 70; union membership
and, 70–1. See also free trade

investment: fixed capital and, 139;
influence on government policy,
17–18

Iraq: post-invasion economic policy,
26; US intervention in, 25–6

Japan, crime rates in, 109
JBC (John Bates Clark) medal winners, 4, 14, 20, 21; comparisons avoided, 154; Dow-Heilbroner-Milberg critique and, 12–13, 147; how research is addressed, 12–13, 153–4; incomes/inequality study, 20; income disparity and, 57–78; individual as center of analysis, 12–13; individual choice, focus on, 141, 142, 145, 154; influence of, 147; mainstream economics, 153–4; microfoundations vs. macrofoundations, 145–6; power analysis, 13, 151, 154, 155; research concentration on US, 13, 154–5; research issues, 12–13; 2001–11 winners, 5; 2003–15 winners, 5
Johnson, Simon, 23
JP Morgan, 122
juvenile crime: causes of (Levitt), 116

Kenyan farmers, 31
Killing Hope (Blum), 25
Knowles, John, 96
Koch, Charles, 18
Koch, David, 18
Krugman, Paul, 7, 50, 53, 78; income inequality, 71; oligarchy of the rich, 150

labor: contractionary monetary policy, 52; guaranteed income and, 51–2; international competition and, 52–3; policy choices and, 52–3
labor market: Danish tax study (Chetty), 62–3, 66; fairness in (Rabin), 60; hours worked (Chetty), 63; information asymmetry (Acemoglu), 67; post–Second World War, 50–7; principal-agent models (Levin), 58; relational contracts (Levin), 58–9; skill-biased technical change (Acemoglu), 67–8, 70, 71–2, 150; two definitions of, 50–1; unemployment and power in, 66, 150; US, *see* labor market, United States
labor market, United States: Golden Age, 52–3; hourly wage growth vs. productivity growth, 54, 57
labor supply: income taxes and (Chetty), 62–3; labor-management strife, 52
labor unions: declining membership (Acemoglu), 68, 70; international trade and membership, 70–1; in US, "Golden Age," 52
laissez-faire capitalism, 5
laissez-faire policy: economic crisis (2008), 10
Lalonde, Marc, 96–7
Latinos: jobs and crime, 108
Lawson, Tony, 9, 13
Leopold II (King of Belgium), 41
Levin, Jonathan, 21, 105, 143; on credit, 137–8, 153; evaluation of, 59–60, 138; ignores broader context, 59; information asymmetry, 58; information and health insurance, 89; principal-agent models of labor market, 58; relational contract, 58–9, 136, 149; timber auctions, 144–5, 153
Levitt, Steven, 4, 20–1; abortion and crime study, 112–15; causes of

decline in US crime, 112–15, *116*, 125, 151; Chicago gang study, 116–17; corporate crime, 122; criticism of his methods, 115–16, 124–5, 151–2; data, reliance on, 111–12, 117; econometrics, 111, 152; economic factors and crime, 117–18, 119–20, 124; economics as toolkit, 111–12; juvenile crime, 116; methodological individualism, 111; methods, 110–11; no international comparisons of crime, 120, 121, 124; organizational crime, 121–2; research, 107; self-interested maximization, 152; social explanations for US crime, dismisses, 116, 117–18, 119–20, 124; US-European Union crime comparison, 120; white-collar crime, 121
liquidity effect: beneficial, of unemployment insurance (Chetty), 63–4, 65
living standards, lagging, 23–4
Lumumba, Patrice, 41

macroeconomics: conservative approaches to, 128, 140–1; instability as shocks, 128–9, 141–2; mathematical modeling and, 9–10; New Keynesian version of, 128
macrofoundations, 10–14; analysis and social forces, 12, 16–17; vs. microfoundations, 145–6 ; of poverty ignored, 46–7, 148
mainstream economics, 6–10; abstraction of the market, 11; Amy Finkelstein, 92–3; broader social forces (macrofoundations) and, 10–14; class as unit of analysis, 6; comparative advantage theory, 6–7; consumer behavior, 6; criticisms, 9–10; development economists and, 23; econometrics and statistical techniques, 8; economic method and, 9–10; four pillars of, 6–8, 147–8; free market criticisms, 10; individual as center of inquiry, 6; individual choice and, 11, 101–2; Levin on credit, 138; mathematical modeling, 7–8, 14; methodological critique of, 14; rational self-interested maximization, 6; timber auctions (Athey), 144–5; recessions (Acemoglu and Saez), 140
Malthus, Thomas, 6; laboring poor, 34
market(s): abstraction of, 11; firms and, 11; inclusiveness, 39; predatory states, 37; shaped by powerful actors, 11
Marmot, Michael, 101
Martin, Andrea, 98–9
Marx, Karl, 127
mathematical deductivist reasoning (Lawson), 9
mathematical modeling, 7–8; criticisms of, 9
Maxwell, Simon, 33–4
Mazzucato, Mariana, 43–4, 46
McCrary, Justin, 119
McKeown, Thomas, 95–6
Medicaid, 81, 90–1; health outcomes and, 92; Oregon experiment, 91–2
Medicare, 81, 82, 83, 90; health outcomes, 92, 94–5; hospital spending, 91; private drug insurance, 90

Mellon empire, 18–19
Merck, 122
methodological individualism:
   Acemoglu and Saez, 140–1,
   Levin, 149; Levitt, 111, 149; Rabin,
   105
Michaillat, Pascal, 139–40
Milberg, William, 10, 11
minimum wage: Acemoglu, 69, 149;
   Chetty, 149, Saez, 76, 149
MNCs. *See* multinational
   corporations
modeling: criticism of, 9; deductivist reasoning and, 9; mathematical, 7–8
monetary policy: used to reduce
   labor costs in US, 52
moral hazard: auto loans
   (Levin), 137; health insurance
   (Finkelstein), 87–8, 89, 91, 93;
   unemployment insurance
   (Chetty), 63
mortality: income and, 100–1; infant, public policy and, 35–6; job
   stress and (Whitehall study), 100;
   Medicare, 94–5; nutrition and, 96
mortgage market, US, 130, 131;
   fraud warning, 138
multinational corporations (MNCs):
   American military intervention,
   25–6; bribery and developing
   nations, 27; developing nations,
   political manipulation, 26–7; ex-
   tractions from developing world,
   42; power of, 24

Navaho-Cornell Health Research
   Project, 96
Navaho health and living condi-
   tions, 96

Ndikumana, Léonce, 24–5, 29–30,
   35–6
Netherlands: crime rates in, 109;
   healthcare spending in, 80
New Keynesian approach, 140, 146;
   Acemoglu, 67; economic crises,
   128, 131, 152–3
Nigeria: Halliburton charges and
   fine, 27
Nobel Prize, 4, 10, 16
Norway, healthcare spending in, 80
nutrition: choices made by poor
   (Duflo), 31–2; mortality and, 96

Obama, President Barack, 88, 94, 128
O'Connor, James, 134
oligopolies, 11
Oregon experiment, 91–2
Organisation for Economic Co-
   operation and Development
   (OECD), 80
organizational crime, 121–2

Peru, 27
Pickett, Kate, 46
Piketty, Thomas, 50, 72–3
police, crime reduction and, 114, 119
policy. *See* economic policy; monetary policy; public policy
policy environment, capitalist
   economies, 148
pollution, 122, 123
poor, choices made by (Duflo), 31
Poor Economics (Duflo and
   Banerjee), 23
Poterba, James, 79
Potter, Wendell, 86
poverty: alleviation and (Duflo),
   32–3; colonialism and extractive
   institutions, 37–8; institutional

reasons for (Acemoglu), 36–9; random control testing and (Duflo), 32–3; social roots, 46–7

power: big business, 39; comparison of modern economic analyses of, 13–14; corporations and, 17–19; development economics and, 23–30; differentials and recessions, 141, 142; in the economic system, 17–19, 148; free market critiques, 13–14; importance of, 16–19; influence on individual preferences, 16–17; institutions and capitalism, 13; labor market post–Second World War, 50–7; of large firms, 17–19; markets, 11; modern international economy, 23–30; multinational corporations, 17–18; political economy and, 13; private investment and policy, 18; role of ignored by RCT, 36; US labor market, 52–7, 59–60; US political economy, 13; whether JBC winners address, 13, 151, 154, 155

Prebisch, Raul, 24

President's Cancer Panel: report (2001), 99

Prisoners' Dilemma, 15

private health insurance: advantageous selection (Finkelstein), 90; bureaucratic costs, 83; consumer choice, 83–4, 85–6, 88; denial of coverage, 82; industry lobbying, 86–7; inefficiencies, 82; vs. Medicare, 83; vs. public insurance, 81–3

privatization, 29

productivity: hourly wage growth, 54, 55, 57; income, 51, 74–5; income gains, 52

profitability: credit and, 130, 131; at expense of labor, 53–4, 57; increases in, 53–4; investment and, 17–18; recovery and, 142

progressive taxation, economic growth and (Saez), 75, 76, 149

property crime, 114; Levitt, 113, 114–15

property rights, 43; cutthroat vs. cuddly capitalist nations, 39; government vs. private sector, 43–5; institutional structure (Acemoglu), 37, 38; predatory states, 37

public health insurance: crowding out private insurance (Finkelstein), 90; Oregon experiment re, 91–2; vs. private insurance, 82–3; rationing, 81–2

public policy: advantageous selection, 90; firms' willingness to invest, 17; inclusive economic institutions (Acemoglu), 37, 39, 43; income inequality and, 74–5; income redistribution (Saez), 140; influence of economics on, 147; infrastructure and health benefits, 96; institutional structure (Acemoglu), 37; labor market re, 52–3; limiting power of big business, 39; solutions to problems in developed countries, 35–6, 148–9; timber industry and, 145; weakening labor in US, 52–3. See also economic policy; monetary policy; tax policy

Public-Private Fair Competition Act (US), 19

Pugh, David: income inequality and homicide, 120

Rabin, Matthew, 20, 101–4; behavioral assumptions, 80, 103, 151; evaluation of, 61–2; evaluation of individual choice research, 103–4; fairness in labor market, 60, 149; methodological individualism, 105; sophisticated vs. naive time inconsistency, 102, 103; time inconsistency vs. rational maximization, 102, 151

random control testing (RCT) (Duflo), 23, 31–3; context, ignoring, 36; criticisms of, 33–6; entrepreneurship vs. secure jobs, 34–5; health policy and, 35; limits questions posed by development economies, 34–5; speculation about motives, 33–4; time inconsistency and, 33–4

RAND study, 85–6, 89

rational self-interested maximization, 6, 92, 102, 103, 105, 151

rationing of health services, 81–2

RCT. See random control testing

recovery: prospects for, 131–2; restored profits and, 142

Reddy, Sanjay, 36

Reich, Robert, 54–5

relational contracts: in labor market (Levin), 58, 59, 149; universal vs. select commitment, 58–9

research and development: government vs. private initiatives, 43–4

Ricardo, David, 6

Right-to-Work Act (US), 19

risk-based pricing, 137

Robinson, James, 23, 36–7, 68

Roe v. Wade, 112, 116

Roubini, Nouriel, 127, 129, 142

Ryan, Paul, 50

Sachs, Jeffrey, 9, 27, 33, 42–3, 124

Saez, Emmanuel, 20, 21, 45, 136; aggregate demand and supply shocks, 142; aggregate demand and unemployment, 139–40; causes of income inequality, 73–4; evaluation of, 76–8; evaluation of recessions research, 140–3; historical income inequality, 73; income inequality, tax study of, 72–3; income transfer programs, 76; interventions to increase demand, 140; methodological individualism, 140, 141; New Keynesian approach, 140–1; progressive taxation, 75–6, 149; public policy and inequality, 74–5; recessions, causes of, 138–40, 146

Scandinavia, 39

Schaife family, 18

SDOH (social determinants of health), 95–101

self-awareness and time inconsistency, 102, 103, 151

Shaikh, Anwar, 14, 133

Shiller, Robert J., 16

shocks, 128–9, 140–1; economic instability as, 141–2

skill-biased technical change and income inequality (Acemoglu), 67–8, 71–2, 150; international trade and, 68

Smith, Adam, 6, 11, 22

smoking: individual vs. social choice, 97–8, 151

social class. See class

social democracies, 13; and concepts of fairness, 61–2

social determinants of health (SDOHs), 95–101

social mobility: intergenerational (Chetty), 64, 65
social welfare, 20
sophisticated vs. naive time inconsistency, 102, 103
South Korea: institutions, 37, 38
Spirit Level, The (Richardson and Pickett), 46
statistical techniques, 8
Stiglitz, Joseph, 28, 29, 50
subprime auto loan market (Levin), 137–8, 153; adverse selection, 137; automated credit scoring, 137–8; information asymmetry, 137, 138, 146; moral hazard, 137; risk-based pricing, 137
subprime credit market, 21
Superfreakonomics (Levitt), 107
supply-induced demand (SID) (healthcare), 84–5, 105, 150
Sweden: crime rates in, 109; innovation ranking of, 46

tax policy: effects on behavior (Saez), 75–6; — (Chetty), 62–3, 66
Thatcher, Margaret, 15, 52
Theocarakis, Nicholas, 154
Thurow, Lester, 44
timber auctions (Athey), 144, 145, 153
time inconsistency: individual health decisions and, 102–3, 151; of poor (Duflo), 34; RCT failure to explain, 33–4
tobacco. *See* smoking
top 1 percent, 71, 73, 77–8
trade, international. *See* international trade
Troubled Asset Relief Program (US), 128

Uganda, 29
underconsumption, economic crises and, 129
unemployment: economic crisis (2008) and, 126, 131; ensuring profitability, 70; firm power and, 66, 150; power differentials and, 141
unemployment insurance: welfare enhancing (Chetty), 63–4, 65, 149
unions. *See* labor unions
United Kingdom: contractionary monetary policy, 52; crime rates in, 109; income and environmental hazards, 100; insurance data, and client riskiness, 104; mortality and income, 100; Whitehall study, 99–100
United Nations Human Development Index, 80
United States: anti-trust movement, 39; capital flight and corrupt regime support, 25; corporate common interests, 18–19; crony capitalism, 39; cutthroat capitalism, 39, 45–6; declining progressivity of tax system (Saez), 75; declining wages in, 54–5, 57; deregulation of financial system, 10; developing nations and, 26; economic efficiency and (Acemoglu), 69; Golden Age of capitalism, 51–2; household debt, 55–6; income inequality, 54, 68; innovation ranking of, 46; intergenerational social mobility (Chetty), 64, 65; and Iraq, 25–6; labor market post–Second World War, 50–7; military intervention, foreign business and, 25–6;

Mobutu, support for, 41; political economy and power, 13; profitability of firms, 53, 54; public works projects to combat high child mortality, 35. *See also* crime, United States; health insurance, United States; healthcare system, United States; labor market, United States

Universal Declaration of Human Rights (UN), 94

universal healthcare, 81, 151

US Forest Services, 144, 145

USAID, 27–8

usurious interest rates, 131

Varoufakis, Yanis, 154

Venezuela, 27

violent crime. *See* crime, violent

Vioxx, 122

Wacquant, Loïc: economic and social context of crime (US), 108–9, 120

wage growth, 54, 57, 73–4; of top earners (Saez), 73–4

wages: productivity and, 54, *55*, 57; stagnant, 130

Wallman, Joel, 119

Walton family, 7–8

Washington Consensus ("Consensus"), 27–8, 147

Weisskopf, Thomas, 51, 132

welfare state: expansion in US, 51

white-collar crime, 121

Whitehall study (Britain), 99–100

Whole Foods, 123

Why Nations Fail (Acemoglu and Robinson), 22, 41–2; on IMF, 42–3

Wilkinson, Richard, 46

work: hierarchy and mortality, 99–100; income, effects on health, 100

Worker's Party, Brazil, 39

workweek, American, 45

World Bank, 29; loans to the Congo, 41

World Economic Forum: Global Competitiveness Report, 45–6

World Health Organization (WHO), 93

World Trade Organization (WTO), 28

Yeager, Peter: corporate crime survey (US), 123–4

Zambia, 27

Lightning Source UK Ltd.
Milton Keynes UK
UKOW02f1108131116

287527UK00004B/129/P